The World of the Roosevelts

Published in cooperation with the Franklin and Eleanor Roosevelt Institute
Hyde Park, New York

General Editors:

William E. Leuchtenburg, Douglas Brinkley, and William J. vanden Heuvel

FDR, THE VATICAN, AND THE
ROMAN CATHOLIC CHURCH IN
AMERICA, 1933–1945
Edited by David B. Woolner
and Richard G. Kurial

FDR AND THE ENVIRONMENT
Edited by Henry L. Henderson and
David B. Woolner

VAN LOON: POPULAR
HISTORIAN, JOURNALIST,
AND FDR CONFIDANT
Cornelis A. van Minnen

FRANKLIN ROOSEVELT'S
FOREIGN POLICY AND
THE WELLES MISSION
J. Simon Rofe

ROOSEVELT AND FRANCO
DURING THE SECOND
WORLD WAR
FROM THE CIVIL WAR TO
PEARL HARBOR
Joan Maria Thomàs

FDR'S WORLD
WAR, PEACE, AND LEGACIES
Edited by David B. Woolner,
Warren F. Kimball, and
David Reynolds

FDR's World
War, Peace, and Legacies

Edited by
David B. Woolner,
Warren F. Kimball, and
David Reynolds

palgrave
macmillan

FDR'S WORLD
Copyright © David B. Woolner, Warren F. Kimball, and
David Reynolds, 2008.

First published in 2008 by
PALGRAVE MACMILLAN®
in the United States—a division of St. Martin's Press LLC,
175 Fifth Avenue, New York, NY 10010.

Where this book is distributed in the UK, Europe and the rest of the world,
this is by Palgrave Macmillan, a division of Macmillan Publishers Limited,
registered in England, company number 785998, of Houndmills,
Basingstoke, Hampshire RG21 6XS.

Palgrave Macmillan is the global academic imprint of the above companies
and has companies and representatives throughout the world.

Palgrave® and Macmillan® are registered trademarks in the United States,
the United Kingdom, Europe and other countries.

ISBN-13: 978–0–230–60938–9
ISBN-10: 0–230–60938–4

Library of Congress Cataloging-in-Publication Data

FDR's world : war, peace, and legacies / edited by David B. Woolner,
Warren F. Kimball, and David Reynolds.
    p. cm.—(The world of the Roosevelts)
    Based on the proceedings of two conferences: "In the shadow of
FDR: how Roosevelt's wartime leadership shaped the postwar world"
organized by the Franklin and Eleanor Roosevelt Institute and the
Franklin D. Roosevelt Presidential Library and Museum and held in
2005; and "Roosevelt and Churchill: the legacy of two statesmen"
organized jointly with the Churchill Centre, Washington, D.C. and
held in 2007.
    Includes bibliographical references and index.
    ISBN 0–230–60938–4
    1. Roosevelt, Franklin D. (Franklin Delano), 1882–1945.
2. Roosevelt, Franklin D. (Franklin Delano), 1882–1945—Influence.
3. World War, 1939–1945—United States. 4. World War,
1939–1945—Diplomatic history. 5. United States—Foreign
relations—1933–1945. 6. United States—Foreign relations—
1945–1989. 7. National security—United States—History.
8. Aeronautics, Commercial—History—20th century. 9. Presidents—
United States—Biography. I. Woolner, David B., 1955– II. Kimball,
Warren F. III. Reynolds, David, 1952–

E807.F346 2008
973.917092—dc22   2008012348

A catalogue record of the book is available from the British Library.

Design by Newgen Imaging Systems (P) Ltd., Chennai, India.

First edition: November 2008

10 9 8 7 6 5 4 3 2 1

To the archivists of the FDR Presidential Library,
whose dedication to scholarship has provided invaluable assistance to
generations of historians.

CONTENTS

FIGURES

ACKNOWLEDGMENTS

Two thousand five marked the sixtieth anniversary of the death of one of the most important figures of the twentieth century—Franklin D. Roosevelt. It also marked the sixtieth anniversary of the end of World War II and the birth of the "postwar" world. FDR never had the opportunity to live in this world. But his tenure as president in the twelve tumultuous years that preceded 1945 left an indelible mark on the generation that lived through the Great Depression and World War II, and, some would argue, an indelible mark on the events that followed.

To honor this occasion and to try to assess the impact of Roosevelt's leadership, the Franklin and Eleanor Roosevelt Institute and the Franklin D. Roosevelt Presidential Library and Museum organized a major conference entitled *In the Shadow of FDR: How Roosevelt's Wartime Leadership Shaped the Postwar World*. As the title suggests, the conference sought to determine the extent to which FDR's efforts to hold together a disparate wartime alliance, while simultaneously trying to secure a better future for the generation that fought the war, have shaped the past six decades.

By all accounts, the conference was a major success. It kindled a great deal of spirited debate about the impact of FDR's leadership. It also raised further questions, particularly about FDR's friendship with Winston Churchill and the wartime "special relationship" between Great Britain and the United States. These questions inspired a second gathering of historians two years later, in a conference organized jointly with The Churchill Centre, Washington, DC, entitled: *Roosevelt and Churchill: The Legacy of Two Statesmen*. Here, the wartime record of both leaders was examined with a special emphasis on the many difficult political, military, and economic issues that Great Britain and the United States wrestled with as they tried to craft and nurture the Anglo-American alliance.

The two conferences attracted some of the best Roosevelt and wartime era historians in the world. They also produced some outstanding scholarship. Together, the two gatherings and the scholarship that went into them represent a serious reassessment of FDR's wartime leadership and its legacy for the twentieth and twenty-first centuries. This book is based on the proceedings of these two conferences.

An intellectual undertaking of this scope and vigor could not have happened without the assistance of many individuals and the support of a number of key institutions. The inspiration for the conference came from professors Warren Kimball and David Reynolds, two of the world's leading FDR scholars, and in the case of Warren Kimball, a member of the Roosevelt Institute's Board of Governors. Without their dedication, determination, and profound desire to gain a more complete understanding of this tumultuous period in our history, these conferences and this book would not have been possible. Special thanks are also due to William J. vanden Heuvel, the founder and chair emeritus of the Franklin and Eleanor Roosevelt Institute, for his welcoming remarks, and for his efforts to help make the two conferences—and the many other activities of the Institute— possible. We are also grateful to Dr. Christopher Breiseth, the president and CEO of the Roosevelt Institute, for his support; to Dr. Cynthia Koch, the director of the Franklin D. Roosevelt Presidential Library and Museum; and to the staffs of the FDR Library and Roosevelt Institute—especially Lynn Bassanese, Elaine Murphy, and Mary McFarland—for their kind assistance. For their help in organizing the Roosevelt–Churchill Conference, we would like to thank William C. Ives, then president of The Churchill Centre, as well as Daniel N. Myers, The Churchill Centre's executive director, who took on much of the burden of organizing this event, ably assisted by Karen Linebarger in the Centre's Washington office.

We wish to extend our heartfelt thanks to the participants of both gatherings who so graciously accepted our invitation to share their knowledge and help us gauge the extent to which FDR's leadership shaped the postwar world. This includes a special thanks to the many commentators and chairs who added so much to the proceedings of both events. For the September 2005 conference, we are grateful to Lt. Col. Lance Betros, the chair of the Department of History at the United States Military Academy at West Point, and David Eisenhower, Public Policy fellow at the Annenberg School of Communication, for providing us with their perspectives on FDR's legacy with respect to the United States Armed Forces; to J. Garry Clifford, professor of Political Science at the University of Connecticut, for his astute observations on the historiographical interpretation of FDR; to historian Frank Costigliola of the University of Connecticut for his comments on FDR's global perspective; to Stephen Schlesinger, the former director of the World Policy Institute at the New School, and Richard Kurial, dean of Arts at the University of Prince Edward Island, for their analysis of FDR's conception of "world order;" to William Roger Louis, Kerr professor of English History and Culture at the University of Texas, for his comments on FDR and colonialism; to Anders Stephanson, James P. Shenton professor of History at Columbia University, and Ann Douglas, Parr professor of Comparative Literature at Columbia, for their views on FDR and "the China question"; to Alan Dobson, professor of Politics and director of the Transatlantic Studies Association at the University of Dundee, and Michael Hopkins, lecturer at the Department of History at the University of Liverpool, for their comments on FDR and the management of the world economy; and finally to Steven M. Gillon, professor of History at the University of Okalahoma and resident historian at the History Channel, and Eric Alterman, distinguished professor of English, Brooklyn College, professor of Journalism at the CUNY Graduate School of Journalism, and columnist for *The Nation*, for their perceptive additions to Professor LaFeber's observations on the overall meaning of the original proceedings.

With respect to the June 2007 conference, we are grateful to Godfrey Hodgson, associate fellow at the Rothermere American Institute at Oxford University, for his astute observations on the legacy of Churchill and Roosevelt; for the stimulating panel discussion on the transition from hot war to Cold War, we extend our thanks to Lloyd Gardner, the Charles and Mary Beard professor emeritus of History at Rutgers University; Deborah Nutter, senior associate dean of the Fletcher School of Law and Diplomacy; David Reynolds, professor of International History at Cambridge University; and Martin Walker, syndicated columnist and editor-in-chief emeritus of United Press International. Finally we also wish to thank Lt. Gen. (Ret) Josiah Bunting III for his fascinating address on the relationship between Winston Churchill, Franklin Roosevelt, and George C. Marshall.

As has been the case with a number of Roosevelt Institute conferences, we are extremely grateful to Michael Gartland and the Charlotte Cunneen Hackett Charitable Trust for their financial support of our efforts; and also to Peter Kovler and the Majorie Kovler Foundation. Without their support, the conference and this book would not have been possible. We would also like to thank Alessandra Bastagli and Christopher Chappell at Palgrave for their assistance in the final preparation of this book.

One final note: In the days since these conferences were organized, the world lost one of its preeminent historians, Arthur Schlesinger, Jr. We are grateful that Arthur was not only able to attend the original conference, but also to give the opening remarks. His sage observations and enthusiasm for our efforts continue to inspire. We miss him deeply.

DAVID B. WOOLNER
Cambridge, England; and Hyde Park, New York

INTRODUCTION

FRANKLIN D. ROOSEVELT WAS ONE OF THE PREEMINENT WORLD LEADERS of the twentieth century. He cast a long shadow over America and the world. Or, to change the metaphor, his presidency was a kind of beacon—illuminating a path for his followers or serving as a stern warning to his critics. Now that we have entered the twenty-first century, perhaps it is easier to take stock. Sixty-plus years after the end of the war, and after Roosevelt's untimely death, what should we make of his policies, his impact, and his legacies? The chapters in this volume assess Roosevelt's role as war leader from the vantage point of the twenty-first century by looking at different aspects of his foreign policy.

By way of a introduction, however, we need to say a little more about the war and the man, to appreciate the magnitude of this unprecedented world crisis and to understand what perspectives and skills FDR brought to bear upon it.

There had been world wars before—the United States was born in one during the eighteenth century—but World War II was the most devastating in history. It left perhaps 55 million dead, half of them in the Soviet Union and maybe another 15 million in China, and it spawned appalling new projects of mass destruction, including the atomic bomb and the attempted genocide of the Jews. It also transformed the world map, by hastening the collapse of European empires around which the world had been shaped for five centuries, and by accelerating the rise of two new "superpowers," the United States and the Soviet Union. Their rivalry spread around the globe, defining history for nearly half a century.

For the United States, the war started with the Japanese attack on Pearl Harbor in December 1941 and ended three and a half years later after the unconditional surrender of Germany and Japan in May and August 1945, respectively. But this was only part of the story, for America's war was only one of a series of regional conflicts that gradually fused into a global conflagration. This began with Japan's invasion of China in July 1937, sparking an eight-year struggle across East Asia. Britain and France declared war on Nazi Germany in September 1939, belatedly trying to stop Hitler's expansion.

The winter of 1939–1940 saw what the Americans called a "Phoney War" but, when fighting began in earnest the following spring, France fell in six weeks and Italy became a belligerent, spreading the war to the Balkans and North Africa. Britain fought on, but Hitler now controlled much of continental Europe and he was free to turn against his visceral enemy, communist Russia, in June 1941. Japan, too, seized its opportunity, attacking not merely America in December 1941, but also toppling the now largely defenseless French, British, and Dutch empires in Southeast Asia.

In a desperate attempt to contain the rampant Axis powers, America, Britain, and Russia forged a wartime alliance—fractious and full of tension but nevertheless a real attempt at cooperation. Even so, it took the Red Army a full year and a half before it turned the tide at Stalingrad in the winter of 1942–1943. Britain and America became bogged down in North Africa and Italy, and could not liberate France until the summer of 1944. Although Germany surrendered in May 1945, Allied planners feared it would take at least another year to conquer the Japanese home islands. In the event, a combination of two atomic bombs and Soviet entry into the Asian war forced Japan to surrender in August 1945.

By then Franklin D. Roosevelt was dead, stricken with a massive cerebral hemorrhage on April 12, 1945. In a clinical sense the war killed him, as is evident from photographs of a gradually ailing president during 1944 and 1945. But politically the war gave Roosevelt a new lease of life; in fact it transformed his presidency and its place in history. In January 1940, with Europe still in the Phoney War, Roosevelt entered the final year of his second term. He was steadily shipping papers from Washington to his new Presidential Library next to his family home in Hyde Park, up the Hudson River from New York. Perhaps he secretly hoped for an unprecedented third term, but this only became practical politics with the Fall of France. Citing the international crisis as justification, he won the election of November 1940 and was reelected yet again four years later, consequently presiding over virtually the whole of America's war. Had FDR retired in January 1941, he would probably have been remembered for pulling his country out of the Depression. Instead, his additional four years in the White House turned him from a domestic president into a war leader, indeed a truly world leader at one of the most decisive moments of twentieth-century history.

What kind of man was this? What traits and attitudes did he bring to bear on the challenges of world war? First, one should mention his social background. Often dubbed a "country squire," he was a member of the upstate New York landed elite, promoted in state politics in the 1920s by Al Smith in the expectation that FDR would help carry the rural vote. Instinctively he thought in terms of hierarchical societies, and his early progressivism was paternalistic in spirit. On the issue of race he was a man of his time and class, who accepted the norms of black–white relations at home and was prone to racist remarks about foreign leaders.

In other ways, too, Roosevelt was a product of the late nineteenth century, nurtured on the heritage of Western civilization, who had travelled extensively around Europe in his youth. It was natural for him to take seriously countries such as Britain, France, and Russia, which had shaped Europe in the past. Conversely, his suspicion of Germany's pretensions as a power, though partly due to boyhood experiences, also reflected the fact that the German nation-state had made a recent and violent appearance on the map of Europe, little more than a decade before his birth in 1882. Although he did not understand the social roots of Nazism, his acute and early sense of the menace of Hitler was rooted in these preconceptions about German militarism.

Taking the old powers of Europe seriously did not mean, however, that he approved of them. His respect for France never recovered from its sudden and catastrophic collapse in 1940. And he entertained a deep antipathy to the colonialism of all the Western European powers, particularly Britain's—which he liked to claim was partly due to his family roots in the seventeenth century Anglo-Dutch rivalry. Although his direct knowledge of current European colonial rule was scanty, one of FDR's deepest convictions was that the world must move on from the era of imperialism. He saw the United States, the first postcolonial nation, as the pioneer and exemplar of this historic rollback of empire. Outside Europe, he took a particular interest in China—also historically a great civilization. By contrast, his dislike of Japan reflected his own experience, since the Sino-Japanese war of 1895, of Japan as a ruthless expansionist power in Asia.

Roosevelt loved the sea. A childhood fascination with ships developed into an adult love of sailing. Some liken his devious, calculating political style to that of a sailor tacking to and fro to exploit the most favorable winds. His appointment as assistant secretary of the Navy in the Wilson Administration (1913–1921) gave him direct experience and firsthand responsibility. The Navy remained a special passion throughout his life and he intervened actively in senior appointments. On an intellectual plane, his early interest in Alfred Thayer Mahan's writings on sea power, coupled with a later sensitivity to the air age provided the bases of a unique geopolitical vision.

Roosevelt travelled extensively in his youth and early manhood, especially to Western Europe. But in 1921 he was stricken with polio. Many were convinced that this marked the end of his political career: his doting mother wanted him to accept the life of a gentleman invalid at Hyde Park. This he refused to do, laboriously developing his torso so he could heave himself around with crutches, but he never walked unaided again. Even for the normal daily tasks—dressing, getting into a chair or bed, going to the toilet—he needed the help of others.

There has been much debate about the effect of his disability on his character and outlook. Did it toughen a previously playboy politician? Did it give the spoilt patrician a new empathy for the suffering of the masses? This is speculation. What can be discussed with greater certainty is the effect of his enforced immobility on Roosevelt the diplomatist. For twenty years he hardly left the United States, and only travelled again extensively abroad in the last couple of years of his life. He did not, for instance, visit Western Europe after 1919, apart from a brief trip in 1931 when his mother was ill and a stopover in Sicily in 1943 en route home from Teheran. His direct knowledge of the world therefore became somewhat dated.

Just as FDR built up his body to compensate for his legs, so in politics he used others to do the legwork for him. His wife Eleanor acted in this way for him in domestic affairs in the 1930s; likewise did trusted advisers such as Harry Hopkins and Averell Harriman abroad during the war. Roosevelt also became a keen, if selective, reader of reports from his ambassadors abroad, especially when these were packaged in a vivid way that suited his preconceptions. The wheelchair president still kept in touch with the world.

Franklin Roosevelt was also a consummate politician, with huge faith in his persuasive powers. These skills were honed over the years in holding together his unlikely New Deal coalition of conservative Southerners, northern liberals, blue-collar ethnic groups, and African Americans, and they were then deployed on the world stage as FDR engaged with other Allied leaders, particularly Churchill and then Stalin. He disliked large, staged conferences, favoring informal meetings with the people that mattered. He also abhorred record-taking—both to maximize his room for maneuver and also to cover his tracks—which has made it hard for historians to pin down his motives and intentions. Such is his fascination, however, that scholars keep coming back to him, and six decades after his death it is also possible to assess his achievements more clearly. That is the aim of this volume.

CHAPTER 1

FDR's Foreign Policy and the Construction of American History, 1945–1955

DAVID REYNOLDS

THE STUDY OF "COLLECTIVE MEMORY" IS ONE OF THE GROWTH AREAS in recent historical writing. This term originated with Maurice Halbwachs, the French sociologist, back in the 1920s, but it gained currency among cultural historians in the 1980s thanks to the massive seven-volume project by Pierra Nora and his collaborators, *Les Lieux de Mémoire*, on how the French had remembered their past. Their essays explored a wide variety of traditions, mentalities, and symbols, but subsequent work on collective remembrance has concentrated on "places" or "sites" of memory, particularly cemeteries and war memorials.[1] Likewise, American scholars have found rich case studies in the struggles to establish a Holocaust Museum and to commemorate Hiroshima and Nagasaki.[2]

The main focus of this work has been on the material and visual—the places and images of memory—and most of the scholarship has been generated by cultural historians. Yet Nora acknowledged that books could also function as *lieux de mémoire*, and Henry Rousso's classic study of French remembrance of the Vichy era included them among what he called "vectors" or "carriers" of memory.[3] Historians are now beginning to take up this theme. Two volumes of essays have been devoted to projects for official history across the Western world, looking particularly at the two world wars.

My own recent study of the writing and impact of Winston Churchill's six volumes of memoirs is intended as a contribution to this field.[4]

Here I wish to offer a provisional sketch about how such an approach might be applied to the way Franklin Roosevelt's wartime strategy and diplomacy were interpreted in the first decade after his death. This period was especially important for the way World War II has been understood; and, although that process owed much to nonwritten forms, particularly films, I believe that memoirs and history books should not be ignored.[5] In the first place, they often established the conceptual framework for popular memory. The titles of Churchill's six volumes—such as *The Gathering Storm, Their Finest Hour,* or *Closing the Ring*—still provide the phases and the phrases by which the conflict has been remembered. Second, these early works often established the agenda for subsequent history, identifying some topics as central and marginalizing others. In American and British writing on the military history of World War II, a case in point is the virtual exclusion of the Eastern Front because of Cold War attitudes and imperatives.[6] In both these ways, I believe that the initial versions of this war helped create a framework within which other "carriers" of collective memory, such as filmmakers, operated. Perhaps the same is true for the recollections of veterans and participants, because their memories are fragmentary and unconnected, needing written history to provide a structure that is otherwise lacking.[7]

To see history under construction in this way requires more than a mere historiographical survey. We need to understand why and how these books were written, to investigate their impact and sales, to research the reviews they elicited and the controversies they aroused. That takes us away from traditional diplomatic history into the domains of intellectual history and the history of the book.[8] I can only scratch the surface in a brief work of this sort. But first, I want to survey the writings of the postwar decade, summarizing the main kinds of work and commenting on their provenance and motivation. Then I take five central themes from that historiography: the Pearl Harbor attack and the so-called "end" of isolationism; the Anglo-American strategic disputes about the Second Front and the conduct of the war in Northwest Europe; the doctrine of Unconditional Surrender and treatment of the Axis; the Yalta conference and policy toward the Soviet Union; and the decision to drop the atomic bomb. I shall briefly examine the main lines of debate in 1945–1955, emphasizing that the arguments during this first postwar decade cast long shadows.

*   *   *

The most striking contrast between the American and British historiographies of the war in this first decade lies at the very top: Winston Churchill published his memoirs whereas Franklin Roosevelt did not. In fact, "memoirs" is not an entirely appropriate term, because Churchill's six volumes, grandly titled *The Second World War*, mixed passages of reminiscence with copious quotations from his wartime documents and lengthy narratives of battles and conferences compiled by his "Syndicate" of research assistants. Moreover, Churchill got in early, publishing his work between 1948 and 1953, and thereby shaping historical debate. This was, of course, his intention: as he liked to say when locked in controversy, "All right, I shall leave it to history, but remember that I shall be one of the historians."[9]

Had Roosevelt survived the war, he would probably have produced his own account. The president's interest in history and his creation of the Roosevelt Library point in that direction. So does the report that on January 27, 1940, when a third term seemed utopian, he signed a postretirement contract with Collier's magazine for an article every two weeks over a three-year period.[10] And in 1943–1944 he was already putting his own spin on events through friendly journalists such as Forrest Davis, whose lengthy articles on "Roosevelt's World Blueprint" and "What Really Happened at Teheran" were based on conversations with the president and approved by the White House prior to publication.[11] So a retired Roosevelt would have been "one of the historians," putting his own spin on events, albeit probably not on a Churchillian scale. But the president's sudden death on April 12, 1945 put paid to any Roosevelt memoirs.[12] Hitler and Mussolini also met their Maker that month, while Stalin was more interested in signing death warrants than in writing books. So this left the historical battlefield very much to Churchill.

Or at least its commanding heights. Although no one could compete with Churchill's blockbuster of nearly two million words, many others were busily occupying the lower slopes. This was particularly true in the United States, whose publishing industry was even more vigorous than Britain's, far more lavishly funded, and not crippled by postwar rationing of paper. Timing also mattered. Churchill required three volumes to get through the 1930s and the first two years of Britain's war, whereas most American books naturally started with Pearl Harbor. As a consequence, Churchill's account of appeasement, which appeared in 1948, was almost first in the field, but on the Second Front debate or the Yalta conference, about which he did not publish until 1950 and 1953, respectively, he had to compete with several well-established American versions.

Nor would it be entirely accurate to say there were no Roosevelt memoirs, because the president's son Elliott was quickly into print in the summer of 1946 with *As He Saw It*. As both the book's title and the dustjacket sketch of a reflective FDR suggested, this purported to be an account of the wartime conferences through the eyes of the president, by someone who acted as aide and confidant at these summit meetings: "I shared his most intimate thoughts and listened to his most cherished aspirations for the world of peace to follow our military victory." An approving foreword by FDR's widow, Eleanor, gave the book added authority. As Elliott made clear, his account of the past was also "impelled by urgent events" in the present— above all his conviction, especially after Churchill's "Iron Curtain" speech in March 1946, that the wartime alliance FDR had built was being torn apart because "a small group of willful men in London and Washington are anxious to create and foster an atmosphere of war hatred against the Russians." This was rooted, Elliott claimed, in Churchill's wartime imperialist strategy and in "British ambitions to play off the U.S.S.R. against the U.S.A." His book was full of barbs by FDR about Churchill, supposedly verbatim, as a "real old Tory, of the old school" with his "eighteenth-century methods" of colonialism.[13]

As He Saw It, also serialized in Look magazine in August 1946, had a wide impact: it certainly infuriated Churchill. But its genesis is still hard to determine. Apparently Elliott, dissatisfied with a couple of drafts that seemed too dull and documentary, recruited a Hollywood scriptwriter of leftist leanings who turned reported speech into dialogue and gave the text its fellow-traveller spin.[14] Close associates of the president were appalled—Felix Frankfurter, for instance, wrote of the book's "complete unreliability"— and the Roosevelt family apologized privately to Churchill, explaining that "Elliott's work had been hotted up by a journalist" and that "Mrs Roosevelt had not seen the final version when she wrote the introduction."[15] Reliable or not, As He Saw It was on the record, establishing a set of influential interpretations with what appeared to be almost autobiographical force.

The nearest thing to an official biography of FDR's wartime leadership was Roosevelt and Hopkins: An Intimate History, published by Robert E. Sherwood in 1948. Harry Hopkins, the president's closest confidant for much of the war, died in January 1946, and Sherwood was asked by his widow to undertake the memoir that Hopkins had been planning to write. The result was, however, a very different book because Sherwood combined the writing skills of a Pulitzer-prize-winning playwright and former White House scriptwriter with an impressive command of the voluminous documentation that Hopkins had accumulated during the war. This included masses of British as well as American official papers, from which Sherwood quoted freely, often on matters in which Hopkins was not personally involved. Chip Bohlen of the State Department considered this to be most improper,[16] but he was the only senior American figure to protest, probably because Sherwood's project enjoyed almost official status, akin to Churchill's memoirs in Britain. President Truman's letter of support—"If I can be of assistance, please do not hesitate to call upon me. I hope also that you will receive the fullest cooperation of all whom you approach"—opened doors at the highest levels.[17] Using it, Sherwood secured extensive interviews with top American and British policymakers, from George Marshall to Anthony Eden. Even Churchill talked with him and sent written answers to detailed questions until their relations turned sour when it seemed that Sherwood's book might scoop his own memoirs.[18] Churchill was right to be alarmed. Although smaller in scale than his own six volumes, *Roosevelt and Hopkins* offered a readable, comprehensive, and semiofficial account of wartime diplomacy, rushed into print in 1948 and therefore well ahead of *The Second World War.*

Most of the president's inner circle of policymakers published their own memoirs between 1945 and 1950, including Sumner Welles (1944) and Cordell Hull (1948) from the State Department, Henry Stimson, FDR's secretary of war (1948), and Admiral William D. Leahy, the president's chief of staff (1950). Among memoirs by senior generals, Dwight D. Eisenhower's *Crusade in Europe* (1948) touched on many issues of high policy, as did the gossipy diary of his aide Harry Butcher, published in 1946. The content of these volumes will be discussed later, but a few general points should be made here.

First, although many of these memoir writers shared Churchill's desire to make a first strike on history, what really persuaded them to devote several years of retirement to such a herculean and unfamiliar task was the financial incentive. Under U.S. tax laws, if an author sold all literary property rights in his memoirs, this would count as the sale of a capital asset and he would be liable to only 25 percent tax, as against nearly 80 percent if he sold book or newspaper rights separately. Much of the residue could be protected from tax by making gifts to family members, particularly grandchildren.[19] Nearly all these authors adopted a tax-avoidance procedure of this sort. Although Churchill pioneered a similar arrangement in Britain, U.S. tax law was unusually beneficial, making it almost folly *not* to go into print if a retired policymaker could command big money. Doubleday paid Eisenhower $635,000 for all the rights to his memoirs, from which he was able to retain $476,250 after tax. Ike was delighted, but his publishers did even better out of the serialization and book sales, not to mention twenty foreign translations.[20]

The importance of serialization in this package raises another general point. Although many of these memoirs sold well in book form, they reached a far wider readership through excerpts in the newspapers or weekly magazines such as *Collier's* or *The Saturday Evening Post.* These excerpts were inevitably the juiciest and most sensational parts of the book, often selectively edited and tendentiously headlined. It was in this form that most Americans derived their impressions of the memoirs and, by extension, of the war. With an eye to serial sales, most memoirists relied on professional writers, some of whom were given full credit. The young McGeorge Bundy was explicitly billed as coauthor of Stimson's memoirs, writer of a text based on Stimson's documents and recollections. For his 1950 book on the Yalta conference, former secretary of state Edward R. Stettinius used Walter Johnson, a historian at the University of Chicago, and the credit "edited by Walter Johnson" appeared on the title page. More usually a journalist acted as ghostwriter in return for a fee and a mention in the acknowledgments. For example, Leahy thanked Charter Heslip for help "in arranging the material contained in my original notes," while Hull, more frankly, admitted that without Andrew Berding "this book could not have been written." Heslip had no compunction about turning reported speech into conversation in an effort to liven up Leahy's *I Was There*, but even a professional ghostwriter could not make Hull's turgid and endless memoirs readable.[21]

Most of these memoirs received little official vetting, some authors even shrugging off the question entirely. *Top Secret* by the journalist and publisher Ralph Ingersoll was an exposé of Anglo-American arguments over grand strategy in 1943–1945 when he served as a senior Allied planner and liaison officer. Ingersoll's acknowledgments included these disarming sentences: "I could never unscramble my sources of information for this book…To the best of my knowledge, what I used in this book does not violate the security of information permanently labelled 'classified'…None of the commanding generals under whom I have served has been burdened with seeing the manuscript."[22] Ingersoll was writing as a civilian-soldier who had left the army; others felt obliged to seek some kind of official approval, but this did not prove very rigorous. Admiral Leahy, for instance, submitted the text to Truman (for whom he had also acted as chief of staff). It was examined "in some haste" by the president's press secretary, Charles Ross, and parts were read by Truman himself, who contributed a fulsome preface. The Security Review Branch of the Office of the Secretary of Defense sent the briefest of notes indicating "no objection to its publication," and Chip Bohlen, on behalf of the State Department, made only a few comments, mostly about the Polish question.[23]

All this was in marked contrast with Britain, where government ministers, civil servants, and officers in the armed forces—serving or retired—were subject to an Official Secrets Act. Furthermore, documents they had written during government service were deemed legally to be Crown Copyright. On both grounds, therefore, the British Government claimed the right to vet publication of memoirs, and during 1946 the Cabinet Office developed elaborate scrutiny procedures to prevent a repeat of the flurry of embarrassing revelations following World War I. Although Churchill successfully asserted that the minutes and telegrams he wrote as prime minister were his "personal" property, even he submitted his manuscript to intense examination by the Cabinet Office and interested government departments. Whitehall was therefore seriously exercised by the use of British documents in books such as *Roosevelt and Hopkins*. Privately the State Department told the British Embassy it regretted the absence of an Official Secrets Act in the United States but, as the law stood, on grounds of both copyright and official secrecy American memoirists and biographers were far less constrained than across the Atlantic.[24]

Official histories of wartime campaigns were also appearing, under much more ambitious publication programs than after World War I. The U.S. Navy and Army Air Forces brought out the first of their multivolume series of histories of the war as early as 1947–1948. The naval volumes were authored by the Harvard historian Samuel Eliot Morison, who volunteered his services to FDR back in March 1942. Rejecting the idea of "an armchair history job after peace is concluded," Morison advocated what he called a "Columbus technique" of sailing in vessels of all types during wartime as well as investigating official files back in Washington. With FDR's blessing, the Navy Department quickly adopted the idea, giving Morison a roving naval commission, and the first of his fifteen volumes appeared as early as February 1947.[25] The Army's Center of Military History was a little slower with its famous "Green Books" on the war—the first volume appeared in 1950—but the next five years saw publication of major studies such as *Cross-Channel Attack* (on the planning and implementation of *Overlord*), *The Supreme Command* (on Eisenhower's direction of the war in Northwest Europe, 1944–1945) and two overview volumes on *Strategic Planning for Coalition Warfare, 1941–5*.[26]

On the diplomatic side, the Council on Foreign Relations obtained funding from the Rockefeller and Sloan Foundations for a history of American foreign policy during the war. It was proposed by William L. Langer, the Harvard diplomatic historian who had served with the wartime OSS; his coauthor was S. Everett Gleason from Amherst College. Although not governmental historians, Langer and Gleason were given almost free run of the archives: through Hull and Acheson they gained access to State Department records, Henry Morgenthau and Sumner Welles made available their own files, and President Truman authorized use of the Roosevelt papers. Even the joint chiefs cooperated, subject to some security closures. Langer's blue-chip establishment contacts, and those of the Council, obviously made a huge difference. But he also made a persuasive pitch for an early and authoritative account of American policy to head off repetition of what he called "the sensationalist journalistic controversies about American policy in 1917 and 1918" and to beat similar projects in other countries. Soviet volumes on the war would certainly "be couched in terms of communistic philosophy . . . Less objectionable, no doubt, would be a British history, but there again we would expect a treatment reflecting an imperial viewpoint which would be quite misleading to an American reader."[27] Increasingly, the Langer and Gleason project came to be seen as an American response to Churchill. After reviewing the draft of volume one, George Kennan said that nothing comparable existed, "not even Churchill's memoirs which, valuable as they are, seem to me to be based on a much narrower foundation of material."[28]

The problem was that Churchill stayed the course, aided by his syndicate of assistants, to cover the whole war in his six volumes. Langer had originally envisaged three volumes on the conflict and its aftermath, running from 1939 to 1948, but the mass of material and the constraints of his four-year leave from Harvard forced a rethink. The result was two massive volumes published in 1952 and 1953, taking the story only up to Pearl Harbor. Although not the comprehensive overview of America's wartime diplomacy that had originally been intended, they proved both influential and controversial.

Langer's fear of another bout of postwar revisionism was widely shared in Establishment circles. There had been wide currency in the 1930s for books arguing that the United States had entered the war in 1917 because of scheming British propagandists or greedy "merchants of death" in the arms industry and Wall Street.[29] Many of America's political and intellectual leaders after 1945 were convinced that this revisionist mood had prevented the country playing its proper role in world affairs in the appeasement decade. This belief helps explain why potentially sympathetic authors were given such extensive access to official and personal papers—another example being the former State Department official Herbert Feis for *The Road to Pearl Harbor* (1950) and for *Churchill, Roosevelt, Stalin* (1957). Moreover, the postwar decade did see several powerful polemics against Administration policy before Pearl Harbor, some of whose authors, such as Charles Callan Tansill and Harry Elmer Barnes, had been leading revisionist writers after World War I. Although Tansill was allowed to use State Department files for his critical study of FDR's foreign policy during 1933–1941, most revisionists were denied special access to government papers in what Barnes stigmatized as a deliberate "historical blackout" designed to benefit the "court historians."[30] He was an obsessive conspiracy theorist, but one has to admit there was something deeply disingenuous about the way that Feis, for instance, could take three pages to itemize his privileged access to archives and interviewees and then assert that "the help given me by many people in the government must not be taken as indicating any kind of official approval, sponsorship, or responsibility."[31] Revisionists therefore had to rely heavily on whatever documents had been published, and this in part explains the attention given to the pre-1941 period because of the material from the Pearl Harbor inquiries. This constitutes the first of my five case studies.

* * *

During the postwar decade the State Department published a series of volumes of documents on prewar diplomacy, especially relations with Germany, Japan, and the Soviet Union, but these were by way of official apologia. It had no desire to open up material relating to the debacle at Pearl Harbor. Immediately after the Japanese attack, the Roosevelt Administration successfully rebuffed demands for a full inquiry, instead, scapegoating the army and navy commanders in Hawaii, General Walter C. Short and Admiral Husband E. Kimmel. But by the fall of 1944, even internal War and Navy Department investigations admitted serious failings in Washington, and, once Japan had surrendered, it was impossible to contain Republican demands for a full congressional inquest. The Democratic leadership in Congress therefore took preemptive action in September 1945, establishing a joint committee of inquiry on which it had a majority, and the resulting report in July 1946 again placed the blame largely on Short and Kimmel. But the 15,000 pages of accompanying documentation—drawing on previous inquiries, official papers, witness testimony, and personal diaries—exposed rich and complex veins of primary material to public scrutiny, and these would be mined assiduously for years to come. Moreover, the dissenting report by two Republican senators, Homer Ferguson and Owen Brewster, offered an alternative view of the evidence, namely, that the Roosevelt Administration, from FDR downward, was equally responsible for Pearl Harbor's lack of readiness.[32]

Thanks to this rich documentation made public by the official inquiries, the controversy over Pearl Harbor became a debate about the Roosevelt Administration's response to Europe and Asia in the period 1937–1941. This debate mirrored the dynamics of both the earlier arguments over U.S. entry into World War I and also the later clash over the origins of the Cold War by setting defenders of the Administration, who portrayed U.S. policy as essentially a prudent reaction to grave foreign threats, against revisionists who argued that American leaders had been assertive and often duplicitous in involving the country in events far beyond the scope of national interest.

The memoirists and "official" historians all insisted that the Axis powers posed a genuine threat to American security and values, which required aid to Britain and eventually entry into the war. But they were not of one mind about the president's tactics. Langer and Gleason, for instance, following Henry Stimson, felt that FDR "tended to underestimate popular support for his foreign policy" and "to exaggerate the strength and cohesion" of the opposition in Congress. On the other hand, Robert Sherwood defended FDR's "cautious policy of one step at a time," arguing that had he engineered a "showdown" on Capitol Hill "he would have been badly defeated and Germany and Japan between them would have conquered all of Europe and Asia, including the Soviet Union, by 1942."[33] Despite differences of emphasis, however, these writers endorsed the priority given by the Administration to events in Europe, highlighting its efforts to delay or deter war with Japan. In so far as America was felt to bear any responsibility for Japan's attack on Pearl Harbor, they usually followed the Administration's wartime line of blaming the local commanders.[34]

Revisionists, by contrast, argued or implied that the Axis, however obnoxious, did not pose any significant threat to the United States. Charles C. Tansill even asserted that in the autumn of 1939 "Hitler had high hopes that America might be induced to accept the role of mediator and thus bring to an early close a war that he had entered with many misgivings." As late as November 1941, said Tansill, "Germany was trying desperately to stay out of war with the United States" whereas Roosevelt wanted to enter the conflict because he espoused the Wilsonian policy of making "the world safe for democracy." With Germany refusing to start a war, FDR reckoned that "perhaps some Japanese statesman would prove more accommodating!"[35] Revisionists therefore attacked FDR for seeking a "back door" to war, and they exploited nuggets of evidence from the Pearl Harbor inquiries, such as the November 25, 1941 diary entry by Henry L. Stimson, FDR's secretary for war, that FDR's Cabinet had to decide how to "maneuver them [the Japanese] into firing the first shot." Revisionists presented Stimson's comment as a military issue, asserting or implying that FDR set up Pearl Harbor, whereas defenders of the Administration claimed Stimson was talking politics: how to represent a likely Japanese offensive in Southeast Asia as a threat to American interests.[36]

As with defenders of the Administration, revisionists did not speak in unison. William L. Neumann, for instance, acknowledged the "errors and fallacies of Japanese policy" but also criticized the Roosevelt Administration for "an exaggerated conception of American political and economic interests in China" and for imposing a total freeze on Japanese assets and trade in July 1941, which left Japan "no alternative but to bow to American demands or fight for the resources by which her economic and military strength was to be maintained." Harry Elmer Barnes, by contrast, focused on Pearl Harbor itself and was quite open in his accusation: "In order to promote Roosevelt's political ambitions and his mendacious foreign policy some three thousand American boys were quite needlessly butchered."[37] But all were agreed that Roosevelt had repeatedly and systematically deceived the American people. The classic indictment came from the progressive historian Charles A. Beard in two massive volumes (1946 and 1948) of highly personalized attack on FDR, a far cry from the analysis of economic interests that had characterized his earlier writings. Beard used copious but selective quotations to compose what Samuel Eliot Morison famously denounced as "a book so full of *suppressio veri* and *suggestio falsi* that it would take one of almost equal length to expose every error, innuendo, or misconception."[38] Whatever the evidential problems, the backdoor-to-war thesis would not go away: there was enough smoke even if no smoking gun. The Administration's clumsy cover-up of the Pearl Harbor attack, plus the forced revelations via the various inquiries, engendered suspicions that have continued to the present in a debate between "conspiracy" and "cock-up" theorists of history.[39]

Defenders of Roosevelt essentially argued that the end justified the means. Such dissimulation as he did practice was necessary, they said, because Americans had been "asleep," indifferent to the nature of the real world. In August 1945 President Truman asserted bluntly that "[t]he country was not ready for preparedness" in 1939–1941 and that it was "as much to blame as any individual in this final situation that developed at Pearl Harbor." In a 1943 preface to a selection of diplomatic documents *Peace and War, 1931–1941*, the State Department claimed that Roosevelt and Hull "early became convinced that the aggressive policies of the Axis powers were directed toward an ultimate attack on the United States and that, therefore, our foreign relations should be so conducted as to give all possible support to the nations endeavoring to check the march of Axis aggression." But because "much of popular opinion" did not share this thesis, State explained, U.S. policy "necessarily had to move within the framework of a gradual evolution of public opinion in the United States away from the idea of isolation."[40]

The terms "isolation" and "isolationist" were used repeatedly for propaganda purpose by defenders of FDR. Thus Walter Johnson, author of a 1944 study about the prewar "Committee to Defend America by Aiding the Allies," entitled his book *The Battle against Isolation*. He asserted that although the United States had been "a world power since the last decade of the nineteenth century," the American people had been "slow to recognize" this fact. According to Johnson, Americans' "stubborn isolationist sleep" resulted in "neglect of their responsibilities to other nations" in the 1930s. In the "One World" of the 1940s, he said, that could only bring about repetition of "the plague of war."[41] Working along parallel lines was the concurrent rehabilitation of President Wilson. Thomas A. Bailey's 1945 volume on *Woodrow Wilson and the Great Betrayal* claimed that "the unwillingness or inability of the United States to carry through the promises made in its behalf" by Wilson at Paris was nothing short of "catastrophic." Bailey produced a rather contorted list of no less than fourteen "betrayals" (perhaps an echo of the Fourteen Points?) to argue that America's failure to break for good with "the ancient path of isolation" meant that the country bore "a very considerable share of the blame" for "the ills that befell Europe from 1919 to 1939."[42] This chimed in with the Administration's campaign in 1943–1945 to sell the United Nations to the American people as the country's "Second Chance" after the fiasco of 1919–1920.

Roosevelt's wartime opponents and his postwar critics vehemently rejected the tag "isolationist," insisting that they favored a policy of "independence" and "non-entanglement," following the tradition of George Washington. Senator Robert Taft said that "isolationist" was a label stuck on "anyone who opposed the policy of the moment;" sociologist George Lundberg called it a means "to attack a position which nobody holds." Fighting smear with smear, Colonel Robert McCormick, owner of the *Chicago Tribune*, declared that "every traitor calls a patriot an isolationist."[43] Such protests were unavailing: the label did stick and, with it, the implication that opponents of Roosevelt's foreign policy had been out of touch with the real world.

A more subtle response was to argue that, for most of the 1930s, FDR had also followed policies otherwise damned as "isolationist." This was the thrust of Charles Beard's first volume. In fact, Beard argued, only once between 1933 and 1940 did FDR make "an open break with the policy of neutrality for the United States in European wars"—his "Quarantine Speech" in October 1937—and even then he quickly backtracked.[44] Beard's argument was later adopted by scholars such as Robert Divine,[45] but during the first postwar decade it attracted little support. In the era of Marshall Aid and NATO, it seemed self-evident that America had finally accepted its historic destiny as a world power. Wilson and Roosevelt were represented as pioneering "internationalists," their critics as head-in-the-sand "isolationists." Within that frame of reference, "the roots of isolationism" were researched rather as a crop scientist might investigate a diseased plant. During the postwar decade, the most popular diagnoses were either geographical or ethnic: isolationism was depicted as an antiquated method of survival in parts of the rural Midwest and the Plains or among introverted groups such as German-Americans—regions and communities that had become somewhat cut off from mainstream national life.[46]

*   *   *

Pearl Harbor and the end of "isolationism" constituted a major strand of early postwar historiography. Another was the debate about Anglo-American strategy, which comprised two main elements—when and where to launch the Second Front and the controversy about the conduct of the war in Northwest Europe.

On the Second Front: the earliest U.S. memoirs depicted this as a fundamental strategic clash between American advocacy of an early, concentrated invasion of France and the British preference for wearing the Axis down in the Mediterranean. Elliott Roosevelt insisted that in 1942–1943 Churchill had "fought an unceasing battle to avoid a cross-channel invasion into Europe...He had tried to shift the weight of the offensive so as to protect British Empire interests in the Balkans and central Europe against his Soviet ally." Ralph Ingersoll concurred, adding that the clash of strategies reflected a deeper difference in approaches to warfare: whereas the Americans only "sought to destroy the armed forces of the enemy in the shortest possible time...the British *always* mix political with military motives." There was "no such thing as a 'pure' British military objective"—using that adjective, he stressed, simply in the "chemical" sense of the word.[47] Here was a new twist to the old theme of innocent Americans and perfidious British.

Not all American writers of the period agreed that Britain advocated an essentially "Balkan" strategy or that it showed particular prescience about the Cold War. Both Henry Stimson and Robert Sherwood argued that Churchill was simply reflecting traditional British interests in the Mediterranean and also following his own preference, dating back to Gallipoli in 1915, for a peripheral strategy rather than direct, frontal attacks on the enemy—what Sherwood in another phrase of studied ambiguity called Churchill's "incurable predilection for 'eccentric operations.'" But they had no doubt that the strategic debate was a story of what Stimson called "persistent and deep-seated differences between partners."[48] So irritated was Churchill by these attacks that he took pains in his memoirs to present himself as a consistent exponent of a cross-Channel attack as soon as it was practicable. He even added a special chapter to his second volume (1949) to suggest that, as early as the grim summer of 1940, he was planning landing craft and artificial harbors in anticipation of D-Day four years later.[49]

There was, however, some fancy footwork on the American side as well. Eisenhower's memoirs in 1948 also depicted Churchill as being preoccupied with the future of the Balkans. "For this concern," said Ike, "I had great sympathy, but as a soldier I was particularly careful to exclude such considerations from my own recommendations." It is therefore interesting that in April 1946—before the Anglo-American debate had set firm and before Ike became a presidential aspirant—he sounded a different note in private. Talking to the military journalist Hanson Baldwin, Eisenhower

stressed that he and Marshall consistently pressed for the invasion of Western France as the final main means of defeating the Germans but he said that he had made two or three great mistakes during the war and that now in retrospect this was one of them. Militarily, he said he was right in insisting that the invasion of Western France was then the proper means of defeating Germany but politically he now felt that because of the Russian attitude perhaps the British were right on insisting upon a Balkans invasion first.[50]

Ike's remark about "two or three great mistakes during the war" may have given Baldwin the title for his *Great Mistakes of the War*, published in 1950. These incisive essays started from the premise that, "unlike the British or the Russians," the American way of war was to fight "for the immediate victory, not for the ultimate peace." But whereas Ingersoll had taken this as evidence of British perfidy, Baldwin considered it a mark of sagacity: "during World War II our political mistakes cost us the peace." He argued that adoption of British strategy for concentrating on "Southern Europe" could have averted Soviet control of Eastern Europe. Instead, the firm commitment at Teheran to operation Overlord "really settled the postwar political fate of Eastern Europe." Baldwin admitted that Churchill "made his share of mistakes" during the war but asserted that on the basic strategic issue "the British were right and we were wrong."[51] Support for this argument came from *The Struggle in Europe*, a full-scale history of the last year of the war in Western Europe published in 1951 by Chester Wilmot, the Australian war correspondent. Wilmot agreed that Stalin always "kept his post-war political objectives in view," in contrast with "the American determination to wage the war to absolute victory without regard to the political consequences," thereby neglecting "opportunities which developed in the Mediterranean and the Balkans."[52] He attracted a particularly ferocious review from Arthur M. Schlesinger, Jr., who called this a "preposterous" book, characterized by a "violent wrenching of the facts of history" in order to shore up the British Empire's "crumbling sense of national self-confidence."[53]

As Schlesinger noted, Churchill's own memoirs did not claim that in 1943 he advocated operations in the Balkans or Italy to preempt the Soviets in Central Europe: his was essentially a military case based on the opportunities he discerned there as against Northern France. In April 1950, when Churchill read the relevant passages in *Great Mistakes*, he was incensed by Baldwin's assertions, many of them lifted from Elliott Roosevelt, that he had wanted to mount a "Balkan invasion" or "jump eastward into the Balkans," and he scrawled angry annotations in the margin—"rubbish," "wrong," even "crazy." *Great Mistakes* argued that Britain was right about strategy and America was misguided, and that it was a refrain of *The Second World War*, but after 1945 the road to Berlin clearly lay across the beaches of Normandy rather than over the mountains of Southern Europe. Churchill therefore used his memoirs to portray himself as a loyal servant of Overlord, once it became militarily practicable.[54]

The other big strategic argument, also informed by the Cold War, was whether the Western Allies could have beaten the Russians to Berlin in

1944–1945. Although not laboring the point, Eisenhower's memoirs made clear his belief at the time, and after, that there was no hope in 1944 "of maintaining a force in Germany capable of penetrating to its capital." They also characterized Montgomery's proposed alternative strategy as a "pencillike thrust" into the Ruhr that was totally unrealistic. Ike's book aroused Monty's defenders in Britain, particularly an anonymous reviewer in the London *Sunday Times* (now identified as Denis Hamilton, writing with Monty's help and encouragement) who set off a major transatlantic row at the end of 1948. Blasting Ike as a "disastrous" field commander, Hamilton insisted that Monty's plan would "have shortened the war" and brought the Western Allies into Berlin, Prague, and Vienna before the Russians, thereby creating "a political balance much more favorable to an early and stable peace than the actual outcome."[55] In 1951 General Omar Bradley, Monty's bitter rival in 1944–1945, entered the lists. His memoir contained several unflattering comments on Monty's arrogance as a person and caution as a commander (except for what seemed the bizarre brainstorm of the Arnhem operation). Bradley described the overall strategic debate as being between the "single" and the "double" thrust, arguing that the latter approach, adopted by Eisenhower, maximized the chance of confusing the enemy and exploiting the Allies' superior mobility.[56]

Wilmot's *Struggle in Europe* was the first major British contribution to this debate, and it was based on special access to some of Montgomery's own papers. It did not whitewash Monty, admitting his "vanity" and dogmatism; a key chapter on "The Lost Opportunity" of Arnhem laid the blame on "the British caution about casualties" as well as "the American failure to concentrate." But, overall, Wilmot had no doubt that Ike, whom he called "a successful Supreme Commander" of a fractious coalition but not "a successful commander in the field," had squandered the chance "to ensure that the great capitals of Central Europe—Berlin, Prague and Vienna—would be liberated from Nazi rule by the West." Wilmot invested this old debate with a mass of detail from the British side and framed it in language much more supportive of Monty. What Ike called a "pencillike" thrust clearly sounded futile; Bradley's "double" thrust was, almost by definition, likely to be more effective than just one. But if, as Wilmot conceptualized it, the alternative to Monty's "single thrust" was Ike's "broad front," that suggested something more ponderous, lacking aggression and drive.[57] Like Baldwin's antithesis between the apolitical Americans, focused only on victory in contrast with their politically savvy Allies, his dichotomy defined debate for years to come.[58]

* * *

These controversies about Allied strategy had their diplomatic counterpart in the row over Roosevelt's doctrine that each Axis power must make an "unconditional surrender," which he announced during a press conference at the Casablanca conference in January 1943. After the war Churchill told Robert Sherwood that he heard the phrase "for the first time from the President's lips at the Conference." He made a similar comment in Parliament in July 1949, adding that FDR had spoken "without consultation with me." But the following November, after checking the records, he admitted that the two of them *had* discussed the matter during the conference and that he had communicated about it with his Cabinet back in London.[59]

Churchill's postwar attempts to distance himself from unconditional surrender reflected the criticism that the policy had by then provoked, especially from members of the German resistance to Hitler and participants in the attempted assassination on July 20, 1944. Ernst von Weizsäcker, state secretary in the German Foreign Ministry but also a closet opponent of the Nazi regime, claimed in his memoirs that the "wretched Casablanca formula...mobilized the forces of despair in Germany behind Hitler," resulting in a fight to the finish and thus "a vacuum in the heart of Europe," which the Russians were partly able to fill.[60] Such criticisms were disseminated in the West via *Germany's Underground* (1947) by Allen W. Dulles—the wartime OSS station chief in Bern, Switzerland, and a prime contact of the 1944 plotters[61]—and through *The German Generals Talk* (1948), a book of interviews conducted by the British military commentator Basil Liddell Hart. Here and in newspaper articles he argued that "war to the bitter end was bound to make Russia 'top dog' on the Continent, to leave the countries of Western Europe gravely weakened, and to destroy any buffer" against the Soviets.[62] For his part, Hanson Baldwin condemned unconditional surrender as "perhaps the biggest political mistake of the war."[63]

Not everyone agreed. Arthur M. Schlesinger noted that the doctrine did not stop the plotters of July 20, and he emphasized the president's diplomatic imperatives at Casablanca: to reassure Stalin that the Allies would not sign a separate peace and to prevent recurrence of Germany's "stab in the back" myth about defeat in 1918.[64] The debate about unconditional surrender has rumbled on inconclusively ever since and lies well beyond the compass of this chapter. The point to underline here is that the main lines of argument emerged soon after the war and in the context of a divided Europe very different from what the Allied leaders had imagined in 1944.

*   *   *

Postwar controversy about the origins of this division came to revolve around the Yalta conference of February 1945. Whereas controversy about

Anglo-American strategy and diplomacy was largely the preserve of retired generals and academic historians, wartime policy toward the Russians became a matter of political polemic in the United States. Initially the charge that FDR had handed over to the Soviets free countries such as Poland and China was confined to a minority of extremist Republicans. But it was taken up by much of the GOP after the defeat in the presidential election of November 1948 made the previous bipartisan foreign policy seem an electoral liability. By the autumn of 1949 the Soviet atomic test and the so-called "fall" of China made the Democrats' policy seem even more dubious, while the exposure of Alger Hiss, a senior State Department official at Yalta, as a probable Soviet agent focused attention on the conference. In the 1952 campaign, Republican slogans included "Repudiate Yalta" and "Liberate the Satellite Countries."[65]

Yalta was also entering the battle of the books. In April 1948, Charles Beard, concluding *President Roosevelt and the Coming of War*, asked whether the ends achieved had justified FDR's duplicitous means. The Four Freedoms and the Atlantic Charter, Beard said, had not been realized in vast areas of Eastern Europe and Asia; victory over Germany and Japan simply ensured "the triumph of another totalitarian regime no less despotic and ruthless than Hitler's system, namely Russia."[66] In the summer of 1948, former Roosevelt adviser William C. Bullitt wrote two articles for *Life* magazine asserting that the president had erred at Teheran and especially Yalta when, exhausted and often unfocused, he "still held to his determination to appease Stalin." *Life*'s accompanying picture of the conference was captioned "High Tide of Appeasement."[67]

As a direct response to Bullitt, Edward R. Stettinius, Jr., FDR's secretary of state at Yalta, published *Roosevelt and the Russians: The Yalta Conference* in 1949, which was serialized in *Life*. Quoting extensively from the official record, Stettinius called Yalta "on the whole, a diplomatic triumph" for America and Britain and argued that "the Soviet Union made greater concessions," citing such issues as the United Nations and German reparations. He claimed that Roosevelt "did not 'surrender' anything significant at Yalta which it was within his power to withhold," given the dominant position of the Red Army in Eastern Europe. The conference was "an honest effort" by America and Britain "to determine whether or not long-range co-operation with the Soviet Union could be attained." Stettinius insisted that subsequent problems were caused not by the Yalta agreements but by "the failure of the Soviet Union to honor those agreements." His defense of FDR was similar to that offered by Chamberlainites for Munich as having been essential to test for the world whether the other side could be trusted to keep its word.[68]

Stettinius did not silence the critics. He was particularly vulnerable on the Far Eastern agreements promising Chinese and Japanese territory to Stalin, where his defense amounted essentially to saying that "the State Department was not a factor" in the negotiations and that "the military insisted that the Soviet Union had to be brought into the Japanese war."[69] In *Roosevelt and Hopkins*, Robert Sherwood had already conceded that the Far East was "the most assailable point in the entire Yalta record," suggesting that FDR made these concessions because, with the conference almost at an end, he was "tired and anxious to avoid further argument."[70] Hanson Baldwin, who castigated FDR for a "personalized foreign policy" marked more "by idealism and altruism, than by realism," described Yalta as "perhaps the saddest chapter in the long history of political futility which the war recorded." The effect of what he called FDR's policy of "appeasement in Asia" was to concede "strategic hegemony in important north-east Asia" and "to make Russia a Pacific power." Yet it was not, said Baldwin, in America's interest to "beg or barter for Russia's entry into the Pacific war."[71] Chester Wilmot, again building on Baldwin, entitled his chapter on Yalta "Stalin's Greatest Victory."[72]

The inquest into Yalta, like that into Pearl Harbor, also generated a major collection of official documents.[73] Although the secret Yalta agreements on the Far East were published in February 1946, the Truman Administration generally managed to hold the line on further revelations about what had happened at the conference. But the situation changed in 1953, with a Republican secretary of state and GOP majorities on key congressional committees. Senators William Knowland and Styles Bridges (now chair of the Senate Appropriations committee) pressed for an increase in the budget of the State Department Historical Office. They wanted to accelerate publication of volumes of documents on twelve wartime conferences and on U.S. policy toward China up to 1949, as well as the regular series *Foreign Relations of the United States* (FRUS) for the years 1935–1941. As Senator John Bricker made clear, the aim was to expose the Democratic cover-ups about Pearl Harbor, the fall of China, and the "secret agreements" made by FDR with Churchill and Stalin.[74] With equal partisanship, Truman, Stettinius, Byrnes, and Harriman all refused to make their papers available for the FRUS projects,[75] while Senate Democrats tried to block the necessary appropriations. In 1954 the Republicans carried the day. The FRUS volume of documents on Yalta, over one thousand pages, was published in March 1955—the preface frankly admitting that it was a response to the "expressions of interest by several Senators and the Senate Committee on Appropriations."[76] The volumes on China for 1942 and 1943 appeared in 1956 and 1957.

The Republicans' window of opportunity soon slammed shut, however. In January 1955 the Democrats regained control, albeit narrowly, of both House and Senate. The FRUS volumes on Potsdam and Teheran did not appear until 1960 and 1961; the 1944 volume on China saw the light of day only in 1967. Among wartime conference, the Yalta volume therefore stood alone. This had two important consequences for diplomatic historians. On the one hand, unlike the Pearl Harbor inquiry, this documentation served to dampen controversy: Roosevelt's critics could not find a smoking gun. On the other hand, Yalta became the focus for writing on wartime diplomacy, arguably to a far greater extent than was historically justified, as would have been clear if the Teheran volume had appeared at the same time.

*   *   *

The final topic of this chapter is the atomic bomb. Although its use was Truman's responsibility not Roosevelt's, the Manhattan Project had been nurtured by FDR. Moreover, the way the American Establishment sought to shape the verdict of history sums up many of the themes of this chapter.

During 1946 the decision to drop two bombs on Japan in August 1945 generated increasing controversy in America. In March a statement by prominent churchmen, including the influential commentator Reinhold Niebuhr, publicly condemned the bombings as "morally indefensible." At the end of August the *New Yorker*, with unwonted earnestness, devoted a whole issue to journalist John Hersey's searing report of interviews with survivors in Hiroshima. At the same time, the published report of the U.S. Strategic Bombing Survey stated that "certainly prior to December 31, 1945, and in all probability prior to November 1, 1945, Japan would have surrendered even if the atomic bomb had not been dropped, even if Russia had not entered the war, and even if no invasion had been planned or contemplated." And in September, the journalist Norman Cousins, in an editorial in the *Saturday Review of Books*, argued that the evidence of the devastation and the doubts about its necessity required Americans to hold their leaders to account. Cousins, who had already claimed in print that the bombs were dropped in an effort to "checkmate Russian expansion," asked: "Have we as a people any sense of responsibility for the crime of Hiroshima and Nagasaki?"[77]

James B. Conant, the president of Harvard and FDR's wartime science adviser, was concerned at the mounting tide of criticism. Recalling that in the 1920s "it became accepted doctrine among a small group of so-called intellectuals who taught in our schools and colleges that the United States had made a great error in entering World War I," he felt in September 1946 that "we are in danger of repeating the fallacy."[78] Conant therefore persuaded MIT president Karl Compton and, even more significant, former secretary of war Henry Stimson to publish articles in support of the decision to drop the atomic bomb, which appeared in the *Atlantic Monthly* in December 1946 and *Harper's* magazine in February 1947. Both were widely read, with Stimson's essay being taken as particularly authoritative. In composing it, he and McGeorge Bundy (in this case acting as ghostwriter rather than coauthor) were assisted by drafts from wartime aides and by material simultaneously being accumulated for his memoirs. Although intended to rebut contrary arguments, the article, at Conant's behest, was couched as a cool recitation of facts, buttressed by extensive quotation from contemporary documents. Stimson said his chief aim in 1945 had been "to end the war in victory with the least possible cost in the lives of the men in the armies which I had helped to raise," at a time when there was "a very strong possibility" of Japan fighting to the bitter end. If it therefore came to a full-scale invasion of the Japanese home islands, victory might be delayed "until the latter part of 1946, at the earliest" and "I was informed that such operations might be expected to cost over a million casualties to American forces alone." That estimate of one million was based on no official documentation: "Mac" Bundy later told his biographer that he and Stimson simply settled on it as a "nice round figure."[79]

Stimson's article did not still all debate. In *Great Mistakes of the War*, Hanson Baldwin accepted that "we used the bomb for one purpose, and one only...to hasten victory." But he argued that as early as the spring of 1945, because of submarine blockade and strategic bombing, "the military defeat of Japan was certain; the atomic bomb was not needed." At most, it accelerated Japanese readiness to surrender by a matter of weeks.[80] Nevertheless, the Stimson article became the definitive statement for the defense, lodging the "nice round figure" of one million in the historical literature. Arthur Schlesinger, debating Chester Wilmot on the ABC radio network's "Town Meeting" in April 1952, cited it no less than four times to justify the Yalta concessions on the Far East.[81] And over the years the word "casualties"—meaning killed, wounded, prisoners, and missing—often became simply "deaths." The last volume of Churchill's memoirs, for instance, suggested that the total conquest of Japan might well have required "the loss of a million American lives and half that number of British."[82] Harry Truman's memoirs (1955), though more circumspect, also opted for a round number: "General Marshall told me that it might cost half a million lives to force the enemy's surrender on his home grounds."[83] The Pentagon's casualty projections in the summer of 1945 have become a matter of vexed debate, but most scholars set them much lower.[84] Suffice it here to say that Stimson's "over a million casualties" was quoted for years to come. This provided a powerful defense for Roosevelt's readiness to buy Russian entry into the Pacific War if the alternative was a holocaust of American lives.

*   *   *

In this brief survey of how the history of FDR's war was constructed in the decade after his death, I have sought to develop a number of themes.

First, to indicate the amount of instant history that appeared so quickly. Although the president was not able to emulate Churchill in being his own historian, many of his entourage rushed their works into print. Lucrative contracts were a major incentive, but most authors were keen to make history as well as to make money. And, in Robert Sherwood's *Roosevelt and Hopkins*, we have something close to an official biography of FDR as war leader, buttressed by an impressive amount of wartime documents. These writers were assisted by the lack of an American Official Secrets Act and of detailed government procedures for the vetting of memoirs by ministers, officers, or officials. Such structures in Britain blocked or delayed would-be memoirists: Monty, for instance, did not publish until 1958, after he had retired from the military—hence his covert cooperation with writers such as Denis Hamilton and Chester Wilmot. Churchill was the exception that proves the rule: he was given special access to official documents and special license to publish them, in part because Whitehall came to view his memoirs as almost *the* official British history of the war.[85]

In the United States, much of the important documentation remained the property of the president's former colleagues, and they made it available to sympathetic scholars, such as Langer and Gleason. Fears of a repeat of the revisionism about World War I prompted Establishment figures to make a preemptive strike on history, most strikingly in Conant's sponsoring of Stimson's essay on the atomic bomb. However, FDR's critics gained two major coups in forcing into print a large amount of material in the Pearl Harbor inquiry of 1946 and in the State Department volume on Yalta in 1955. In both cases, publication was a response to partisan politics, but as a consequence, historical debate became permanently skewed. The duplicitous way the Roosevelt and Truman Administrations tried to manage the Pearl Harbor documents encouraged conspiracy theorists who remained obsessed with December 1941, while the early appearance of the Yalta documents helped perpetuate an exaggerated emphasis on Yalta as against the Teheran conference of 1943.

In other areas, new documentation from overseas also opened up debate. Memoirs and documents about the German resistance to Hitler, for instance, proved grist to the mill for critics of FDR's policy of unconditional surrender. But probably the biggest influence on the early historiography of Roosevelt's foreign policy was current diplomacy. Debates about the Mediterranean strategy, unconditional surrender, and the Yalta conference intensified in 1949–1950 against the backdrop of a divided Europe, the Chinese revolution, and the Korean War. On all these matters, the developing Cold War enabled Roosevelt's critics such as Hanson Baldwin to cast plausible doubt on his policies. In other areas of historical debate, however, the Cold War had the opposite effect. For instance, "isolationism" came to seem almost incredible in the era of an Atlantic alliance, global American bases, and a Soviet atomic bomb. In general, the controversy about Pearl Harbor faded fairly quickly in the late 1940s, other than among a group of diehard revisionists, in contrast to growing debate about FDR's conduct in 1943–1945.

Since 1955, of course, a vast amount more has been written about Roosevelt's war. During the 1960s the official archives were opening up, though many early scholars followed the patterns and issues framed by this first decade of historiography—revisiting isolationism, unconditional surrender, or Yalta. But the so-called New Left approach to American diplomatic history offered a different way of looking at the whole story, and an early example of its application to the Roosevelt era was Lloyd Gardner's *Economic Aspects of New Deal Diplomacy*. Whereas earlier writings had generally claimed or implied that American policy from Pearl Harbor to Yalta was reactive to international conditions, these historians argued that the Roosevelt Administration had its own expansionist agenda. This strongly ideological approach to American foreign policy effected a paradigm shift in the historiography, though one that was, and still remains, controversial.[86]

The light of history is, of course, ever-changing. As Churchill observed in 1940: "In one phase men seemed to have been right, in another they seem to have been wrong. Then again, a few years later, when the perspective of time has lengthened, all stands in a different setting. There is a new proportion. There is another scale of values."[87] In that sense, Arthur Schlesinger was surely right in 1949 when he said that the contemporary writings on Roosevelt were rather like trying to pronounce "a final judgment" on Lincoln at the beginning of Reconstruction.[88] Nevertheless, what this chapter suggests is that it helps to write history soon after the events in question, because the early light often endures, illuminating a path for future generations. As Henry Stimson put it in his 1948 memoirs, "history is often not what actually happened but what is recorded as such."[89]

NOTES

1. The English translation, problematically titled, is Pierre Nora, ed., *Realms of Memory: Rethinking the French Past*, trans. Arthur Goldhammer, 3 vols. (New York: Columbia University Press, 1996–1998). For European examples see Jay Winter and Emmanuel Sivan, eds., *War and Remembrance in the Twentieth Century* (New York: Cambridge University Press, 1999); T.G. Ashplant, Graham Dawson, and Michael Roper, eds., *The Politics of War Memory and Commemoration* (London: Routledge, 2000); Jan-Werner Müller, ed., *Memory and Power in Post-War Europe: Studies in the Presence of the Past* (New York: Cambridge University Press, 2002).

2. For a survey, see Robert D. Schulzinger, "Memory and Understanding U.S. Foreign Relations," in *Explaining the History of American Foreign Relations*, ed. Michael J. Hogan and Thomas G. Paterson, 2nd ed. (New York: Cambridge University Press, 2004), 336–52.

3. Nora's general introduction in *Realms of Memory*, 1:17; Henry Rousso, *The Vichy Syndrome: History and Memory in France since 1944*, trans. Arthur Goldhammer (Cambridge, MA: Harvard University Press, 1991), 241–70.

4. Keith Wilson, ed., *Forging the Collective Memory: Governments and International Historians through the Two World Wars* (Oxford: Berghahn, 1996); Jeffrey Grey, *The Last Word? Essays on Official History in the United States and British Commonwealth* (Westport, CT: Greenwood, 2003); David Reynolds, *In Command of History: Churchill Fighting and Writing the Second World War* (New York: Random House, 2005).

5. Emily S. Rosenberg, *A Date Which Will Live in Infamy: Pearl Harbor in American Memory* (Durham, NC: Duke University Press, 2003), 3, 5, who argues that "in recent American culture, historical memory . . . is inseparable from the modern media, in all their forms" and that the distinction between "memory" and professional "history" has "little significance" when studying the place of World War II in American culture in the late twentieth century.

6. A theme I have explored further in "How the Cold War Froze the History of World War Two," the Liddell Hart Lecture for 2005 (Liddell Hart Centre for Military Archives, King's College, London).

7. Cf. Alice M. and Howard S. Hoffman, *Archives of Memory: A Soldier Recalls World War II* (Lexington: University of Kentucky Press, 1990), chapter 1.

8. For some reflections on methodology, see the essay on "Culture, Discourse, and Policy: Reflections on the New International History," in David Reynolds, *From World War to Cold War: Churchill, Roosevelt, and the International History of the 1940s* (Oxford: Oxford University Press, 2006), chapter 18.

9. See Reynolds, *In Command of History*, 39, 68–77.

10. John Gunther, *Roosevelt in Retrospect: A Profile in History* (London: Hamish Hamilton, 1950), 335, citing a photocopy of the contract. I have been unable to discover confirmatory evidence in the Franklin D. Roosevelt Library (henceforth FDRL).

11. Davis did not conceal his role as FDR's mouthpiece, for instance when summarizing the president's tentative postwar blueprint "which I have had the privilege of learning from the highest authority." Forrest Davis, "Roosevelt's World Blueprint," *Saturday Evening Post*, April 10, 1943, 20–21, 109–110, quoting 109. See also "What Really Happened at Teheran," ibid., May 13 and 20, 1944; correspondence in FDRL, OF 4287, esp. FDR to Welles, February 16, 1943, and PPF 1493 indicating meetings with Davis on February 10, 1943, and March 8, 1944.

12. Though journalist Bernard Asbell tried to fill the gap with his imaginative book *The F.D.R. Memoirs* (Garden City, NY: Doubleday, 1973), constructed around the idea that Roosevelt was a loner who always tried to be "one of the boys" but never succeeded (55).

13. Elliott Roosevelt, *As He Saw It* (New York: Duell, Sloan & Pearce, 1946), quoting xiii, xvii, 36, 38, 42, 256.

14. As reported in Arthur M. Schlesinger, Jr., *A Life in the Twentieth Century: Innocent Beginnings, 1917–1950* (Boston: Houghton Mifflin, 2000), 435–6, from conversation with Elliott, and in the earlier investigative article by Joseph and Stewart Alsop, *New York Herald Tribune*, December 2, 1946. See also Joe Alsop to Eleanor Roosevelt, December 17, 1946, Eleanor Roosevelt papers, box 3248: Alsop (FDRL).

15. Felix Frankfurter to Robert Sherwood, October 7, 1946, Frankfurter papers, box 102, folder 2112 (Library of Congress, Washington, DC); Beaverbrook to Churchill, draft telegram, no date [September, 1946], Beaverbrook papers (House of Lords Record Office, London). The telegram, based on a conversation with FDR Jr., is marked "unsent" but it is likely that Beaverbrook communicated its contents verbally to Churchill.

16. Bohlen to Sherwood, July 8, 1948, Robert E. Sherwood papers, folder 94 (Houghton Library, Harvard University, bMS Am 1947).

17. Sherwood later told the president's secretary that the letter had been of "incalculable value" in obtaining information for the book. See Truman to Sherwood, May 23, 1946, and Sherwood to Matthew J. Connelly, January 23, 1948, President's Personal Files PPF 1685: Hopkins (Harry S. Truman Library, Independence, Missouri—henceforth HSTL).

18. See Reynolds, *In Command of History*, 53–54, 156–9.

19. See Willis D. Nance to Don Maxwell, memo on Admiral Leahy's memoirs, March 11, 1946, William D. Leahy papers, box 10: Book Correspondence, General (Library of Congress, Washington, DC).

20. Stephen E. Ambrose, *Eisenhower*, 2 vols. (New York: Simon and Schuster, 1983–1984), vol. 1, 473–5.

21. *The Memoirs of Cordell Hull*, 2 vols. (New York: Macmillan, 1948), vol. 1, vi and vol. 2, 1726–7; William D. Leahy, *I Was There* (New York: Whittlesey House, 1950), acknowledgment; cf. Heslip to Leahy, April 14, 1949, Leahy papers, box 10: Heslip.

22. Ralph Ingersoll, *Top Secret* (New York: Harcourt, Brace & Co., 1946), vii.

23. Ross, memo to Truman, May 9, 1949, and Shepard to Kelly, May 13, 1949, Leahy papers, box 10: Distribution of MS., and Bohlen to Kelly, May 11, 1949, ibid., box 10: General.

24. For the State Department, see Washington Chancery to FO Library, November 23, 1949, FO 370/1759, L5326/39/405 (The National Archives of the UK: Public Record Office, Kew—henceforth TNA); also generally David Reynolds, "Official History: How Churchill and the Cabinet Office Wrote *The Second World War*," *Historical Research* 78, 201 (August, 2005): 400–23.

25. Morison to FDR, March 23, 1942, Samuel Eliot Morison papers, series 33.41, box 37/1 (Harvard University Archives). See generally Samuel E. Morison, *History of United States Naval Operations in World War II*, 15 vols. (Boston: Little, Brown & Co., 1947–1962); Wesley F. Craven and James L. Cate, eds, *The Army Air Forces in World War II*, 7 vols. (Chicago: University of Chicago Press, 1948–1958).

26. On the Army series see Edward J. Drea, "Change becomes Continuity: The Start of the U.S. Army's 'Green Book' series," in *The Last Word*, ed. Grey, 83–104.

27. Quotations from Langer memos, "Projected History," February 12, 1946, and "The United States in the Second World War," October 1, 1945, in Council on Foreign Relations papers, box 49: Langer Project, files on "Access to Government Materials" and "Langer Appointment" (Seeley G. Mudd Library, Princeton University). These two paragraphs draw generally on material in box 49.

28. Kennan to H. Freeman Matthews, September 29, 1950, and similarly Mallory to Langer, October 10, 1950, ibid., files on "State Dept. Clearance" and "Correspondence with Langer."

29. On the earlier era, see Warren I. Cohen, *The American Revisionists: Lessons of Intervention in World War I* (Chicago: University of Chicago, 1967).

30. Harry Elmer Barnes, ed., *Perpetual War for Perpetual Peace: A Critical Examination of the Foreign Policy of Franklin Delano Roosevelt and its Aftermath* (Caldwell, ID: The Caxton Printers, 1953), 15–16. Barnes glossed over Tansill's access to State Department documents—cf. 46–47.

31. Herbert Feis, *The Road to Pearl Harbor* (Princeton: Princeton University Press, 1950), viii–ix.

32. The various inquiries in 1941–1946 are surveyed in Martin V. Melosi, *The Shadow of Pearl Harbor: Political Controversy over the Surprise Attack, 1941–1946* (College Station: Texas A & M Press, 1977). The texts may be found on the Internet at http://www.ibiblio.org/pha/pha/invest.html

33. Robert E. Sherwood, *Roosevelt and Hopkins: An Intimate History* (New York: Harper & Brothers, 1948), 133, 151; William L. Langer and S. Everett Gleason, *The Challenge to Isolation, 1937–40* (New York: Harper & Brothers, 1952), 5–6.

34. Wayne S. Cole, "American Entry into World War II: A Historiographical Appraisal," *Mississippi Valley Historical Review* 43 (1957): 595–617, still offers a useful summary of the debate from both sides (esp. 603–10).

35. Charles Callan Tansill, *Back Door to War: The Roosevelt Foreign Policy, 1933–1941* (Chicago: Henry Regnery Co., 1952), 606, 614–15.

36. See the discussion by Richard N. Current, "How Stimson Meant to 'Maneuver' the Japanese," *Mississippi Valley Historical Review* 40 (1953): 67–74.

37. Quotations from Barnes, ed., *Perpetual War*, 263–4, 651.

38. Charles A. Beard, *American Foreign Policy in the Making, 1932–1940: A Study in Responsibilities*, and *President Roosevelt and the Coming of War, 1941: A Study in Appearances and Realities* (New Haven: Yale University Press, 1946, 1948); Samuel Eliot Morison, "Did Roosevelt Start the War? History through a Beard," *The Atlantic*, August 1948, 95.

39. For more recent "back door" texts, see John Costello, *Days of Infamy* (New York: Pocket Books, 1994); and Robert B. Stinnett, *Day of Deceit: The Truth about FDR and Pearl Harbor* (New York: Free Press, 1999).

40. *Public Papers of the Presidents of the United States: Harry S. Truman, 1945* (Washington, DC: Government Printing Office, 1961), 249, press conference

of August 30, 1945; U.S. Department of State, *Peace and War: United States Foreign Policy, 1931–1941* (Washington, DC: Government Printing Office, 1943), 2–3.

41. Walter Johnson, *The Battle against Isolation* (Chicago: University of Chicago, 1944), vii, 239.

42. Thomas A. Bailey, *Woodrow Wilson and the Great Betrayal* (Chicago: Quadrangle Books, 1945), 356, 361.

43. Quotations from Barnes, ed., *Perpetual War*, 561, and Justus D. Doenecke, *Not to the Swift: The Old Isolationists in the Cold War Era* (Lewisburg, PA: Bucknell University Press, 1979), 11–12.

44. Beard, *American Foreign Policy in the Making,* 157; *President Roosevelt and the Coming of War,* 6.

45. Robert A. Divine, *Roosevelt and World War II* (Baltimore: Pelican Books, 1970), 7, argued that Beard's first volume was "a sound study" and that in the 1930s the president "pursued an isolationist policy out of genuine conviction."

46. Ray Allen Billington, "The Origins of Middle Western Isolationism," *Political Science Quarterly* 60 (1945): 44–64; Samuel Lubell, *The Future of American Politics* (New York: Harper & Brothers, 1952), chapter 7. A rare exception was Wayne S. Cole's scholarly study of the main anti-interventionist pressure group *America First: The Battle against Intervention, 1940–1941* (Madison: University of Wisconsin Press, 1953).

47. Roosevelt, *As He Saw It*, 253; Ingersoll, *Top Secret*, 46, 348. Cf. Admiral Leahy in 1950: "We were concentrating on the early defeat of Nazi Germany. The British wished to defeat the Nazis but at the same time to acquire for the Empire postwar advantages in the Balkan States" (Leahy, *I Was There*, 242).

48. Sherwood, *Roosevelt and Hopkins,* 590–1; Henry L. Stimson and McGeorge Bundy, *On Active Service in Peace and War* (New York: Harper & Brothers, 1948), 445–7.

49. See Reynolds, *In Command of History*, 154–6.

50. Dwight D. Eisenhower, *Crusade in Europe* (Garden City, NY: Doubelday, 1948), 194–5, 283–4; "Notes on General Eisenhower," April 26, 1946, Hanson W. Baldwin papers, 101/754 (Sterling Library, Yale University).

51. Hanson W. Baldwin, *Great Mistakes of the War* (New York: Harper & Brothers, 1950), quoting 1, 36, 45.

52. Chester Wilmot, *The Struggle for Europe* (London: Collins, 1951), 708, 714–15.

53. Arthur M. Schlesinger, "Wilmot's War, Or, 'Churchill Was Right,'" *The Reporter*, April 29, 1952, 35–40. An edited version of this essay, less caustic about the British, was published in *The New Statesman and Nation*, May 10, 1952, 557–9.

54. WSC's annotations appear on 31–44 of a copy of Baldwin's book that he forwarded to Deakin on April 3, 1950. I am indebted to the late Sir William Deakin for showing this to me. See also Churchill to Ismay, June 17, 1949, dismissing claims that he favored "the large-scale invasion of the Balkans"

as "absolutely without foundation" (Ismay papers, 2/3/160, Liddell Hart Centre for Military Archives, King's College, London). More generally see Reynolds, *In Command of History*, chapter 24.

55. Eisenhower, *Crusade in Europe*, 306; *Sunday Times* (London), November 21, 1948. On the background, see G.E. Patrick Murray, *Eisenhower versus Montgomery: The Continuing Debate* (Westport, CT: Praeger, 1996), chapters 3 and 4.

56. Omar N. Bradley, *A Soldier's Story* (New York, 1951), 434–5. Bradley acknowledged Monty's "brilliant record" in the war but argued that those who advanced "the myth of the infallible military commander" did Monty "the greatest disservice," xi. For specific criticisms see especially 208–9, 299–300, 416–19 (Arnhem), and 476–89 (the Bulge).

57. Wilmot, *Struggle for Europe*, 13, 460–1, 464–5, 468, 528.

58. Even the maps in subsequent books are often evidently based on Wilmot's stark depiction of the alternatives—see *Struggle*, 461.

59. Sherwood, *Roosevelt and Hopkins*, 696; Churchill, *Second World War*, 4: 685–8. See also Reynolds, *In Command of History*, 322–3.

60. *Memoirs of Ernst von Weizsäcker*, trans. John Andrews (London: Victor Gollancz, 1951), 274, 297.

61. Allen W. Dulles, *Germany's Underground* (New York: Macmillan, 1947); see also Franklin L. Ford, "The Twentieth of July in the History of the German Resistance," *American Historical Review* 51 (1946): 609–26, esp. 625 on unconditional surrender.

62. Quotation from B.H. Liddell Hart, "Two Words: The War's Greatest Blunder," *The Sunday Pictorial* (London), December 7, 1947, 11 (copy in Liddell Hart papers, LH 10/1947/22c, Liddell Hart Centre). See also Liddell Hart, *The German Generals Talk* (New York: William Morrow, 1948), 292–3—the British edition was entitled *The Other Side of the Hill*.

63. Baldwin, *Great Mistakes*, 14. Likewise Chester Wilmot concluded it was "both unnecessary and unwise" (*Struggle for Europe*, 713).

64. Arthur M. Schlesinger, Jr., "Roosevelt and His Detractors," *Harper's Magazine*, June 1950, 62–8, esp. 66.

65. For a fuller discussion see Athan G. Theoharis, *The Yalta Myths: An Issue in U.S. Politics, 1945–1955* (Columbia, MO: University of Missouri Press, 1955).

66. Beard, *President Roosevelt and the Coming of War*, 576–7. The journalist William Henry Chamberlin enlarged and updated this indictment after the communist takeover of China to demonstrate, in his words, the "bankruptcy" of Roosevelt's foreign policy, "complete and irretrievable." Quotations from Barnes, ed., *Perpetual War*, 542.

67. William Bullitt, "How We Won the War and Lost the Peace," *Life*, August 30, 1948, 91–94, and September 6, 1948, 86–90.

68. Edward R. Stettinius, Jr., *Roosevelt and the Russians: The Yalta Conference* (Garden City, NY: Doubleday, 1949), quoting from 295, 306, ix–x.

69. Stettinius, *Roosevelt and the Russians*, 95–96.

70. Sherwood, *Roosevelt and Hopkins*, 867.

71. Baldwin, *Great Mistakes*, 7, 77–78, 87.

72. Unlike Baldwin, who blamed FDR for all this, Wilmot rightly pointed out that Churchill was implicated in the Asian concessions: see *Struggle for Europe*, 628, 650–5.

73. This paragraph draws on Theoharis, *The Yalta Myths* and material in FDRL, Administrative Files, State Department Correspondence, 1952–1955.

74. *Congressional Record*, Supplemental State, Justice, and Commerce, 1954, 25–29; *Congressional Record*, Senate, April 21, 1954, 5044–6.

75. Herman Kahn, Director FDRL, memo, March 5, 1954, FDRL, Admin., State Dept., 1954.

76. U.S. Dept. of State, *Foreign Relations of the United States: The Conferences at Malta and Yalta, 1945* (Washington, DC: Government Printing Office, 1955), iii.

77. For background, see Barton J. Bernstein, "Seizing the Contested Terrain of Nuclear History: Stimson, Conant, and their Allies Explain the Decision to Use the Atomic Bomb," *Diplomatic History* 17 (1993): 35–72, quoting 38; James Hershberg, *James B. Conant: Harvard to Hiroshima and the Making of the Nuclear Age* (New York: Alfred A. Knopf, 1993), chapter 16, quoting 284, 291–2.

78. Conant to Harvey H. Bundy, September 23, 1946, James B. Conant, presidential papers, box 296 (Harvard University Archives).

79. Henry L. Stimson, "The Decision to Use the Atomic Bomb," *Harper's Magazine*, February 1947, 97–107, quoting 102, 106–7. On the figures, see Bernstein, "Seizing the Contested Terrain," 48, and Kai Bird, *The Color of Truth: McGeorge Bundy and William Bundy: Brothers in Arms* (New York: Simon & Schuster, 1998), 93, 97–98, 419–20.

80. Baldwin, *Great Mistakes*, 88–107, quoting from 95 and 101.

81. "Was Yalta Stalin's Greatest Victory?"—transcript of ABC's "Town Meeting," April 29, 1952, 8–10—copy in Arthur M. Schlesinger, Jr., papers, box W-33 (John F. Kennedy Library, Boston).

82. Winston S. Churchill, *The Second World War*, 6 vols. (Boston: Houghton Mifflin, 1948–1953), vol. 6, 638. Churchill did, however, say later (in an addition drafted by his adviser on naval history), "It was a mistake to suppose that the fate of Japan was settled by the atomic bomb. Her defeat was certain before the first bomb fell, and was brought about by overwhelming maritime power." Ibid., 646.

83. Harry S. Truman, *1945: Year of Decisions* (New York: Signet Books, 1965), 460.

84. Some writers have supported Truman's claim, most cite estimates of 40,000 to 50,000 American fatalities (still a very real consideration if one remembers that the country's total combat deaths in the war were some 300,000). On the historiography, see Barton J. Bernstein, "The Atomic Bomb and American Foreign Policy, 1941–1945: A Historiographical Controversy," *Peace and Change* 2 (1974), 1–16; J. Samuel Walker, "The Decision to Use the Bomb: A Historiographical Update," *Diplomatic History* 14 (1990), 97–114; J. Samuel Walker, "Recent Literature on Truman's Atomic Bomb

Decision: A Search for Middle Ground," *Diplomatic History* 29 (2005), 311–34, where the casualty debate is examined at length.

85. A theme developed in David Reynolds, "Official History: How Churchill and the Cabinet Office Wrote *The Second World War*," *Historical Research* 78, 201 (August 2005): 400–22.

86. Lloyd C. Gardner, *Economic Aspects of New Deal Diplomacy* (Madison: University of Wisconsin, 1964). See more generally the valuable histo-riographical articles by Mark A. Stoler, "World War II Diplomacy in Historical Writing: Prelude to Cold War," in *American Foreign Relations: A Historiographical Review*, ed. Gerald K. Haines and J. Samuel Walker (Westport, CT: Greenwood Press, 1981), 187–206, and "A Half-Century of Conflict: Interpretations of U.S. World War II Diplomacy," *Diplomatic History* 18 (1994), 375–403.

87. Quoted in Reynolds, *In Command of History*, 37.

88. Arthur M. Schlesinger, Jr., "The Roosevelt Literature," *ADA Yearbook* 1 (1949), 26, copy in Schlesinger papers, box W-33 (JFKL).

89. Stimson and Bundy, *On Active Service in Peace and War*, xi.

CHAPTER 2

FDR AND THE "WORLD-WIDE ARENA"

ALAN K. HENRIKSON

FRANKLIN D. ROOSEVELT WAS THE ONLY WORLD WAR II LEADER to fight a truly global war. He had an exceptionally integrated concept, and understanding, of what he termed the "world-wide arena"—and of the central place, and central role, of the United States in it. It was an ideological role as well as a geopolitical role. In an address at the University of Virginia in Charlottesville on June 10, 1940, the day Italy declared war on France, with Nazi German forces already approaching Paris and seemingly capable of driving through to the Atlantic, the president said: "Perception of danger, danger to our institutions, may come slowly or it may come with a rush and a shock as it has to the people of the United States in the past few months. This perception of danger, danger in a worldwide area—it has come to us clearly and overwhelmingly—we perceive the peril in a worldwide arena, an arena that may become so narrowed that only the Americas will retain the ancient faiths." He warned—especially those still inclined to think and vote as "isolationists"—that the United States could "become a lone island, a lone island in a world dominated by the philosophy of force," with "the contemptuous, unpitying masters of other continents" feeding it through the bars of its hemispheric "prison." Its "freedom," of movement and even of intellect and spirit, would be lost.[1] This was Roosevelt's basic geographic-cartographic frame—his "mental map," so to speak.[2] Neither Winston Churchill, despite the wide (though fragmented) area of the British Empire, nor Josef Stalin, despite the many time zones that the U.S.S.R. spanned across the Eurasian continent, had a comparable "global" view. Nor did most Americans have such a view when the war in Europe and then in the Pacific—after the Japanese attack on Pearl Harbor on December 7, 1941—began. By the end of

Figure 2.1   The President's Globe.
Source: Courtesy Franklin D. Roosevelt Presidential Library.

the war, they did. This carried over into their view of the future world order
in general. President Roosevelt's geographical vision *and its associated ideals*
framed, and also morally fired, theirs.

There were many elements in Roosevelt's global strategic imagination. A
key element was his transcendence of the traditional "landsman's view" and
also his own "seaman's view," conventionally represented for most Americans
as well as the U.S. Navy by the Equator-based Mercator's projection. He welcomed, and espoused, the new "airman's view" that had already entered into
so much of American popular culture. The aerial frontier was still mostly
to be conquered, although American aviator heroes, notably Charles A.
Lindbergh, had flown into the empyrean unknown and had stepped out
safely on foreign shores. President Roosevelt, catching the enthusiasm, had
in 1934 designated December 17—the date of Wilbur and Orville Wright's
historic first flights at Kitty Hawk in 1903—as National Aviation Day. It
was a day of remembrance but also of "feasting and rejoicing," in the words
of Senator Hiram Bingham—an almost religious reconsecration of man's
effort to reach, through further technological miracles, a higher plane of
being as well as a higher national vantage.[3]

North to the Orient, the title of a recounting by Anne Morrow Lindbergh of a flight that she and her husband Charles made, by stages, from Washington, DC, to Japan and China, helped to focus American popular attention in a new direction: up toward and over the Arctic, and beyond.[4] The most direct routes from the continental United States to the countries of Asia, as can readily be seen by looking at the top of a globe, extend on great-circle lines across the north polar region. As the involvement of the United States in the war against Germany, Italy, and Japan increased, a new unifying "picture" of the different theaters of present and future U.S. military battles was needed.

This need for a sharper visualization was filled by the North Pole-centered azimuthal equidistant projection. Polar projections appeared in magazines, most prominently in *Fortune*, and also in many newspapers. These exhibited, as words alone never could, the interconnection of continents, "closely" arrayed around the Arctic Ocean, and also the continuity of the war's operations—especially from an American perspective, as the United States occupied a newly "central" position.[5] This was truly "One World, One War," as the wartime cartographer Richard Edes Harrison titled one of his vivid

Figure 2.2 One World, One War.

Source: From Richard Edes Harrison, *Look at the World* ©1944. Courtesy of *Fortune* and Richard Edes Harrison by permission of Ross Granville Harrison III and Samuel Edes Harrison.

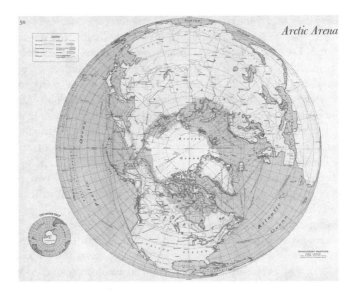

Figure 2.3   Arctic Arena.

Source: From Richard Edes Harrison, *Look at the World* ©1944. Courtesy of *Fortune* and Richard Edes
Harrison by permission of Ross Granville Harrison III and Samuel Edes Harrison.

Fortune maps.[6] These were seen by many Americans and were adapted by
the U.S. government for training and other purposes.[7] Americans learned
that the shortest supply lines to Europe as well as to Asia were northward
ones, traveled by air, via Newfoundland and up to Alaska and beyond toward
Siberia. A much wider panorama now opened across the world's top. The new
northerly supply routes, although they could not and did not carry the large
volume of weapons and other heavier materials, or of course the thousands
of personnel, that were carried across the traditional Atlantic and Pacific
shipping lanes, did carry vital items that needed to be transported quickly—
and also important emissaries from and to the United States. The limited,
though growing use of the new routes suggested nothing less than a future
revolution in the world's transportation system and traffic pattern. The prospect of transpolar air travel created expectations of postwar commerce and
social exchange, as well as military and political communication, that would
make the world's North a global "Arctic Mediterranean." Even during the
war, there were futuristic graphic imaginings of direct nonstop flights from
cities in the United States to Tokyo, Singapore, Moscow, and Zanzibar! I
have called this projective way of thinking "Air-Age Globalism."[8]

The first objective, certainly that of the president, was to win the war.
It was not clear to Americans, whose geopolitical tradition was one of

hemispheric isolation and reliance on the European balance of power, how this actually could be done. Roosevelt's own "grand strategy" was, at first, mostly reactive. He was defensive and, though defiant, somewhat imitative. He initially attempted to match, conceptually as well as militarily, what Japan, Germany, and Italy appeared to be attempting with their global linkup, making operational their 1936 Anti-Comintern Pact and 1940 Tripartite Pact. To an extent, his world strategy—though its geographical scope and practical detail were probably greater—mirrored their's. World policy *contra* world policy.[9]

In a fireside chat on December 9, 1941, two days after Pearl Harbor, President Roosevelt said: "The course that Japan has followed for the past ten years in Asia has paralleled the course of Hitler and Mussolini in Europe and Africa. Today, it has become more than a parallel. It is a collaboration so well calculated that all the continents of the world, and all the oceans, are now considered by the Axis strategists as one gigantic battlefield." The United States, as part of this single world arena, was no longer insulated and secure. "We have learned," Roosevelt said, "that our ocean-girt hemisphere is not immune from severe attack—that we cannot measure safety in terms of miles on any map any more." Germany and Japan were conducting their military and naval operations according to "a joint plan." All peoples and nations not helping the Axis powers were "common enemies," each and every one of them. "That is their simple and obvious grand strategy. That is why the American people must realize that it can be matched only with similar grand strategy." Just as Japanese successes against the United States are "helpful" to German operations in Libya, so is the United States helped by guerrilla warfare against the Germans in Serbia or Norway, by a successful Russian offensive against the Germans, and by British successes on land or sea "in any part of the world."[10] How U.S. forces would fit into, and even "join," these distant and diverse efforts had yet to be defined.

In fact, as we now know better, the leaders of Japan, Germany, and Italy did not see the world as an integrated strategic whole, or "one gigantic battlefield." Their efforts, and even their designs, were more segmented. But *Roosevelt* came to see the world this way, and through him, so did many Americans, and, progressively, also the leaders and publics of countries that were allied with the United States. That is part of his legacy.

THE SOURCES AND NATURE OF
ROOSEVELT'S GLOBAL UNDERSTANDING

One cannot know, ultimately, what made Franklin Roosevelt the global thinker that he was or became. His boyhood interests and early career surely contributed to his mature outlook. As a teenager he read the works of

Admiral Alfred Thayer Mahan on British and American "sea power." He was an avid recreational sailor and, even before becoming assistant secretary of the navy during World War I, a traveler, mainly to Europe. He had served as a councilor of the American Geographical Society and worked closely with its director, Isaiah Bowman—"Roosevelt's Geographer," a recent biographer has called him.[11] As president, he was the world's most famous stamp collector— possibly a solace, given his physical infirmity, but also, very probably, a supplier of his historical-geographical imagination. "Since you collect stamps," William Bullitt once wrote to him, "you don't need to look at the map."[12] He was in fact a skilled map reader, fancier, visualizer, and sketcher—as his creation of the Map Room in the White House attests. The huge 50-inch "President's globe" that he had in his office also attests to geographical and cartographic interests and facility. This globe, the largest detailed military globe ever made, was prepared in the Map Division of the Office of Strategic Services and was given to the president by General George C. Marshall as a Christmas present in 1942.[13] Apart from its unprecedented size, it was unusual in not being mounted in the standard way on a fixed or swiveled axis. Instead, it was cradled so as to be capable of "universal" movement at the flip of a hand—ideal for obtaining a "flexible" view, a literally global view.

Roosevelt's mind was filled with specific geographical knowledge. His knowledge of places—those he had visited or otherwise knew about—was formidable. Some commentators, rather amazingly, have said: "Geography was not Roosevelt's strong point."[14] Indeed he could sometimes be vague about particular locations and features—for example, the Ljubljana Gap, of whose significance a British observer thought he was only too dimly aware. (The observer was Churchill's assistant, William Deakin, a Balkan specialist.)[15] Nonetheless, even by the standards of European leaders, officials, and experts, Roosevelt was exceptionally well informed about world geography—and the relationships between continents and places on them. He was not just informed, he was inform*ing*. With his exceptional knowledge and understanding, he *shaped* his colleagues', the country's, and, eventually, as can be demonstrated, even mankind's worldview.

He did so with enjoyment as well as purpose. His children used to play games with him, to try to stump him with names of places he had never heard of. They rarely succeeded. He, too, played geography games, sometimes even in public. Once, when leaving on a short cruise, he told a group of newspaper reporters "a cock and bull story" about visiting the Andaman Islands, the Celebes Islands, and the South Shetland Islands. "To this I added the possibility of visiting the 'Cherable Isles,'" as he confessed in a note to Archibald MacLeish, Librarian of Congress. "One or two of the newspaper men sent the story in just as I had given it to them and it was printed in a number of papers by desk editors who had never learned geography." FDR was actually "in a bit of a quandary himself" over this. His "dim recollection" was that the name "Cherable Isles" came from one of Edward Lear's Nonsense poems. But he couldn't find it in Lear. The Library of Congress staff couldn't either, in Lear or elsewhere.[16]

Whatever blind spots that may have occurred when it came to pinpointing places or recalling their names, Franklin Roosevelt was geographically phenomenal in his spatial understanding and factual awareness. What is even more remarkable is that this characteristic of his mind communicated itself, at a distance, to people who did not know him. As one visiting European scholar remarked, Roosevelt's understanding of "the relationships of climate, geography, economics, soil, politics, and cultural tradition almost by instinct [make] the President a 'one-man Institute of Geopolitics.'"[17]

Those who knew him best readily testify on this point. Sumner Welles, his longtime family friend and his closest diplomatic collaborator as under secretary of state, stated simply: "His knowledge of geography was exceptional and his grasp of the principles of geopolitics almost instinctive."[18] Vice President Henry A. Wallace, the former secretary of agriculture and wartime head of the Board of Economic Warfare recalled that perhaps

> the most startling of all the intimate qualities of his mind was his spectacular spatial memory. He could remember strange streets, bays, oceans, harbors, countrysides with almost total visual recall. During the war his knowledge of maps, distances and physical barriers was invaluable. (Usually, he was right, but sometimes he was wrong.) He remembered the depths of waters on marine charts, the heights of mountains, the quality of roads and highways. He loved to draw plans of buildings; he drew rough ones for the construction and placing of many a new building in Washington. Some he loved; others, like the Pentagon, he loathed.
>
> This quality he extended to his vision of America, as a country. No man saw the nation more clearly as a geographic whole than Roosevelt did. He thought of it in terms of watersheds and rivers rather than in terms of states. He could catch great geophysical ideas quicker than any other man with whom I worked in the government.[19]

This matter of Franklin Roosevelt's observed "*instinct*" for geographical thought and action merits analysis. Clearly, he seems to have had a remarkable spatial sense, but more than that: an expansiveness of thought, an ability to extrapolate from his knowledge, and to extend in scope the ideas he held. His was far from being only a passive knowledge. It was active knowledge, gained and expressed dynamically.

He had an uncanny sense of orientation. In a sense, he didn't *need* a map—at least he often felt he didn't. "FDR was proud of his skill as a dead-reckoning navigator among the rocks, shoals, swirling currents, and fickle winds of the northeastern United States and eastern Canada—a skill involving intuition, the intangible feel for conditions, inspired guesswork, and luck," as the historian Gaddis Smith has written.[20] His was not just a situational awareness, a feeling for local conditions. It was spatial imagination on a grand scale, an ability to conceive of the larger dynamics of things and to anticipate their movement, nearby and also far away. His was truly a kind of projective-imaginative genius.

One cannot help but speculate about what effect Roosevelt's partial physical paralysis may have had on his natural mental gifts. There may have been a mutually supportive relationship, a synergism, at the level of psychology as well as of physiology. His enforced relative immobility may actually have reinforced the remarkable mobility of his spatial imagination, and also his desire for action and to see action—despite his handicap. "On many trips," recalled White House physician Vice Admiral Ross T. McIntire, "where his eager interest insisted on seeing some place that could not be reached by car or boat, we made a cradle of our hands and carried him, but even then it never occurred to any of us to think of him as helpless."[21]

Nonetheless, after contracting polio, he could not so easily go out into the world—a constraint imposed also by the presidency and living in the White House. He thus had to *remember* the places he had been, what he had seen, and what he had done. He conjectured knowingly from his past, sometimes much earlier experience. He also eagerly gathered current news and intelligence, often from personal reports he received from visitors who came to see him. These visitors not only included his ambassadors stationed abroad or internationally informed government officials such as Welles. They also included myriad complete outsiders, including a number of foreign correspondents—the left-oriented American journalist-scholar-adventurer Louis Fischer being one example. Of course, his principal "eyes and ears" were those of his wife, Eleanor Roosevelt, who traveled frequently and famously.[22]

It should not be forgotten that the president, despite his infirmity, himself traveled across much of the globe during World War II—by ship, to Argentia Bay off Newfoundland for his "Atlantic" conference with Churchill, for example, but mostly by air, to the much more distant meeting sites of Casablanca, Cairo, Teheran, and Yalta. He also traveled in the vast Pacific theater where he once journeyed by sea to Hawaii to meet General Douglas MacArthur and Admiral Chester Nimitz. Somewhat amused but also irritated by the recurrent speculation as to why he didn't appoint a single supreme commander for the whole Pacific, as was done in Europe with General Dwight D. Eisenhower, and instead worked with the two commanders MacArthur and Nimitz, Roosevelt stressed the enormous difference in scale. "Our typewriter strategists," he remarked, "ought to take a primary course in oceanography. None of them seems to realize that the Pacific covers 66,634,000 square miles." After the Pearl Harbor consultation, he sailed on to the remote Adak in the "stormy, fog-bound" Aleutian Islands. When his party finally returned to Washington, "after journeying 13,912 miles, he was in better shape than when we left," his physician Dr. McIntire observed. By contrast, his trip to Malta, by sea, and then onward to Yalta, by air, at the beginning of 1945 clearly was taxing for him. Nevertheless, though for the first time choosing to sit when he spoke to Congress to report afterward, he insisted: "Yes, I returned from the trip refreshed and inspired—the Roosevelts are not, as you may suspect, averse to travel. We seem to thrive on it."[23]

For the United States more than for any other country, World War II was a war of distances, and the president himself traveled many of them. So, too, did his various emissaries—Harry Hopkins, Wendell Willkie, Henry Wallace, and others. Military strategy and foreign policy and their conduct require a profound mastery of distance—not just physical distance but also political distance, economic distance, cultural distance, and psychological distance.[24] Franklin D. Roosevelt was a unique master of them all.

Among the American presidents before him, he had no peer in this respect. Not even George Washington, a professional surveyor. Not Thomas Jefferson, who sent out Lewis and Clark across the continent, and John Ledyard on a failed mission to encircle the world. Not even John Quincy Adams, whose well-stocked and expansive intellect combined with prior diplomatic experience in France, England, Prussia, the Netherlands, and Russia, enabled him to see the North American continent "from the outside in," from various angles. None grasped the essentials of global strategy as Franklin Roosevelt did.

Even his cousin Theodore, who was perhaps the first U.S. president to have a genuine sense of a global balance of power and of how regional power balances fitted within it, was not so multidimensionally cognizant in his understanding of the world's essential unity, not merely of the "arena" of military strife. Certainly President Woodrow Wilson, though he too had to lead the fight in a world war with operations in the Atlantic and some in the Pacific as well, was not truly "globally" minded, for all of his studiousness and universalist principles. Franklin Roosevelt, of course, learned from all of these predecessors, especially his Republican cousin and his Democratic chief, but he outlearned and, particularly, outtaught them all.

FROM A WORLD-PICTURE TO
A WORLD-PHILOSOPHY

What is most important *historically*, in terms of Roosevelt's continuing legacy, is that he shared his geographically based global understanding and imagination with the peoples of the United States and the world. At the very base of his thinking was a global mental map, as described above. On this foundation lay a blueprint of world order, as yet somewhat inchoate in Roosevelt's mind but already definite in its essential content. The two—the map and the vision—were connected. His global idealism had a solid basis in world realities as he knew and experienced them.

During the war, he drew a world map for Americans and others with his words as well as through his travels. The photographic and cinematic record of the presidential trips, as well as the journalistic cartography occasioned by them, supplemented the powerful reportage by war correspondents and military analysts of the "world-wide arena" of the president's rhetoric. His chosen medium was the airwaves—the newest way of mastering distance and reaching others' minds. He would draw sound-pictures of the globe in the heads of a mass listenership.

In a radio talk on February 23, 1942, six weeks after Pearl Harbor, President Roosevelt gave the country what can only be called a geography lesson. In planning this fireside address, he decided to use maps—not just his own, mounted behind him as he spoke from the White House, but those in the hands of his remote audience as well. "I love maps," he once said. "I have a map mind and I can explain things."[25] FDR's reasoning, in

Figure 2.4   "Progress of the War," Fireside Chat, February 23, 1942.
Source: Courtesy Franklin D. Roosevelt Presidential Library.

giving a graphically explanatory war message to the country, was that if the American people could be made first to visualize the basic geostrategic necessities of the conflict, they would later be much more likely to understand, and to approve, his conduct of it—in particular, sending American boys to fight outside the continental United States, far beyond the expansive (and expandable) limits of the Western Hemisphere—the policy sphere of the Monroe Doctrine.[26]

To one of his speechwriters, Judge Samuel Rosenman, the president outlined his lesson plan:

> I'm going to ask the American people to take out their maps. I'm going to speak about strange places that many of them never heard of—places that are now the battlefield for civilization. I am going to ask the newspapers to print maps of the whole world. I want to explain to the people something about geography—what our problem is and what the overall strategy of this war has to be. I want to tell it to them in simple terms of ABC so that they will understand what is going on and how each battle fits into the picture. I want to explain this war in laymen's language; if they understand the problem and what we are driving at, I am sure that they can take any kind of bad news right on the chin.[27]

Roosevelt's radio message, delivered on February 23, was probably the most effective fireside chat he gave during his wartime presidency. When he delivered his preannounced lecture, millions of American families where sitting near their radios prepared to follow his words on maps spread out before them.[28] "This war is a new kind of war," he told them. "It is different from all other wars of the past, not only in its methods and weapons but also in its geography. It is warfare in terms of every continent, every island, every air lane in the world." Repeatedly telling his listeners, "Look at your map," he pointed out to them "the world-encircling battle lines" of the war and explained their importance. "We must all understand and face the hard fact that our job now is to fight at distances which extend all the way around the globe," he declared. "We fight at these vast distances because that is where our enemies are."

If the Southwest Pacific were entirely cut off and taken over, he went on to explain, Japan would then be in a position to launch attacks against South, Central, and North America and also could move in the other direction through the Indian Ocean into India, Africa, and the Near East, there to join hands with Germany and Italy. If the Mediterranean fell to the fascists, the whole coast of West Africa would be overrun—"putting Germany within easy striking distance of South America." These potential aggressions, which were intercontinental in scope, obviously could not be prevented by adopting the isolationists' strategy of pulling American ships and planes into home waters and concentrating on "last-ditch defense," he emphasized.

For anyone who continued to think in these outmoded terms, the president had nothing but ridicule and scorn. "Those Americans who believed that we could live under the illusion of isolationism," he said, with mockery in his voice,

> wanted the American eagle to imitate the tactics of the ostrich. Now, many of those same people, afraid that we may be sticking our necks out, want our national bird to be turned into a turtle. But we prefer to retain the eagle as it is—flying high and striking hard.
>
> I know that I speak for the mass of American people when I say that we reject the turtle policy and will continue increasingly the policy of carrying the war to the enemy in distant lands and distant waters—as far away as possible from our home grounds.[29]

In this speech, despite its "offensive" thrust and tone, the president was in fact covering for major military setbacks that had been suffered by the Allies—most recently, the fall of the key British base at Singapore to Japanese forces. His geography lesson did not yet express a real grand strategy, well thought-out and ready to be implemented, but, rather, his opposition to the residue of isolationism in the United States and to the apparently global designs of the Axis powers. In that respect his outline was negative rather than positive. In another sense, however, as a framework of understanding for the worldwide struggle that was to come, with the various theaters integrated in an emerging U.S. global geostrategy, it was as concrete a statement as he then could make. It was powerfully graphic—*ideo*graphic as well as geographic.

Roosevelt's linkage, in his February 23 fireside chat, of the words "battlefield" and "civilization," in the unified phrase "the battlefield for civilization," makes the key transition, which I have underscored at the outset, *from geography to ideology*. For him, the map was an "idea." In his speeches he set out a geospatial framework—a worldwide one—for the higher, longer-term, even planetary "goals" of the war, far beyond its military objectives. This subject, relatively unstudied by historians, of the relationship of geographical thinking to higher diplomatic, political, and philosophical thinking, particularly that concerning international "peace aims"—or "Purposes" such as those articulated later in the United Nations Charter (Chapter I, Article 1)—is demonstrated by the statesmanship of Franklin Roosevelt with particular force and clarity. Through FDR's rhetoric, his *global* thinking, on a geographical plane, reemerged as *universal* thinking on an ideological plane. His world-*picture* thus became his, and others', world-*philosophy*.

PROCLAIMING THE FOUR FREEDOMS
"EVERYWHERE IN THE WORLD"

Let me briefly illustrate this imaginative and rhetorical-linguistic process by referring to a specific text, one that antedates the entry of the United States into the war but nevertheless carried its meaning into the postwar period and serves as an inspiration for mankind even today. This was Roosevelt's "Four Freedoms" speech—his annual message delivered to Congress on January 6, 1941. The ideas in it were abstract. Listeners, however, knew what he meant; they could relate his large ideas to their lives. They were assisted in this soon afterward by the *Saturday Evening Post* artist Norman Rockwell, whose magazine illustrations of the "Four Freedoms" gave these very American blessings a homely near-universality.[30]

In redrafting this text, Roosevelt modified the language in a way that enlarged its geographical scope, making its field of application more truly global—by emphasizing its relevance "everywhere in the world." His editing, which can be seen in his hand, broadens the text's philosophical-moral meaning, even though he was, no doubt, in part just using his device of verbal repetition for greater aural effect. His substitution of the term "world" for the word "international" when referring to his third and fourth freedoms—"freedom from want" and "freedom from fear"—was significant. It was not just a rhetorical but a substantive change. It had the effect of expanding these ideas, generalizing them, lifting them from the lower-level context of *interstate* relations to a *global* level. It connoted comprehensiveness, or all-inclusiveness, and not only worldwide physical extent. Individuals and peoples along with places—nations as well as governments—would be encompassed.

The following is the pertinent passage from the fifth draft of the president's speech. It shows the changes that he made in pencil—again, as noted, partly for rhetorical effect but also to highlight the broader uniformity of his vision:

> The third is freedom from want – which translated into *international* [crossed out by FDR and changed by him to "world"] terms means economic understandings which will secure to every nation *everywhere* [crossed out] a healthy peace time life for its inhabitants – *everywhere in the world* [dash and phrase added].
>
> The fourth is freedom from fear – which translated into *international* [crossed out by FDR and changed by him to "world"] terms means a worldwide reduction of armaments to such a point and in such a thorough fashion that no nation *anywhere* [crossed out] will be in a position to commit an act of physical aggression against any neighbor –*anywhere in the world* [dash and phrase added].

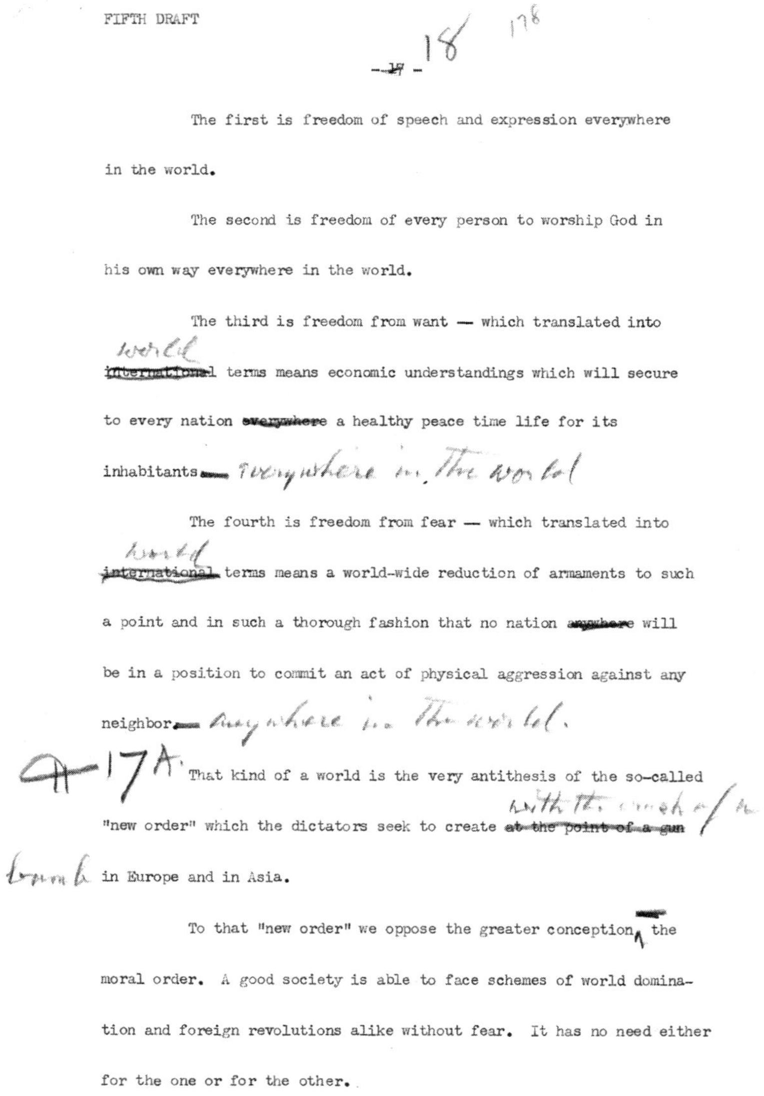

The first is freedom of speech and expression everywhere
in the world.

The second is freedom of every person to worship God in
his own way everywhere in the world.

The third is freedom from want — which translated into
~~international~~ *world* terms means economic understandings which will secure
to every nation ~~everywhere~~ a healthy peace time life for its
inhabitants. *Everywhere in the world*

The fourth is freedom from fear — which translated into
~~international~~ *world* terms means a world-wide reduction of armaments to such
a point and in such a thorough fashion that no nation ~~anywhere~~ will
be in a position to commit an act of physical aggression against any
neighbor. *Anywhere in the world.*

17A That kind of a world is the very antithesis of the so-called
"new order" which the dictators seek to create ~~at the point of a gun~~ *with the crack of a bomb*
in Europe and in Asia.

To that "new order" we oppose the greater conception, the
moral order. A good society is able to face schemes of world domination and foreign revolutions alike without fear. It has no need either
for the one or for the other.

Figure 2.5   Fifth Draft of FDR's "Four Freedoms" Speech.
Source: Courtesy Franklin D. Roosevelt Presidential Library.

That kind of a world is the very antithesis of the so-called "new order" which the dictators seek to create *at the point of a gun* [crossed out and replaced with "with the crash of a bomb"] in Europe and in Asia.

To that "new order" we oppose the greater conception, [– dash replacing a comma] the moral order. A good society is able to face schemes of world domination and foreign revolutions alike without fear. It has no need either for the one or for the other.[31]

President Roosevelt's "freedom from fear"-throughout-the-*world* notion became an ideological, as well as a merely geographical, basis for his administration's plans for a postwar order—a new, *world* order. Most of these concepts, somewhat further specified and differently enumerated, were expressed by President Roosevelt and Prime Minister Winston Churchill in the Atlantic Charter, an eight-point statement produced at their meeting off Newfoundland on August 14, 1941.[32] When asked afterward if there also would be a "Pacific Charter," addressing the concerns of Asia, Roosevelt said that it was called the Atlantic Charter because it was concluded in the Atlantic but that the scope of its meaning was universal. This was true, and it remains so to this day. When on January 1, 1942, following Congress's declaration of war against Japan and its recognition that war existed with Germany and Italy (when on December 11 those two countries declared war on the United States), the text of the Atlantic Charter was easily transformed into the Declaration by United Nations, a set of principles for a much broader coalition. As such, it was subscribed to by a majority of the countries of the world, not just the wider "Free World," as it was already then often being called, but also a world including Soviet Russia. The fact that Joseph Stalin would, and did, sign the Atlantic Charter's democratic principles—not just "the final destruction of the Nazi tyranny" but also an assurance of peace afterward in which "all the men in all the nations may live out their lives in freedom from fear and want"—was a hopeful sign, considering Soviet territorial designs and demands.[33] The possible long-term global significance of the Atlantic Charter's principles, incorporating most of the Four Freedoms, was, at least for Franklin Roosevelt, clear beyond doubt.

"ONE WORLD" PROGRAMS OF
THE ROOSEVELTIANS

President Roosevelt's perception, so well articulated by him in many wartime statements, of the essential unity of the earth and its relation to mankind's problems can also be seen as a strong influence upon the thinking of Rooseveltians, both in and out of government. Among the most notable are Henry Wallace, vice president in Roosevelt's third term, and Sumner Welles, under secretary of state until late 1943. It is no accident that their own global proposals had a strong Rooseveltian frame, for they were both, though very different minds, inspired and instructed by him. Even the "One World" of the title of the best-selling book by the Republican Wendell Willkie, published by Willkie following his round-the-world trip, has a Rooseveltian provenance, for it was President Roosevelt who sent his 1940 political challenger on that mission. "When I say that peace must be planned on a world basis," Willkie wrote in *One World*, "I mean quite literally that it must embrace the earth. Continents and oceans are plainly only parts of a whole, seen, as I have seen them, from the air."[34]

While the ideas of some of these personalities, particularly the sometimes utopian Wallace, were mocked by Clare Boothe Luce and others as "globaloney," their globalist concepts were nonetheless usually given logical, strategic, and even organizational expression, if sometimes only in blueprint form. Some of their notions had real, practical applicability.

Here are just two examples. First, Vice President Wallace's proposal, made to Roosevelt in the middle of the war, for a postwar United Nations Organization that would include: "Internationalization of worldwide airports for use by the United Nations."[35] In introducing this quintessentially Air-Age proposal, Wallace wrote: "Dear Mr. President: Most schemes for postwar organizations of the United Nations take in so much territory that it is difficult to see how they will work. I want to make this suggestion for your thinking."[36] (One is here reminded of perhaps the main reason why FDR, rather surprisingly, chose the visionary and experimental Wallace, a secretary of agriculture, to run with him as vice presidential nominee in 1940. "He's not a mystic," Roosevelt said. "He's a philosopher. He's got ideas. He thinks right. He'll help the people think."[37])

In a June 1943 article in the *New York Times*, "Freedom of the Air—a Momentous Issue," Vice President Wallace declared: "The inescapable fact is that solution of the air problem is absolutely indispensable to solution of the problem of world peace." He repeated the suggestions he recently had been making for "creation of an international air authority to regulate the air commerce between nations, internationalizing of large airports, relying upon the air arm of an international security force as the most effective means of keeping the peace, and utilizing personnel already trained in military aviation in the operation of commercial airways." His suggestions were "not intended to be final answers," he wished to make clear, but rather were intended "to indicate the general direction in which our own aviation policies and those of other countries ought to go when we reach the stage of post-war reconstruction."[38]

The idea that Wallace outlined for a postwar international air authority, though very considerably curtailed, both by the opposition of the British and other governments and by the resistance of U.S. private air carriers, did have consequences. It contributed, in part because of his own persistent advocacy both as vice president and as chairman of the Board of the Economic Warfare, to the deliberations leading to the negotiation of a limited international regime for civil aviation at the 1944 Chicago Aviation Conference. There was even considerable wartime interest, though not emanating directly from Wallace, in creating under the auspices of a United Nations Organization an "international" air force.[39] One can see a faint remnant of this idea in the provision of the eventually adopted UN Charter, in Chapter VII, for member countries, on the initiative of the Security Council, to make "special agreements" to contribute for the maintenance of international peace and security "armed forces, assistance, and facilities, including rights of passage." To date, however, no such practical "special agreements," though occasionally proposed, have been concluded.[40]

From Sumner Welles, even after his complete falling out with Secretary of State Cordell Hull in 1943, which led to his resignation, came some magisterial, powerfully coherent ideas, inspired by FDR but even more liberal than his chief's, for a postwar international organization. Welles, along with Leo Pasvolsky, initiated the State Department's planning for peace.[41] It was a process that President Roosevelt initially resisted for fear of having his hands tied politically, in case the course of the war should necessitate a shift of policy. Nonetheless, they communicated and collaborated closely. What the two men in particular shared was an enthusiasm for Pan American cooperation, strengthened on the president's part by his voyage to the Buenos Aires Conference at the end of 1936 and for Welles by his long diplomatic experience and earlier administrative responsibility for relations with the American republics. Where they differed was over Roosevelt's belief that only the major powers (the "Big Four") could deal with possible future military aggression. Welles, by contrast, tended to champion the interests and virtues of small countries. When Welles and his fellow planners presented a scheme for a United Nations "Authority," they attempted to blend his and the president's views. Their proposed UN "Executive Committee" would combine the Big Four and other small countries. To the four top powers of the United States, Soviet Union, United Kingdom, and Republic of China in the Executive Committee would be added "approximately five representatives from the regions of eastern Europe, the western democracies of Europe, the [Latin] American republics, the Far East and, possibly, the Mohammedan peoples."[42]

The United Nations Organization that in time emerged, from the Dumbarton Oaks meeting and later San Francisco Conference, joined big power and small country interests in a somewhat different, less geographically and culturally specific way. But the essential unity of the U.S. organizing concept—the Roosevelt *global* image of it—remained. The identity of the person primarily responsible for this new world construction, though he did not quite live to witness its birth in June of 1945, was unquestionable. As Sumner Welles wrote later, in his book *Seven Decisions That Shaped History*, "One man, and one man alone, made it possible for us to have a working United Nations organization before the end of World War II. That man was Franklin Roosevelt."[43]

POSTWAR DIVISION OF THE "GLOBAL" EARTH AN UNDERLYING CAUSE OF THE COLD WAR

The dreary Cold War story cannot be fully explained without attention to the transformation of our global understanding that Franklin D. Roosevelt, more than any other wartime political leader, produced in our thinking. As early as the November 1944 International Conference on Civil Aviation at Chicago, which he himself opened, he espoused, as Vice President Wallace earlier had done, the principle of "freedom of the air"—if not, so clearly as Wallace, the international control of it. "I hope you will not dally with the thought of creating great blocs of closed air," he said, "thereby tracing in the sky the conditions of possible future wars. I know you will see to it that the air which God gave to everyone shall not become the means of domination over anyone."[44]

Powerfully sustaining the argument for future freedom of world air travel was, as President Roosevelt's metaphysical language at Chicago suggests, the notion of the world as a sphere enveloped by a unifying ethereal ocean. It seemed unrealistic, unreasonable, unfair, even immoral to require the airships that would sail around this vast supraterrestrial sea to conform in their increasingly rapid movements to the political configurations of the earth's low, uneven, partitioned surface. Recent progress in stratospheric flying seemed to make this old territorial logic especially senseless. High above the clouds the geographical dividing lines between nations on earth were invisible and, to that extent, insignificant.

The fluffy illusions of the aerialist, which had become widely shared by the general public in 1945, made the case for the complete postwar freedom of communication and transportation almost self-evident. The earth seemed simply too whole and too small a place to permit the existence of political spheres of influence—either in the air or, by implication, on land. An appropriate symbol for this globalist, universalist, and pacific sentiment was the official emblem of the new United Nations Organization: "A map of the world representing an azimuthal equidistant projection centered on the North Pole, inscribed in a wreath consisting of crossed conventionalized branches of the olive tree; in gold on a field of smoke blue with all water areas in white."[45] On the United Nations emblem and flag, no political boundaries are shown.

Figure 2.6   Flag of the United Nations Organization.

Despite these image-related hopes of the Air-Age Globalist, spheres of influence continued to exist. Those of the United States and the Soviet Union were, as a result of the war and the revolution in transport technology that accompanied it, *considerably* expanded. Each nation, grown absolutely and relatively more powerful, cast a longer shadow. For the first time in history, the American and Russian shadows seemed to fall across one another. They did so, as a revealing postwar cartoon by "Herblock" in the *Washington Post* shows, not just because "Uncle Sam" and "Uncle Joe" had grown to the stature of giants or because they chose to confront one another, but because they now stood on a world (a "One World") that had been reduced to the size of a ball. The caption—Uncle Sam's warning to Stalin, "I'm here to stay too"—reflects this uneasy consciousness of a contracted territorial base.

Because of the virtual elimination of other empires on this shrunken footing, the United States and the U.S.S.R. were in direct as well as closer contact with one another, not only on the European continent and in the Far East but also over the world's top, the Arctic. This mental transformation and shrinkage of shared Earth during World War II was a major underlying cause of the Cold War, a factor of no less significance than the well-known military, political, economic, and ideological causes. Both sides continued to obey more or less the same national imperatives they always had obeyed, but in a radically altered real and imagined spatial context. Of the great influence of this new geographical condition, Americans, and probably the Russians too, were imperfectly aware, although their maps and even their cartoons vividly manifested it.

Roosevelt's "world-wide arena," of which he first had spoken in 1940 when denouncing Mussolini and Italy for opportunistically joining in the

Figure 2.7   "The Realization of the Shrinking World."

Source: Copyright 1947 by Herblock in *The Washington Post*.

Nazi attack on France, had changed. He and his ideas, more than the think-ing and actions of any other statesman of the Second World War period, had changed it. Always conscious, as a geographically literate person, of the importance of great-circle routes, he was intellectually receptive to the new northward orientation of wartime American cartography, though he did not exaggerate it. He was a promoter of the technological and organiza-tional advances that made Air-Age Globalism plausible. More importantly,

Franklin Roosevelt changed an essentially negative picture of the pre-Pearl Harbor world—a worldwide arena full of "peril" for Americans—into a positive world-image of possible international collaboration and greater hope for mankind.

FROM YESTERDAY'S GLOBALISM TO
TODAY'S GLOBALIZATION

President Roosevelt's idea-filled mental maps have had a continuing influence through the Cold War era into the present. In the military security field, very little true global cooperation was possible in the immediate postwar decades because of the East–West ideological divide and a "balance of terror" resulting from the stockpiling, forward deployment, and intimidating effect of atomic weapons. The fear of a Pearl Harbor-like atomic "surprise attack," felt on both sides of the Cold War divide, did, however, generate a few remarkable proposals that had the potential to relieve international tension and even engender trust between Washington and Moscow and their respective camps.

One such idea that in 1992 resulted in a workable treaty between the NATO and Warsaw Pact countries was President Dwight Eisenhower's 1955 Open Skies proposal. This scheme, had it been adopted, would have entailed the exchange of detailed maps of military installations on both sides of the Iron Curtain. It also would have enabled the carrying out of extensive surveillance overflights, using landing facilities reciprocally made available for that purpose. Considered by many, even some officials of the U.S. government, to have been a dangerous disarmament plot or just a propaganda ploy, Eisenhower's Open Skies plan—not wholly unlike President Roosevelt's vaguer "freedom of the air" proposition, which may have caused the Soviet delegation to depart from the Chicago Aviation Conference—was a carefully thought-out and technically advanced proposal, even if controversial, and, at the time, internationally unacceptable.

I cannot prove that the Eisenhower administration's Open Skies proposal owed anything to Roosevelt's or the Rooseveltians' "open skies" concepts—both being Air-Age Globalist approaches to international peace and security. But, surely, there is a connection.[46] An essential optimism lay at the base of both leaders' outlooks, that of President Roosevelt and the general he picked to lead the fight in Europe. The example that Roosevelt gave of placing confidence in the other side—assuming a risk for peace—was memorable, and inspiring. President Eisenhower, too, reasoned that trust would beget trust, and that the Free World versus Slave World dynamic could be ended. As Eisenhower said at the conference in Geneva where he presented his Open

Skies plan to the British, French, and Russians: "Likewise we will make more easily attainable a comprehensive and effective system of inspection and disarmament, because what I propose, I assure you, would be but a beginning."[47]

In the nonmilitary security field, one can actually trace the influence, and even the very wording, of Franklin Roosevelt's globalizing ideas. An important recent example is the "Millennium Report" of UN Secretary-General Kofi Annan.[48] "If one word encapsulates the changes we are living through, it is 'globalization,'" Secretary-General Annan said in presenting this report to the UN General Assembly. "We live in a world that is interconnected as never before—one in which groups and individuals interact more and more directly across State frontiers, often without involving the State at all."[49] One is here reminded of President Roosevelt's crossing out the word "international" and replacing it with "world" in his Four Freedoms address. Drafted principally by John Ruggie, a historically reflective political science professor then serving as an assistant secretary-general at the UN, this major Annan report, titled 'We the Peoples': The Role of the United Nations in the 21st Century, contained as its chapters three and four, "Freedom from Want" and "Freedom from Fear." Taken together, these Rooseveltian phrases, and the ideas behind them, constitute the best definition we have of the influential new concept of "human security." To these, Secretary-General Annan added a third element: the environment. "Freedom from want, freedom from fear, and the freedom of future generations to inherit a healthy natural environment—these are the interrelated building blocks of human—and therefore national—security."[50] This, too, has a Rooseveltian antecedent: the president's interest in conservation, as well as his broader knowledge and awareness of geography—the land, the earth's waters, and the air.

In the 'We the Peoples' report, it is stated: "Extreme poverty is an affront to our humanity."[51] One can imagine FDR saying much the same. With his keen and sympathetic appreciation of the interconnection of things and peoples, one can easily see him nodding assent to Secretary-General Annan's words: "every step taken towards reducing poverty and achieving broad-based economic growth is a step towards conflict resolution."[52] That is to say, there must be an integrated approach to development, security, and human rights in the world.

Only thus, as the UN secretary-general concluded in a follow-on set of recommendations that he hoped would become the basis for decision by heads of states and governments at their World Summit in September 2005, fifty years after the founding of Roosevelt's dreamed-of and planned-for United Nations, would it be possible for mankind to live, as he stated, "In larger freedom."[53]

NOTES

1. *Roosevelt's Foreign Policy, 1933–1941: Franklin D. Roosevelt's Unedited Speeches and Messages*, compiled by O. I. Dodge (New York: Wilfred Funk, 1942), 251.

2. For an elaboration, with examples, of this concept as applied to the scale of international relations, see Alan K. Henrikson, "Mental Maps," in *Explaining the History of American Foreign Relations*, ed. Michael J. Hogan and Thomas G. Paterson (Cambridge: Cambridge University Press, 1991), 177–92. On the logic of actual maps, including their construction and interpretation, see the compendious recent treatment by Alan M. MacEachren, *How Maps Work: Representation, Visualization, and Design* (New York: The Guilford Press, 2004).

3. Joseph J. Corn, *The Winged Gospel: America's Romance with Aviation, 1900–1950* (New York: Oxford University Press, 1983), 60–61.

4. Anne Morrow Lindbergh, *North to the Orient*, with maps by Charles A. Lindbergh (New York: Harcourt, Brace, and Company, 1935).

5. Alan K. Henrikson, "America's Changing Place in the World: From 'Periphery' to 'Centre'?" in *Centre and Periphery: Spatial Variation in Politics*, ed. Jean Gottmann (Beverly Hills, CA: SAGE Publications, 1980), 83–86.

6. Richard Edes Harrison, *Look at the World: The FORTUNE Atlas for World Strategy* (New York: Alfred A. Knopf, 1944), 8–9. See also Harrison's article, "The War in Maps," *The Saturday Review of Literature* 26, 30 (August 7, 1943): 24–27.

7. For a comprehensive examination of this subject, see Alan K. Henrikson, "The Map as an 'Idea': The Role of Cartographic Imagery During the Second World War," *The American Cartographer* 2, 1 (April 1975): 19–53.

8. Henrikson, "The Map as an 'Idea'": 24.

9. David Reynolds has pointed out, in a comparative survey of the major powers' wartime rhetoric, that "world war" or "*Weltkrieg*" was most characteristic of American and of German thinking, though this was so for historically and situationally quite different reasons. David Reynolds, "The Origins of the Two 'World Wars': Historical Discourse and International Politics," *Journal of Contemporary History* 38, 1 (2003): 29–44.

10. *Roosevelt's Foreign Policy, 1933–1941*, 559–65.

11. Neil Smith, *American Empire: Roosevelt's Geographer and the Prelude to Globalization* (Berkeley: University of California Press, 2004). See also Isaiah Bowman, "Franklin Delano Roosevelt," *The Geographical Review* 35, 3 (July 1945): 349–51.

12. William Bullitt to FDR, February 22, 1939, PSF: France: Bullitt, Franklin D. Roosevelt Library (FDRL), Hyde Park, New York.

13. The globe was manufactured by the Weber Costello Company of Chicago Heights under the direct supervision of the Office of Strategic Services and the War Department. It was prepared by a specially organized section (headed by Arch C. Gerlach) of the O.S.S.'s Map Division. Prime Minister Churchill, whose own war maps facility inspired the Map Room in the

White House, was also given one of the globes. Copies were placed in the House and Senate Chambers of the Capitol. The publicizing of the President's globe surely stimulated the design, manufacture, and sale of smaller globes and ingenious globe substitutes, including R. Buckminster Fuller's geometric, foldable "Dymaxion" globe. See Henrikson, "The Map as an 'Idea'": 26–27, 49 (note 28).

14. Francis L. Loewenheim, Harold D. Langley, and Manfred Jonas, *Roosevelt and Churchill: Their Secret Wartime Correspondence* (New York: Saturday Review Press/E. P. Dutton, 1975), 139n.

15. C.L. Sulzberger, *A Long Row of Candles: Memoirs and Diaries [1934–1954]* (Toronto: The Macmillan Company, 1969), entry for July 27, 1951: "Bill said one of the great difficulties was that Roosevelt was very ignorant of the geography of Eastern Europe. He did not even seem to know where the Balkans were. He did talk vaguely of the Ljubljana Gap, but didn't know what it was. Churchill always wanted to mount an offensive through the Ljubljana Gap. As a compromise, it was finally agreed this should come after the Italian campaign was over" (664).

16. F.D.R. to Archibald MacLeish, Hyde Park, November 22, 1940, in *F.D.R.: His Personal Letters, 1928–1945*, ed. Elliott Roosevelt (New York: Duell, Sloan and Pearce, 1950), II, 1082. David C. Mearns, Superintendent of the Reading Room of the Library of Congress, replied to FDR's inquiry with a "Progress report," attached to MacLeish's reply to the President, an excerpt from which is:

> To hunt for an island named Cherable,
> Is a job that is almost unbearable;
> Pray accept our apologies,
> But nonsense anthologies
> Are giving us hemorrhages cerebral.

(Archibald MacLeish to F.D.R. at the White House, December 3, 1940, in *F.D.R.: His Personal Letters, 1928–1945*, II, 1082–83).

17. Forrest Davis and Ernest K. Lindley, *How War Came: An American White Paper; From the Fall of France to Pearl Harbor* (New York: Simon and Schuster, 1942), 272.

18. Sumner Welles, *Seven Decisions That Shaped History* (New York: Harper and Brothers, 1951), 66.

19. Henry Wallace, "The Man We Remember," *New Republic* 116, 15 (April 14, 1947): 14–15.

20. Gaddis Smith, "Roosevelt, the Sea, and International Security," in *The Atlantic Charter*, ed. Douglas Brinkley and David R. Facey-Crowther (New York: St. Martin's Press, 1994), 34.

21. Vice Admiral Ross T. McIntire, in collaboration with George Creel, *White House Physician* (New York: G. P. Putnam's Sons, 1946), 4. Admiral McIntire also notes of FDR: "His idea of a rest was a change of activity, a switch from one eager interest to another," 7–8.

22. Joseph P. Lash, *Eleanor and Franklin: The Story of Their Relationship Based on Eleanor Roosevelt's Private Papers* (New York: W. W. Norton, 1971); Doris Kearns Goodwin, *No Ordinary Time: Franklin and Eleanor Roosevelt: The Home Front in World War II* (New York: Simon and Schuster, 1994).

23. McIntire, *White House Physician*, 21, 199, 201–2, 235–6.

24. Alan K. Henrikson, "Distance and Foreign Policy: A Political Geography Approach," *International Political Science Review/Revue internationale de science politique* 23, 4 (October 2002): 439–68.

25. Quoted in Smith, "Roosevelt, the Sea, and International Security," 35.

26. It had been illegal for him under the Selective Service Act, which had been renewed by the bare majority of 203 to 202 in the House of Representatives in August 1941, to deploy American conscripts outside the "Western Hemisphere." Roosevelt cartographically redefined this to allow him to place U.S. troops in Iceland, in order to replace British troops sent there to preclude a German takeover of the Danish-controlled country after Denmark was overrun by Germany in 1940. On Roosevelt's creeping hemispherism, see Henrikson, "The Map as an 'Idea' ": 28–31.

27. Samuel I. Rosenman, *Working with Roosevelt* (New York: Harper and Brothers, 1952), 330.

28. Many were using the National Geographic Society's new "world map," fortuitously issued by the Society to its 1,165,000 member families with the December 1941 *Magazine*. The map showed the earth in two hemispheres drawn on azimuthal equal-area projections; thus it did not really show "one gigantic battlefield." Nonetheless, the Society was pleased with the national service it had rendered. Gilbert Grosvenor, "Maps for Victory: National Geographic Society's Maps Used in War on Land, Sea, and in the Air," *The National Geographic Society Magazine* 81, 5 (May 1942): 660–90.

29. Samuel I. Rosenman, comp., *The Public Papers and Addresses of Franklin D. Roosevelt*, Vol. 1942 (New York: Harper and Brothers, 1950), 105–17. Roosevelt's point about keeping the enemy at a distance was driven home, even while he was speaking, by a Japanese submarine that surfaced off Santa Barbara and fired some shells at a ranch. This taught him and his staff never to have his speeches announced more than two or three days ahead of time, which perhaps limited the effectiveness of some of his future messages. James MacGregor Burns, *Roosevelt: The Soldier of Freedom* (New York: Harcourt, Brace, Jovanovich, 1970), 213; Robert E. Sherwood, *Roosevelt and Hopkins: An Intimate History*, rev. ed. (New York: The Universal Library, 1950), 504.

30. Stuart Murray and James McCabe, *Norman Rockwell's Four Freedoms: Images That Inspire a Nation* (Stockbridge, MA: Berkshire House Publishers, 1993).

31. From page 18 of the "FIFTH DRAFT" of FDR's message, reproduced on the back cover of the Roosevelt Library publication, *Freedom from Fear*, and also in Murray and McCabe, *Norman Rockwell's Four Freedoms*, 4.

32. There was some criticism of the fact that there was no counterpart point in the Atlantic Charter for Roosevelt's second "freedom," the "freedom of

every person to worship God in his own way everywhere in the world." This failure to specify a religious freedom, as the journalists Davis and Lindley note, led conservative isolationist skeptics to suppose that the President "had omitted it 'out of consideration for the new ally, Joe Stalin.'" They add, however: "In submitting the charter to Congress, the President disposed of that quibble." Davis and Lindley, *How War Came*, 270n.

33. The text of the Atlantic Charter, on which the Declaration by United Nations is based, may be found in *Roosevelt's Foreign Policy, 1933–1941*, 450–51. Regarding the tension between the Soviet government's formal subscription to the Charter's principles and actual Soviet territorial interests, see Herbert Feis, *Churchill, Roosevelt, Stalin: The War They Waged and the Peace They Sought* (Princeton, NJ: Princeton University Press, 1957), 22–28.

34. Wendell L. Willkie, *One World* (New York: Simon and Schuster, 1943), 203. Inside the front cover of the book is a global map in light blue, "Flight of *The Gulliver*," with "Side trips," showing the vast, globe-circling route that Willkie followed. "I had traveled a total of 31,000 miles, which—looked at as a figure—still impresses and almost bewilders me. For the net impression of my trip was not one of distance from other peoples, but of closeness to them. If I had ever had any doubts that the world has become small and completely interdependent, this trip would have dispelled them altogether" (p. 1).

35. Consider what this might have meant, for example, for the prosecution of the current "War on Terror," for international cooperation against airplane hijacking, and so on, as well as in the conduct of UN peace operations, and also as an overall confidence-building measure in regions of the world where there are still balance of power uncertainties and security threats.

36. Henry A. Wallace to Franklin D. Roosevelt, February 5, 1943, in *The Price of Vision: The Diary of Henry A. Wallace, 1942–1946*, ed. John Morton Blum (Boston: Houghton Mifflin Company, 1973), 182.

37. James A. Farley, *Jim Farley's Story: The Roosevelt Years* (New York: Whittlesey House, McGraw-Hill Book Company, 1948), 293–4. See also John C. Culver and John Hyde, *American Dreamer: A Life of Henry A. Wallace* (New York: W. W. Norton and Company, 2000), 209–10, 217–18.

38. Henry Wallace, "Freedom of the Air—a Momentous Issue," *The New York Times*, June 27, 1943.

39. Ruth B. Russell, assisted by Jeannette E. Muther, *A History of the United Nations Charter: The Role of the United States 1940–1945* (Washington, DC: The Brookings Institution, 1958), 470–72.

40. A noteworthy revival of the idea—to activate Article 43 of Chapter VII of the Charter—was the advocacy of it by the U.S. Permanent Representative to the United Nations at the time of the 1991 Gulf War, Ambassador Thomas R. Pickering, speaking personally rather than in an official capacity. For a discussion of the idea, see Alan K. Henrikson, "The United Nations and Regional Organizations: 'King Links' of a 'Global Chain,'" *Duke Journal of Comparative and International Law* 7, 1 (1996): 35–70, especially 63–70.

41. Robert A. Divine, *Second Chance: The Triumph of Internationalism in America During World War II* (New York: Atheneum, 1967), 49–50.

42. Quoted in Benjamin Welles, *Sumner Welles: FDR's Global Srategist* (New York: St. Martin's Press, 1997), 330.

43. Sumner Welles, *Seven Decisions That Shaped History* (New York: Harper and Brothers, 1951), 172. Prime Minister Churchill, Welles correctly emphasized, preferred starting by "building up purely regional organizations which could collaborate if need arose, but which should remain autonomous for an indefinite time, or at least until it was clear whether a supreme international authority could be successfully set up over them."

44. Franklin D. Roosevelt, "Freedom of the Air," in *The Impact of Air Power: National Security and World Policy*, ed. Eugene M. Emme (Princeton, NJ: D. Van Nostrand Company, 1959), 81–83. The Russians opted for "closed air." Foreign planes would be allowed to transport goods to the Soviet Union only indirectly, by carrying them to agreed interchange points outside the U.S.S.R., such as Cairo, where the cargo would be picked up and carried onward by Soviet planes.

45. United Nations, Department of Public Information, *Yearbook of the United Nations, 1946–47* (Lake Success, NY: United Nations, 1947), 251.

46. It is worth noting here that the driving force behind the Open Skies proposal was a former Roosevelt assistant, Nelson A. Rockefeller, who was brought into the Eisenhower White House as a special assistant for psychological warfare. In that capacity and as a member of the Operations Coordinating Board, Rockefeller with a team of experts meeting in Quantico, Virginia, generated the mutual aerial inspection plan—outside the regular bureaucracy, in a manner that FDR might have tolerated and even encouraged! Cary Reich, *The Life of Nelson A. Rockefeller: Worlds to Conquer, 1908–1958* (New York: Doubleday, 1996), chapter 34, "Open Skies."

47. Quoted in W.W. Rostow, *Concept and Controversy: Sixty Years of Taking Ideas to Market* (Austin: University of Texas Press, 2003), 139. Rostow, a Massachusetts Institute of Technology professor, was the chairman of Rockefeller's Quantico panel.

48. *'We the Peoples': The Role of the United Nations in the 21st Century* (New York: United Nations, 2000).

49. Secretary-General's Statement to the General Assembly, April 3, 2000, www.un.org/millennium/sg/report/state.htm. Accessed November 10, 2007.

50. Kofi A. Annan, "Secretary-General Salutes International Workshop on Human Security in Mongolia," Two-Day Session in Ulaanbaatar, May 8–10, 2000, Press Release SG/SM/7382.

51. *'We the Peoples'*, 19.

52. Ibid., 45.

53. Report of the Secretary-General, *In larger freedom: towards development, security and human rights for all*, United Nations General Assembly, March 21, 2005, A/59/2005.

CHAPTER 3

FDR AND THE ORIGINS OF THE NATIONAL SECURITY ESTABLISHMENT

MARK A. STOLER[1]

FRANKLIN D. ROOSEVELT'S LEGACY IN MILITARY AFFAIRS would appear to be obvious: under his leadership the United States during World War II created, almost from scratch, the largest and most powerful war machine the world had ever seen. In late 1939 the U.S. Army had numbered approximately 175,000 enlisted men and had ranked 19th in the world in size.[2] By 1945 total U.S. armed forces consisted of more than 12 million personnel deployed around the world and totally triumphant over their Axis enemies. These forces included the largest army in U.S. history (nearly 8.3 million), the largest navy in world history (nearly 3.4 million plus 475,000 marines), and an air force of unsurpassed size and in sole possession of the atomic bomb.[3] They also included some of the most successful and famous military commanders of the twentieth century, one of whom—Dwight D. Eisenhower—would himself be elected president a scant seven years after Roosevelt's death.

Despite their awesome size and power, these forces do not constitute Franklin D. Roosevelt's legacy for the postwar era in military affairs. Indeed, they were largely demobilized after Axis surrender, and by mid-1948 stood at less than one and a half million.[4] What was not demobilized were a series of ad hoc wartime institutional innovations and arrangements that would be formalized in the immediate postwar years within a new National Security Establishment. Along with that National Security Establishment came the virtual replacement of foreign and military policies with the concept of national security policy, as well as an enormous expansion of executive power in this realm. These constitute Roosevelt's true legacies in military affairs for the postwar era.

The most important of these institutional innovations and arrangements focused on the service chiefs of staff, whose power and influence increased enormously during the war. Soon after Pearl Harbor they were reorganized as the Joint Chiefs of Staff (JCS), the predecessor to the contemporary body that still bears that name. Along with this organization came a plethora of joint service committees to advise the chiefs, and a massive expansion of the War and Navy Departments—so massive as to require the creation of, and wartime movement into, a new and enormous building in Arlington, Virginia—the Pentagon—whose name has become virtually synonymous with American military power. The war also witnessed expanded military contact and coordination with the State Department and with numerous wartime agencies responsible for the awesome economic mobilization that would supply America's allies as well as its own forces and produce two-third of all Allied war material;[5] and the creation of a national intelligence service, the Office of Strategic Services (OSS), which was the predecessor of the postwar and contemporary Central Intelligence Agency (CIA).

All of this clearly resulted from the requirements of global war from 1941 to 1945. But the inception of such new institutional arrangements preceded formal U.S. entry into the war and was also the result of two additional factors: the so-called managerial revolution in warfare that had been underway for decades and that reached an apogee during World War II; and the ideas and activism of Franklin D. Roosevelt in his role as commander in chief. The fact that a president notorious for his chaotic institutional arrangements and decision-making processes would be at least partially responsible for such a legacy may rank as one of the great ironies of American history.

*   *   *

The late nineteenth and early twentieth centuries witnessed dramatic changes in the organization, as well as the size and weaponry, of the world's armed forces. In what Walter Millis aptly labeled "the managerial revolution" in warfare, the industrialized powers began to apply the principles of large-scale corporate organization and expertise to their armies and navies. Although the United States lagged far behind its European counterparts in this development, by World War I it did possess, albeit in skeleton form, the key components associated with this managerial revolution: army and navy general staffs headed by uniformed service chiefs of staff, and a Joint Army–Navy Board composed of those chiefs and their key strategists.[6]

One of the principle goals of these organizations was rational, long-term planning for the armed forces so that they would be prepared for any contingency. Control over both field forces and existing service bureaucracies was a necessary prerequisite for such planning and preparedness, and throughout the early decades of the twentieth century the service chiefs and their staffs fought a series of bitter battles to obtain such control. The process was well under way before Roosevelt's election as president, but it was far from complete. It would be completed under FDR.[7]

With this rise of the service chiefs and their staffs came requests for greater civil–military coordination in both foreign and military policies and a role for the military in what would become known after World War II as national security policy. Such requests flowed logically from both the nature of their work and significant changes in U.S. foreign policy during these years. The managerial revolution in the armed forces coincided with the rise of the United States as a world power with extensive overseas possessions and interests. The army and navy staffs viewed the protection and promotion of these possessions and interests via appropriate contingency war planning as one of their primary functions. Such planning required clear understanding of the objectives and priorities of the government policies they were supposed to defend and promote, as well as an appropriate matching of military means with political ends. Consequently the service chiefs and their staffs consistently requested both policy guidance from and consultation with the State Department regarding the formulation, prioritization, and implementation of U.S. foreign policies.

The secretaries of state and their subordinates just as consistently ignored or rejected these requests on the grounds that they constituted a challenge to civilian prerogatives in the policymaking process, and thus to civilian supremacy over armed forces—forces whose leaders should be consulted only after diplomacy had failed and war ensued. As Secretary of State William Jennings Bryan stated in 1913, "Army and Navy officers could not be trusted to say what we should or should not do till we actually get into war." Bryan's successors modified this policy and agreed to consult with the armed forces on the arms limitation treaties of the 1920s and early 1930s, but they often ignored the military advice they received. The service chiefs fared no better when they attempted to bypass the State Department by going directly to the White House for policy guidance and coordination. Indeed, President Woodrow Wilson was so angered by their efforts to influence his policies in 1913 that he suspended the Joint Board and threatened to abolish it as well as the Navy's General Board. While far less belligerent, his Republican successors also showed little interest in consultation with the armed forces.[8]

This situation changed during the mid- and late 1930s under the impact of both world events and Roosevelt's leadership. The emerging European and Far Eastern crises finally led the State Department to agree to limited coordination, first with Far Eastern expert Stanley Hornbeck in 1935 and then in 1938 with the formation of a Standing Liaison Committee composed of Under Secretary of State Sumner Welles and the army and navy chiefs of staff. At the same time, Roosevelt responded to the appeals of the armed forces by agreeing to direct consultation—without any State Department intermediaries.

Roosevelt entered the White House in 1933 with a keen interest in and knowledge of military affairs that dated to his service in World War I as assistant secretary of the Navy. By this point he had become known as one of the leading exponents of the expansive naval doctrines of Alfred Thayer Mahan, and interestingly, greater civil–military coordination. In 1919 Roosevelt submitted one of the first formal proposals that called for better cooperation between high level officials of the State Department and those of the War and Navy Departments—a proposal never acted upon, or apparently even opened within the State Department.[9] Although initially preoccupied with the Great Depression and the New Deal, Roosevelt from 1936 onward provided the armed forces with unprecedented direction, guidance, and coordination. He began by supporting increased powers for the army and navy chiefs within their respective services so as to give them control over their field forces as well as their staffs. In 1937 he examined existing war plans, requested the creation of new ones, and initiated secret naval staff conversations with the British. By 1938 he was requesting congressional authorization and funding for extensive expansion of the U.S. armed forces. And in 1939, before the outbreak of war in Europe, he carefully and personally selected both a new chief of naval operations and a new army chief of staff: Admiral Harold R. Stark and General George C. Marshall.

Roosevelt also provided these new service chiefs with a direct link to him in 1939 by transferring the Joint Army–Navy Board on which they served from the existing Navy and War Departments to the newly created Executive Offices of the President. This shift enabled the board to become a true national strategy body for the first time and, in bypassing the service secretaries, made its members the president's foremost and immediate strategic advisers. It also made FDR himself, as former Roosevelt Library Director William Emerson accurately pointed out many years ago, the "sole coordinating link" between U.S. military strategies and foreign policies.[10]

These consequences were far from accidental or coincidental. Roosevelt had originally appointed his secretaries of War, Navy, and State primarily for domestic political reasons and had little faith in their opinions. Secretary of State Cordell Hull was useful for maintaining good relations with Congress, where he had previously served for many years as a Tennessee congressman and senator; but FDR held both him and his department in low esteem, regularly disagreed with or just plain ignored their conclusions, and was determined to be his own secretary of state. He was also determined to be a very strong and active commander in chief of the armed forces.[11] Furthermore, by 1939–1940 he was having serious policy disagreements with his cautious if not isolationist secretary of war, Harry H. Woodring, and Secretary of the Navy Charles Edison.

In June of 1940, Roosevelt replaced Woodring and Edison with Henry L. Stimson and Frank Knox, but this shift only reinforced his urge to bypass the service secretaries as much as possible. Stimson and Knox were highly respected, and the former possessed enormous experience as a former secretary of war under President William Howard Taft and secretary of state under Roosevelt's predecessor Herbert Hoover. Both were Republicans, however (Knox had been the Republican vice presidential nominee in 1936), albeit internationalist Republicans whom Roosevelt had appointed primarily to prevent military preparedness and aid to England from becoming partisan issues, and whom he neither could nor would trust with his innermost thoughts. While they dealt with Congress and the public, he would deal directly with his chief admiral and general, Stark and Marshall.

During the ensuing rearmament campaign of 1940–1941, Roosevelt established very close and direct working relationships with both chiefs. He came to rely upon them and their staffs for war plans, strategic and rearmament advice, legislative initiatives for the armed forces, and getting those initiatives through Congress. So successful were Marshall and Stark in this latter responsibility that members of Congress often voted for requests that they would have voted against if those requests had come from Roosevelt, thereby making continued close relations with them mandatory.[12] Indeed, by mid-1940 the president could provide Britain with military equipment only if one or both of the service chiefs certified that such equipment was not essential for national defense. Neither the sending of aircraft, guns, and ammunition to Great Britain, nor the famous Destroyer–Bases Deal of 1940, would have been possible without such close relations and agreement.[13]

This relationship grew even closer after Pearl Harbor and official U.S. entry into the war. At the same time, the powers of the service chiefs expanded enormously. The reasons were simple. As Roosevelt himself stated, "Doctor Win-the-War" had replaced "Dr. New Deal," and the new "physicians" would by definition wear military uniforms and receive priority over their civilian colleagues. The head doctors would be chiefs of staff rather than field commanders not only because of the powers those chiefs had recently obtained, but also because World War II was a global conflict requiring U.S. planning for, as well as participation in, multiple theaters: only chiefs of staff stationed in Washington could properly plan for and coordinate such an effort. Furthermore, unlike theater commanders such as General Douglas

MacArthur, these chiefs of staff had no personal political ambitions and therefore did not constitute a potential threat to Roosevelt's leadership (as a matter of principle, Marshall did not even vote in U.S. elections; and when asked about his "political faith" he would respond that "my father was a democrat, my mother a republican, and I am an Episcopalian").[14] The chiefs close relations with Congress was further reason to rely heavily upon them, for in positions of power they could keep war-related issues out of the partisan arena and hold congressional interference—something both the president and the chiefs disliked and feared—to a minimum.

Official U.S. entry into the war also expanded the chiefs' scope of interests, especially in regard to political factors. U.S. wartime strategy, for example, was part of a coalition effort that had to take into account the differing strategies and policies of America's numerous allies—especially the British and the Soviets. Furthermore, the global and total nature of the war led to an unprecedented fusion of military and political issues, making continued separation impossible. As General Marshall stated, "Any move in a global war has military implications."[15]

Highly illustrative of the expanded political interests and power of the chiefs, and indeed reinforcing that expansion and power, was the transformation of the Joint Army–Navy Board into the Joint Chiefs of Staff in early 1942 via the addition of army air forces chief, Lieutenant General Henry H. Arnold and commander in chief of the U.S. Fleet, Admiral Ernest J. King. This new structure paralleled to an extent the British Chiefs of Staff Committee (COS) that fell within the newly formed Anglo–American Combined Chiefs of Staff (CCS)—an extraordinary body created and charged at the December–January ARCADIA Conference with all strategic planning for both nations and responsible only to Roosevelt and British Prime Minister Winston S. Churchill.[16] Soon thereafter Admiral Stark departed to command U.S. naval forces in Europe and King assumed the title of CNO while retaining his previous title of commander in chief of the U.S. Fleet, thereby completing the unification of naval staff and field forces under a single chief that the army had previously accomplished and that was now reinforced via a major reorganization of the War Department.

Undertaken at Marshall's direction via an executive order from Roosevelt, this reorganization resulted in the most dramatic changes within the War Department since the reforms of Elihu Root forty years earlier had first created the general staff. The reforms included a reduction in the number of individuals with direct access to the chief of staff from sixty-one to six; the creation of three new "super commands" (Army Ground Forces, Army Air Forces, and Services of Supply); and the replacement of the old General Headquarters and War Plans Division with a new Operations Division that would plan global strategy, staff the interservice and Anglo–American committees that served the JCS and CCS, and serve as Marshall's "Washington Command Post."[17]

In July 1942, Roosevelt, upon Marshall's constant urging, finally agreed to appoint his former chief of naval operations and recent ambassador to Vichy France Admiral William D. Leahy to the Joint Chiefs in the new position of chief of staff to the commander in chief. This position was parallel to that of Lieutenant General Sir Hastings Ismay on the British Chiefs of Staff Committee and would evolve after the war into the contemporary position of Chairman of the Joint Chiefs of Staff. That Marshall had recommended the admiral for this important post was far from accidental. Leahy and Roosevelt had known and worked with each other extensively in the past. Equally important, interservice politics required another naval officer on the JCS to replace Stark and balance the presence of Arnold, who technically remained Marshall's subordinate as head of the Army Air Forces.[18]

During and immediately after the ARCADIA Conference, a host of joint Army–Navy and combined Anglo–American committees were also formed and staffed by appropriate officers from each service and nation to advise the chiefs on a host of matters ranging from war plans and logistics to intelligence and postwar planning. In the aftermath of their bitter defeats at the hands of the British regarding European strategy in 1942 and at the January 1943 Casablanca Conference, the U.S. joint committees also underwent a major expansion and reorganization in the spring of 1943.

The Joint Chiefs of Staff, along with many of the officers on these committees, would accompany Roosevelt on every one of his numerous wartime conferences with Churchill as well as the less frequent but equally important conferences with Soviet leader Josef Stalin and Chinese leader Chiang Kai-shek. At these conferences the chiefs would meet directly with their British counterparts as the Combined Chiefs of Staff and with these political leaders. At all other times during the war they would meet weekly in Washington with representatives of the COS from the Washington-based British Joint Staff Mission headed by former chief of the imperial general staff, Field Marshal Sir John Dill, who became a close personal friend of General Marshall and whose presence in Washington played a major role in the effective functioning of the entire CCS organization. According to Leahy, the JCS dealt with 1,457 separate subjects during the war, the CCS with 902.[19]

A great deal of mythology surrounds the relationship between Roosevelt and these chiefs of staff. According to that mythology, the president and his foremost military advisers worked very well together from the start, at least partially because the chiefs eschewed political judgments and provided only "purely military" advice that FDR then accepted without question because of the primacy of military victory during the war. Consequently, an advisory vacuum on political issues emerged, with the chiefs refusing to make political assessments and the president, relying so much upon them and distrusting the State Department, refusing to seek it elsewhere. The result was a series of U.S. blunders regarding postwar issues, and a massive, unnecessary increase in Soviet power by war's end. The president's chaotic decision-making style, including his refusal to institutionalize channels and delegate authority, only made matters worse.[20]

The historical reality of the relationship between Roosevelt and his military chiefs does not support such Cold War era conclusions. The relationship developed very gradually. In this respect, FDR's decision-making process was neither chaotic nor apolitical. Rather, the president created a very personal and informal process in which he consistently demanded military opinions but felt free to overrule those opinions on political, and on military, grounds, something he did on numerous occasions. Moreover, the advice FDR received from the chiefs was itself often quite political and not "purely military" by any means.

Even at its best, however, it was a relationship marked by profound differences in methods and temperaments as well as ideas. Accustomed to working with very specific plans and within a rigid and detailed chain of command, the chiefs were often unnerved, disappointed, and frustrated by the president's refusal to be tied to such plans as well as his informal methods and style. Highly illustrative of that informality was Roosevelt's reply when the formidable Admiral King reminded him in a 1942 note that he was reaching the mandatory retirement age of 64. "So what, old top?" Roosevelt wrote at the bottom of the note. "I may send you a birthday present!" (He did—a framed photograph).[21]

Throughout the war the chiefs fought against such informality. Marshall in particular would not bend for fear of losing his independence and integrity, insisting that he be addressed by last name (at least in public) and refusing all invitations to "drop in" to the White House "for a chat," to visit the president at Warm Springs or his home in Hyde Park (he did not make such a trip until Eleanor Roosevelt asked him to direct FDR's funeral and burial in April of 1945). Indeed, he even refused to laugh at FDR's jokes.[22]

Marshall had an advantage over his naval colleagues Stark and King in this regard in that Roosevelt, as a former assistant secretary of the navy, felt much closer to and more knowledgeable of that service, and therefore much freer to badger its chiefs and intervene in its affairs—on matters ranging all the way from officer selection to fleet movements. While Marshall humorously asked the president to stop referring to the navy as "us" and the army as "they,"[23] FDR's different behavior toward the services provided each chief with different problems. For Stark and King, FDR was often overbearing and controlling; for Marshall he was insufficiently attentive and understanding.

The extent to which each service and its chief suffered or gained as a result of this presidential bias is, of course, a matter of interpretation. The naval chiefs had easier and more frequent access to the White House, for example, but also more frequent presidential pressure and interference in their affairs. According to navy rumors, Roosevelt had to threaten Stark with relief before obtaining the CNO's agonized acquiescence in the 1940 destroyer-bases trade that most naval officers opposed.[24] And a few months later the president did relieve Admiral James O. Richardson as commander in chief of the U.S. Fleet for his vehement and apparently intemperate objections to moving the fleet from its California base to Pearl Harbor. Throughout 1941, FDR also ordered specific ships moved from one ocean to the other, and his constant shifts required the creation of four different hemispheric defense plans for the Atlantic within four months. Stark spent a great deal of time that year, according to one of his planners, "knocking down the harebrained schemes of the President in regard to the Navy," some of which Stark himself bluntly labeled "childish." And when his successor Admiral King attempted a reorganization and centralization of authority over the bureau chiefs within the Navy Department similar to the War Department reorganization of early 1942, Roosevelt refused to agree. While Marshall faced little or no such interference in army affairs, Roosevelt in 1939–1941 flatly rejected many of the army chief's pleas and plans for an expanded and balanced army, and even considered a late 1941 reduction in its size. Until Pearl Harbor, Roosevelt apparently remained convinced that he could limit the U.S. role in the war to naval and air forces as well as military supplies to the Allies. Marshall and his planners disagreed totally, resulting in a series of tense confrontations between the president and his army chief.[25]

Waldo Heinrichs has effectively shown that there was actually a very conscious method and policy to many of these presidential moves, which were based upon the very limited military forces available in 1941; the numerous and constantly shifting diplomatic, political, and military pressures in the Atlantic, Pacific, and at home; and a fundamental shift at this time from a hemispheric to a global policy.[26] That is not the way it appeared to the frustrated service chiefs, however, who viewed presidential behavior as provocative, erratic, unfocused, and dangerous as well as contrary to their recommendations.

The chiefs attempted on numerous occasions to create more formality and structure in their relationship with the president, pressing for a wartime JCS charter, for regular meetings with FDR that included formal note-taking, and for a chairman to represent them in the White House. Most of these efforts were unsuccessful. Roosevelt rejected the idea of a wartime charter as "too restrictive," preferring the Joint Chiefs to exist solely at his personal discretion.[27] He also rejected regularly scheduled meetings, felt free to see the chiefs individually as well as in a group and as frequently or infrequently as he desired, and objected to formal note-taking during their meetings. Indeed, on one occasion he "blew up" when Major General John R. Deane, the JCS secretary, brought a "big notebook" to one of their meetings. "Put that thing up," he ordered. Deane complied but at the next meeting tried a smaller notebook that the president would not notice; unfortunately it was "so little," Marshall later recollected, "that he couldn't use it."[28]

Roosevelt did eventually agree to appoint Admiral Leahy as a de facto chairman of the JCS, with his own office in the White House and almost daily meetings with the president. But he may very well have done so primarily to halt calls by his critics for the appointment of MacArthur to head a unified army–navy–air general staff and, in effect, run the war. Furthermore, FDR would not allow Leahy to function as a true military adviser, JCS chair and representative of the chiefs, relegating him instead, as he told the press in July of 1942, to the role of his "leg man." And that meant "leg man" for the president *in* the White House, and *from* the White House *to* the JCS— virtually the opposite of what the chiefs had desired. As Leahy himself put it, "The Joint Chiefs of Staff was an instrument of the Commander in Chief and was responsible to him. I was his representative on that body."[29]

Roosevelt clearly stated his primary reason for this very limited definition of responsibilities when Marshall first raised the idea of a JCS chairman and explained that individual's theoretical functions. "But you are the chief of staff," the president said. "There is no chief of staff of all the military services," Marshall responded. "Well," FDR shot back, "I'm the chief of staff. I'm the commander in chief."[30] He expressed similar sentiment in objecting to King's title as commander in chief of the U.S. Fleet, arguing that there was only one commander in chief. Clearly, Roosevelt intended to jealously guard and use extensively his military prerogatives. Just as clearly he intended to remain the "sole coordinating link" between U.S. military strategies and foreign policies that William Emerson accurately noted he had become in 1939 when he moved the Joint Board into the Executive Offices of the President.[31]

Roosevelt exercised these functions whenever he overruled his chiefs of staff during their numerous disagreements, disagreements that ranged from rearmament legislation and the size and composition of the armed forces through aid to the allies and global strategy. Army chief historian Kent Roberts Greenfield counted 22 occasions between late 1938 and 1944 in which FDR overruled his military advisers. He also noted an additional 13 strategic decisions that Roosevelt, rather than those advisers, initiated from 1941 to 1943.[32] Roosevelt did admit to Marshall, who quickly emerged as "first among equals" and the real leader of and spokesman for the JCS, that he could not sleep at night with the army chief out of the country.[33]

But that comment was not made until December of 1943. Furthermore, to say one could not sleep at night with the general out of the country is not to say that one is ready to follow everything that officer recommends. And Roosevelt clearly did not do so.

The chiefs could and did on numerous occasion influence or alter Roosevelt's views, and they would do so more frequently as the war progressed, both by direct and by indirect methods. The direct methods included not only written and oral recommendations, but also a willingness to openly disagree with the president to his face. Roosevelt, to his great credit, accepted such disagreement, at least from his service chiefs and when respectfully presented.[34] Indeed, FDR appointed Marshall as army chief of staff only five months after the latter had in late 1938 openly disagreed with him at a White House meeting, replying to FDR, "Mr. President, I'm sorry, but I don't agree with that at all." When called to the White House in April of 1939 to be informed of his selection over thirty-three senior general officers, Marshall told the president that he "wanted the right to say what I think and it would often be unpleasing." Roosevelt responded affirmatively. "You said *yes* pleasantly," Marshall warned, "but it may be unpleasant." On numerous occasions it was. Similarly, the crusty King had a wartime reputation for being able to "raise holy hell with FDR."[35]

The most notable and effective indirect method was the frequent use of presidential adviser and confidante Harry Hopkins as an informal intermediary. In that role he was of invaluable assistance to the chiefs on numerous occasions. But Hopkins' ultimate loyalty was of course to Roosevelt, a fact that clearly emerged during some of the serious disagreements between the chiefs and the president. "Hopkins and I had an unspoken understanding," Marshall later admitted in regard to one such case—China policy: "He was representing the president's interest and I was not in agreement with it." That held true for other issues as well. This was vividly illustrated, as will be shown, in the 1942 debate over cross-Channel versus North African operations.[36]

Leahy's loyalty was also to FDR. Indeed, the official JCS minutes reveal the admiral often acting as a "watchdog" for presidential prerogatives in the linkage of strategy with policy, even balking at the inclusion of the term "grand strategy" within a JCS committee charter and pointedly asking his colleagues exactly what the term meant. He also objected to any JCS concern with postwar political issues, and consistently took exception to JCS committee reports that he believed dealt with "purely political" matters.[37] Admittedly, this might have been the result of a personal belief in a strict division between military and political affairs. More likely it reflected Leahy's recognition of the fact that Roosevelt jealously guarded his prerogatives in the policy realm and expected the admiral to do the same.

Many if not most of Roosevelt's conflicts with the chiefs were due to their different military *and* political perspectives. Roosevelt was, of course, more attuned to domestic and international political realities, while the chiefs were more attuned to military realities. Roosevelt was also willing to act on the basis of intuitive "hunches," whereas his hardheaded chiefs had been trained to see the world as it appeared on the basis of hard facts. And throughout the war the president's political impulses and intuition as well as his military judgments usually emerged triumphant, as they should have via both the Clausewitzian doctrine that war is an instrument of policy and the American tradition of civilian supremacy.

In 1940, for example, Roosevelt pressed material aid to Britain onto an army and navy that doubted London's ability to survive the German onslaught and that insisted their own forces had to be expanded and supplied first in this crisis. As one of Marshall's staff officers pointedly warned in June, "if we were required to mobilize after having released guns necessary for this mobilization and were found to be short in artillery materiel...everyone who was a party to the deal might hope to be found hanging from a lamp post." Consequently Marshall and Stark recommended what David Reynolds has aptly described as "a virtual ban on further arms sales to Britain"[38]—a recommendation the president flatly rejected. A similar conflict emerged over the wisdom of moving the fleet to Pearl Harbor in 1940, with the vehement and intemperately stated objections of Admiral James O. Richardson, leading to his relief as commander in chief of the U.S. Fleet, and in 1941 over aid to the Soviet Union—a nation British and American expert military opinion insisted would not survive two months against the German *Wehrmacht*.

Then in 1942, FDR with Hopkins' connivance forced the Joint Chiefs to agree to an invasion of North Africa that they loathed instead of cross-Channel operations that they clearly preferred, primarily for political reasons: British refusal to cross the Channel in 1942 made the North African operation necessary to maintain the alliance, mollify the Soviets who had been "promised" a 1942 operation and thereby keep them in the war, mollify public opinion that was demanding offensive action, and refocus that opinion on the European theater and away from its Pacific preoccupation. When the CCS during the June 1942 summit conference in Washington asserted a preference for no action over North Africa that year, they were directly overruled by Roosevelt and Churchill, who insisted that offensive action in the European theater was mandatory in 1942. And when Marshall and King in the following month suggested turning to the Pacific instead of North Africa, Roosevelt angrily rejected the idea as a bluff, a "red herring," the equivalent of "taking up your dishes and going away," and "exactly what Germany hoped the United States would do following Pearl Harbor."

Instead he ordered the army and navy chiefs to go to London with Hopkins and reach agreement on North Africa. He also reminded them that the defeat of Germany first was basic Anglo–American strategy and that such defeat "means the defeat of Japan, probably without firing a shot or losing a life." And for emphasis he signed his orders "Commander-in-Chief."[39]

According to Marshall, FDR also suggested that the historical record on the matter "should be altered so that it would not appear in later years that we had proposed what amounted to abandonment of the British." Thankfully the Joint Chiefs did not do so. But they did bow to his wishes, with Hopkins torpedoing one final late-July effort in London to postpone final decision on cross-Channel versus North African operations until mid-September. The Joint Chiefs well understood the political nature of these decisions, noting in their official minutes that the president and "our political system would require major operations this year in Africa." Marshall was even blunter after the war, telling his biographer Forrest C. Pogue that "the leader in a democracy has to keep the people entertained. That may sound like the wrong word, but it conveys the thought," he added. "People demand action."[40]

As these quotes illustrate, the Joint Chiefs were well aware of the political aspects of strategy making, and their strategic assessments and recommendations to the president usually included consideration of political factors and were by no means "purely military" in nature. Indeed, one dual biographer of Roosevelt and Marshall has astutely noted that their highly successful wartime partnership partially rested on an ironic paradox whereby Roosevelt the great politician became one of the strongest and most active military commanders in chief while Marshall, the supposedly quintessential "nonpolitical" soldier, became one of the nation's most effective politicians.[41] "Nothing could be more mistaken," Dean Acheson later wrote in this regard, "than to believe that General Marshall's mind was a military mind in the sense that it was dominated by military considerations.... When he thought about military problems, nonmilitary factors played a controlling part."[42] The same was true for other members of the JCS. That neither their British counterparts on the CCS nor others with whom they dealt perceived this was a conscious JCS policy. As Marshall later told biographer Pogue,

> I doubt there was any one thing, except the shortage of LSTs, that came to our minds more frequently than the political factors. But we were very careful, exceedingly careful, never to discuss them with the British, and from that they took the count that we didn't observe those things at all. But we observed them constantly, with great frequency and particular solicitude.... We didn't discuss it with them [the British] because we were not in any way putting our neck out as to political factors, which were the business of the head of state—the President—who happened also to be the Commander-in-Chief.[43]

Such reticence did not usually extend, however, to the State Department or the president. The chiefs and their planners consulted with State Department officials as well as FDR throughout the war, had State Department personnel assigned to individual theater commanders, and placed high-level representatives on the department's important Advisory Committee on Postwar Foreign Policy. Simultaneously the secretaries of state, war, and navy met as a special committee, and in late 1944 a State–War–Navy Coordinating Committee composed of uniformed officers as well as high-level civilians in all three departments began to function. The comments made by the uniformed officers on these committees, and by the Joint Chiefs themselves to both Roosevelt and the State Department, reveal substantial political sophistication by individuals who supposedly thought in "purely military" terms.

In late 1940 and early 1941, for example, Stark, Marshall and their key planners proposed a "Europe first" strategy based on the fact that British survival and the European balance of power were crucial to American security. To insure that survival and balance of power, they argued, the United States would have to become an active belligerent in the European war, and it should therefore relegate the Pacific to secondary consideration and avoid immediate conflict with Japan at all costs. Implicit within these conclusions, and partially motivating their enunciation at this time, was a recommendation that the president reverse what the armed forces considered a provocative and dangerous State Department policy vis-à-vis Japan.[44]

In 1942 and 1943, the chiefs and their planners asserted that the Anglo–American strategic conflict over cross-Channel versus Mediterranean operations was only part of a broader and global strategic conflict between the two nations, one based upon their very different national policies and postwar interests that they explicitly identified. Protection of U.S. interests, they further argued, required not only cross-Channel operations but also a higher priority for the Pacific at the expense of the Mediterranean.[45]

And from late 1943 through early 1945, the Joint Chiefs and their senior military advisers argued that close collaboration with the Soviet Union both during and after the war had to be a fundamental U.S. policy objective. Without close wartime collaboration, they warned, Germany could not be defeated and U.S. casualties would reach enormous and unacceptably high levels. Furthermore, such collaboration had to continue into the postwar era because once the Axis Powers had been beaten, Moscow would possess "assured military dominance" in Central and Eastern Europe, the Middle East, and northeast Asia. This dominance, they warned, "could not be successfully challenged eastward of the Rhine and the Adriatic." This massive expansion of Russian power, which the chiefs and their senior military advisers bluntly labeled "phenomenal" and "epochal," coincided with a precipitous decline in British power that heralded a shift in the world balance of power unparalleled since the fall of Rome.[46]

In short, the chiefs were predicting the rise of two postwar superpowers and insisting that conflict between the two had to be avoided. They did not naively ignore the possibility of future conflict; they merely warned against it. Indeed, they simultaneously prepared in their postwar plans for just such a contingency by insisting that postwar security be based upon national forces rather than an international police force, and by pressing for the acquisition of a worldwide system of air and naval bases as well as a central intelligence agency. This time, they insisted, there would be no complete postwar demobilization: sufficient forces and bases would have to be maintained to provide security suitable for a global superpower, with suitability defined in global terms and potential enemies including a possibly hostile Soviet Union a s well as a resurgent Germany or Japan.[47]

The extent to which Roosevelt agreed or disagreed with such politico—military assessments by his military chiefs varied with both the issues and the period. The chiefs' 1940–1941 recommendations regarding the Europefirst strategy and Japan made perfect sense in light of political and military realities as perceived by the chiefs and their planners, but it ignored the possible negative reaction of America's Far Eastern allies as well as the problems with American public opinion that Roosevelt would face if he tried to pursue a highly aggressive policy in Europe in conjunction with what amounted to appeasement of Japan. Consequently, although he fully accepted the Europe-first strategy and the logic behind it, he rejected the change in policy toward Japan that the chiefs considered mandatory to achieve success in their strategy as well as their late 1941 call for at least a temporary agreement with Tokyo to postpone if not avoid war.[48] Similarly, and as previously noted, FDR rejected the chiefs' Pacific proposals in 1942 as counterproductive to both the alliance and the war effort.[49] In 1943, however, with more American resources and power at his command vis-à-vis the British as well as the Axis, he accepted JCS arguments, resulting in both cross-Channel operations in 1944 and a higher priority for the Pacific campaigns. As for JCS 1943–1945 policy recommendations regarding the Soviets, they mirrored Roosevelt's policy exactly, leaving open the question as to who had influenced whom. Most likely the president and his military chiefs simply agreed, and in a symbiotic relationship reinforced each other—until April of 1945, when Roosevelt's death, the post-Yalta breakdown in Soviet–American relations, and the looming final defeat of Germany led to increasing calls within the armed forces as well as the administration for a policy shift. That shift began with an April 1945 alteration in previous JCS policy regarding the Soviets.[50]

* * *

Two additional and related aspects of Roosevelt's record in regard to American military power deserve brief analysis here: intelligence and Anglo–American military relations. As previously mentioned, the Joint Chiefs of Staff had been formed in early 1942 so as to parallel the British Chiefs of Staff Committee within the Combined Chiefs of Staff that would run the unprecedented Anglo–American global war effort. Intelligence gathering would be a key component of that war effort. So would Anglo–American sharing of such intelligence.

Roosevelt took a strong interest in both. As David Stafford has aptly noted, FDR and Churchill were both "Men of Secrets" who were deeply interested in wartime intelligence gathering.[51] Furthermore, such intelligence gathering expanded enormously during World War II. In the United States it centered not only in the intelligence divisions of the army and navy staffs, but also in the Office of the Coordinator for Information, William J. Donovan, which evolved during the war into the Office of Strategic Services (OSS). Personally selected by FDR, Donovan maintained throughout the war a very close relationship with the president and created within the OSS an enormous bureaucracy that involved not only extensive intelligence gathering, but also "black" operations, academic research and analysis, and liaison with and training of anti-Axis resistance movements.

Intelligence-gathering expanded not only quantitatively and bureaucratically, but also technologically during World War II. Particularly noteworthy in this regard was the development of Signals Intelligence (SIGINT), whereby critical military information was sent via encryption over radio waves and often intercepted and deciphered. While the successful American breaking of the Japanese codes became publicly known soon after the war, other extensive and very high-level signals intelligence remained the last and best-kept secret of the war until the mid-1970s. Particularly noteworthy in this regard was the British "Ultra Secret," the deciphering at Bletchley Park of the highest level German military intelligence from the so-called Enigma enciphering machine.[52]

Intelligence ties between the United States and Great Britain were first established informally in 1941 and then formally in early 1942 via the formation of a Combined Anglo–American Intelligence Committee under the CCS. Despite intense competition and suspicion between the two nations in the intelligence realm, those ties grew stronger as the war progressed. By June of 1942 American code breakers had joined the British at Bletchley

Park, and in late 1942/early 1943 the two nations agreed, in the so-called BRUSA accord, to a sharing of intelligence results and personnel, which was unprecedented in modern history. "Never before," Bradley F. Smith aptly concluded "had two countries agreed to share the most profound secrets they possessed about their enemies. Even more significant, no governments previously had obligated themselves to carry out an exchange of personnel within such sensitive and secret operations." So sensitive and extensive were these wartime exchanges, Smith maintains, that they virtually guaranteed a continuation of the alliance into the postwar era, since any break would compromise the security of both countries.[53]

Weapons development was another important aspect of the war effort in which extensive Anglo–American sharing took place. It was also one in which Roosevelt took a strong interest. Most notable in this regard was the sharing he proposed to Churchill as early as October of 1941 regarding development of an atomic bomb. This proposal would eventually lead to a series of secret Churchill–Roosevelt wartime agreements for full collaboration in atomic research and a postwar Anglo–American monopoly on any weapon that might result from that research. However, Churchill had to prod Roosevelt in 1943 to fulfill his commitments in regard to sharing research results. And unlike the BRUSA intelligence-sharing accord, which remains in effect as of this writing, these nuclear agreements did not survive the war itself. Indeed, the United States in effect abrogated them via both presidential and congressional action in 1945–1946.[54]

*　*　*

What then, was the Roosevelt legacy in military affairs?

On the positive side the United States under FDR created one of the greatest war machines in history, an enormous force that played a pivotal role in the total defeat of the Axis Powers in World War II and that made the United States a global military superpower. That force was largely created and led by outstanding chiefs of staff whom Roosevelt personally selected, granted greatly expanded powers, and organized into a body directly responsible to him. During the war they and he worked together in some of the closest and most effective civil–military relations in U.S. history, relations in which Roosevelt personally and consistently maintained control and thereby preserved one of the oldest and most important traditions in American civil–military relations. FDR was also responsible for an enormous qualitative as well as quantitative expansion of American intelligence gathering and scientific research geared to warfare, and for the establishment of exceptionally close ties with Great Britain in these realms as well as in the area of global military planning.

On the negative side, however, Roosevelt maintained control over the U.S. armed forces in what many labeled a haphazard, chaotic, and seriously defective manner. He also seriously diminished the power of the civilian service secretaries and the secretary of state over those armed forces, while simultaneously increasing his own executive power and that of the armed forces and their chiefs enormously—and dangerously. Equally dangerous, some critics maintain, was the huge intelligence apparatus he oversaw but did not sufficiently control.

What all of this would mean for postwar America emerged soon after Roosevelt's April 1945 death and the end of the war itself five months later. That end led to the rapid demobilization of the massive war machine that had been created during the war. It did not lead to the demise of the Joint Chiefs of Staff organization, however, or many of the other informal institutions that had sprung up to coordinate the American war effort. To the contrary, many of those institutions were formalized only a few years later when Congress, in the National Security Act of 1947 and its 1949 amendment, created the basics of the National Security Establishment we still live with today. Included within that establishment was a fully chartered Joint Chiefs of Staff with a chairman and representatives from a now independent air force as well as the army and the navy, a nascent Department of Defense to replace the old War and Navy Departments, and a Central Intelligence Agency to replace the wartime OSS. To insure full coordination in the formulation and execution of national security policy, the act also established a series of joint military schools; special boards for munitions, resources, and research/development; a War Council consisting of the JCS and the military secretaries; a National Securities Board to keep the president informed on the coordination of civilian and military mobilization; and a National Security Council (NSC) to which the CIA was to report directly. The predecessor to the body that still bears its original name, the NSC was to consist of the president, the secretary of state, the secretary of defense, the three service secretaries, the chairman of the National Securities Board, and others the president might wish to appoint.

The full history of the National Security Act of 1947 and its amendments is extraordinarily complex. It involved numerous and often savage political conflicts, both military and civilian, whose details are not appropriate subjects for this chapter. What is important to note is the paradoxical impact of Roosevelt's legacy on the 1947 act. On one hand, in its establishment of formal institutional structures, the act was partially motivated by a desire to avoid a repetition of what was generally perceived to have been Roosevelt's overly personal, informal, and inadequate processes. It ironically did so, however, by formalizing and expanding many of the ad hoc institutional arrangements that Roosevelt had created during the war years at the very moment that the massive armed forces of those years were being largely demobilized. Most important in this regard was the fact that the powerful Joint Chiefs of Staff organization created during the war years was formalized and made a central feature of the postwar defense establishment.

That National Security Establishment also expanded and institutionalized the wartime intelligence service that Roosevelt had established with the OSS and the wartime structures for economic mobilization that had played so important a role in Allied victory. And within the very concept of national security policy as defined in the years immediately following the end of World War II, it also institutionalized a view of the world and a response to threats that echoed in many ways the views and policies of the Roosevelt Administration from 1940 to 1945.

Most notable in this regard was the belief that a hegemonic European power, be it Germany or Russia, constituted a potential threat to American security that could not be tolerated. Along with that conclusion went a belief that the threat should be met in Europe rather than in the Western Hemisphere, and that the United States should therefore continue to remain deeply involved with European allies, particularly, but far from exclusively, Great Britain, in international affairs and organizations. By 1947 this "forward" strategy had been defined in terms of the "containment" of the Soviet Union.

Interestingly, the strategy was at first largely economic via the Economic Recovery Plan—and in that sense similar to Roosevelt's 1940–1941 strategy of Lend-Lease aid to Britain. Also interesting is the fact that it was first publicly proposed by none other than wartime army chief of staff George C. Marshall, now serving as secretary of state. By 1950–1951, however, containment had become largely military, as had Roosevelt's policy after Pearl Harbor. The 1947 act and 1949 amendment provided the institutional framework within which to make it so and to rebuild the American World War II arsenal and forces, at the same time the United States agreed to join the states of Western Europe in a formal peacetime military alliance—the North Atlantic Treaty Organization.

Actually the U.S. World War II arsenal and forces had never been totally dismantled. As the wartime JCS had insisted, U.S. military forces were not fully demobilized after German and Japanese surrender. At their low point in 1948, they admittedly had been decreased from over 12 million in 1945 to fewer than one and a half million personnel. But that latter number nevertheless constituted by far the largest peacetime force in U.S. history—and more than four times the size of the force that had existed in 1939. The United States also stood in sole possession of the atomic bomb and had an industrial base unscathed by wartime attack, unsurpassed in size and power, and fully capable of another wartime conversion. Furthermore, the 1947 act provided the structure for that conversion and, along with the 1948 reinstitution of the draft, for the massive expansion of the U.S. armed forces whenever such an expansion was considered necessary—something that occurred only a few years later. Indeed, that expansion originated in an early 1950 National Security Council Paper, NSC 68, calling for a major U.S. rearmament effort and a national security policy based upon a militarized and global containment policy in response to the communist triumph in the Chinese civil war and Soviet acquisition of an atomic bomb.

The Truman Administration illustrated soon thereafter the enormous war powers now housed in the White House when it committed the United States to a war in Korea without any congressional declaration of war. Interestingly, it made use of the same tool the Roosevelt Administration had used in 1940 for the first time in U.S. history—a peacetime draft—to create the force necessary to fight that war. Equally interesting is the fact that the individual most responsible for the creation of that force was once again George Marshall, this time as the new secretary of defense rather than army chief of staff or secretary of state. But it would be largely up to Marshall's wartime protégé and Truman's successor as president, Dwight D. Eisenhower, to make full use of the National Security Council and National Security Establishment that had been created in the war's aftermath. That he did so indirectly, in what Fred Greenstein aptly labeled, the "hidden-hand presidency," would probably have appealed to an FDR famous for indirection.[55]

As previously noted, much of this postwar National Security Establishment can be considered a reaction to one of the negative aspects of the Roosevelt legacy—his informality and apparently chaotic, haphazard decision-making style. All his informal institutional arrangements of the war years were now, in the postwar era, formalized and given legal charters—something FDR had studiously avoided. Also formalized was a special new body to coordinate foreign, economic, and military policies into a global national security policy. No longer would such coordination be blocked by a state department jealous of its prerogatives. Nor would it ever again depend solely upon the whims of one man in the White House.

Yet that man had ironically provided in nascent form many of the key components for this institutional revolution and for postwar U.S. security policy itself. In seeking to avoid any repetition of Roosevelt's behavior, his successors had ironically been forced to formalize and expand what he had begun. The National Security Establishment thus stands simultaneously as a reaction to Roosevelt, as his institutional replacement, and as his legacy. Whether its postwar record has been superior to his wartime record in terms of positive versus negative consequences is an interesting question to ponder. The answer is by no means clear. As Eric Larrabee noted, the post-Roosevelt years "witnessed catastrophic failures of coordination between politics and the military that his years in office did not. Perhaps there was more method to his maneuverings than appeared."[56]

In this regard, it is interesting to note that Roosevelt during World War II opposed the creation not only of a true JCS chairman, but also the unified army–navy–air staff that many called for during the war—be it under MacArthur or under anyone else. Each of the Joint Chiefs remained a service chief as well as a member of this interservice body, representing the interests of his branch rather than the armed forces as a whole. While critics have consistently bewailed the inefficiency of and inherent conflicts within such a system, it effectively created checks and balances within the armed forces high command that matched the checks and balances within the U.S. government. As a result, it may well have precluded the assumption of even more power by the armed forces in the postwar years and a fundamental threat to civilian control of the military.

It is also interesting to note how the post-World War II Joint Chiefs behaved when such a threat did emerge in 1951, with MacArthur's challenge to President Truman's limited war policy in Korea. Those chiefs backed the president rather than the general. So did Marshall as secretary of defense. Despite the enormous growth in the power of the service chiefs during Roosevelt's presidency, they remained properly subordinate to civil authority.

NOTES

1. Portions of this paper were originally published as "U.S. Civil–Military Relations in World War II" in *Parameters* 21, 3, the U.S. Army War College Quarterly (Autumn, 1991): 60–72. See also my *Allies and Adversaries: The Joint Chiefs of Staff, the Grand Alliance, and U.S. Strategy in World War II* (Chapel Hill: University of North Carolina Press, 2000).

2. House Appropriations Committee, *Emergency Supplemental Appropriations Bill for 1940, Hearings on H.R. 7805*, 76th Cong., 3rd sess., Nov 29, 1939, 21. Army officers added another 14,486 to this figure, with navy and marine forces numbering 125,202 and 19,432, respectively, for a grand total of 334,473. *The Statistical History of the United States: from Colonial Times to the Present* (commercial edition of Bureau of the Census, *Historical Statistics of the United States, Colonial Times to the Present*) (New York: Basic Books 1976), 1141.

3. Ibid., 1141. The actual figures for 1945 were 8,267,958 in the army, 3,380,817 in the navy, and 474,680 in the marine corps, for a total of 12,123,455. More than 16 million Americans actually served during the war.

4. Ibid., 1141.

5. During World War II American industry produced a staggering 297,000 aircraft; 193,000 artillery pieces; 86,000 tanks; 2.4 million army trucks and

Jeeps; 1,200 combat vessels and 8,800 total naval vessels; 87,000 landing craft; 3,300 merchant ships and tankers; and 14 million shoulder weapons. The percentage of U.S. Gross National Product devoted to defense and the war effort rose from 2 in 1939 to 42 in 1945, with military spending increasing 8,000 percent. Richard Overy, *Why the Allies Won* (New York, 1995), 192; Allan R. Millett and Peter Maslowski, *For the Common Defense: A Military History of the United States of America* (New York, 1984), 430–33; Allan R. Millett, "The United States Armed Forces in the Second World War," in *Military Effectiveness*, ed. Allan R. Millett and Williamson Murray (Routledge: Boston, 1988), Vol. 3: 47–52.

6. Walter Millis, *Arms and Men: A Study of American Military History* (New York: G.P. Putnam's Sons, 1956), 131–210. See also James L. Abrahamson, *America Arms for a New Century: The Making of a Great Military Power* (New York: Free Press, 1981), 105–27; Louis Morton, "Interservice Co-operation and Political–Military Collaboration, 1900–1938," in *Total War and Cold War: Problems in Civilian Control of the Military*, ed. Harry L. Coles (Columbus: Ohio State University Press, 1962), 133–8; Louis Morton, "War Plan ORANGE: Evolution of a Strategy," *World Politics* 11 (January, 1959): 221–5; Ray S. Cline, *Washington Command Post: The Operations Division* (Washington, DC: U.S. Government Printing Office, 1951), 44–45; and Mark S. Watson, *Chief of Staff: Prewar Plans and Preparations* (Washington, DC: U.S. Government Printing Office, 1950), 57–84. These latter two works are volumes within the massive 79-volume *United States Army in World War II* series.

   The army obtained a general staff and chief of staff in 1903; the navy in 1915. Their powers were originally quite limited, and not until the 1930s and early 1940s did the chiefs obtain full operational control over their forces. The original Joint Army–Navy Board was also created in 1903 and similarly possessed very limited powers. It was essentially an advisory body composed of U.S. Army general staff officers and members of the Navy's general board, a group of retired naval officers established in 1900 to provide advice on broad matters of strategy and policy.

7. The most famous, or infamous, of these battles took place in 1912. It pitted Army Chief of Staff General Leonard Wood and Secretary of War Henry L. Stimson against Adjutant General Frederick Ainsworth and resulted in the latter's forced retirement under threat of court-martial for insubordination. But Ainsworth's numerous friends in Congress obtained their revenge by legislation that blocked virtually all of Wood's ensuing proposals for general staff expansion and Army reform.

8. See *Allies and Adversaries*, 1–3 and 273–4, notes 7 and 8.

9. William L. Neumann, "Franklin Delano Roosevelt: A Disciple of Admiral Mahan," *United States Naval Institute Proceedings* 78 (July 1952): 713–14; Morton, "Interservice Co-operation and Political–Military Collaboration," 142–3; Ernest R. May, "The Development of Political–Military Consultation in the United States," *Political Science Quarterly* 70 (June 1955): 167–8; Frank Freidel, *Franklin D. Roosevelt: The Ordeal* (Boston: Little Brown, 1954), 19–20.

10. William R. Emerson, "Franklin D. Roosevelt as Commander-in-Chief in World War II," *Military Affairs* 22 (Winter 1958–1959): 183–5. See also Lester H. Brune, *The Origins of American National Security Policy: Sea Power, Air Power and Foreign Policy* (Manhattan, KS: MA/AH Publishing, 1981), 106–10.

11. For Roosevelt as activist Commander-in-Chief, see Emerson, "Franklin D. Roosevelt as Commander-in-Chief," 181–207, and his "F.D.R." in *The Ultimate Decision: The President as Commander in Chief,* ed. Ernest R. May (New York: George Brzilier, 1960), 133–77; Kent Roberts Greenfield, *American Strategy in World War II: A Reconsideration* (Baltimore: Johns Hopkins University Press, 1963), 49–84; and Eric Larrabee, *Commander in Chief: Franklin Delano Roosevelt, His Lieutenants, and Their War* (New York: Harper & Row, 1987), 1–39.

12. Larry I. Bland, ed. *The Papers of George Catlett Marshall, 2: "We Cannot Delay," July 1, 1939–December 6, 1941* (Baltimore: Johns Hopkins University Press, 1986), 214.

13. In the Destroyer Bases Deal, Stark asserted that the acquisition of British hemispheric bases in exchange for overage destroyers constituted a net strategic gain for the United States. See page 71.

14. Ibid, 2: 616.

15. Cline, *Washington Command Post*, 319.

16. The COS consisted of the service chief of an independent Air Force as well as the Army and Navy chiefs, plus a fourth member who served as liaison between the three chiefs and Churchill. The U.S. Air Force was still part of the Army and not independent, but Arnold as its commander was nevertheless appointed to the JCS at this time so as to parallel the British organization within the CCS. As explained directly below, Stark would soon depart and a liaison to Roosevelt paralleling the COS liaison to Churchill would be added in July.

17. Forrest C. Pogue, *George C. Marshall, 2: Ordeal and Hope* (New York: Viking, 1966), 289–96; and Larrabee, *Commander in Chief* , 142–3. See also Cline, *Washington Command Post*. Interestingly, Roosevelt did not allow Admiral King to complete a similar reorganization and centralization of power within the Navy Department. See Thomas B. Buell, *Master of Sea Power: A Biography of Fleet Admiral Ernest J. King* (Boston: Little, Brown, 1980), 235–9; and Larrabee, *Commander-in-Chief,* 171, 194–5.

18. Larry I. Bland, ed., *George C. Marshall Interviews and Reminiscences for Forrest C. Pogue* (Lexington, VA: George C. Marshall Research Foundation, 1991), 431–3, 623–4.

19. Alex Danchev, *Very Special Relationship: Field-Marshal Sir John Dill and the Anglo–American Alliance, 1941–1944* (London: Brassey's, 1986); William D. Leahy, *I Was There: The Personal Story of the Chief of Staff to Presidents Roosevelt and Truman Based on His Notes and Diaries Made at the Time* (New York: Whittlesey House, 1950), 103.

20. See, for example, Hanson W. Baldwin, *Great Mistakes of the War* (New York: Harper and Brothers, 1948); and Samuel P. Huntington, *The Soldier and the*

State: The Theory and Practice and Civil–Military Relationships (New York: Vintage, 1957), 315–44.

21. Ernest J. King and Walter M. Whitehill, *Fleet Admiral King: A Naval Record* (New York: W. W. Norton, 1952), 412–13; Buell, *Master of Sea Power*, 187, 222–3.

22. Bland, *Marshall Interviews*, 108–9, 418, 620; Forrest C. Pogue, *George C. Marshall, 1: Education of a General, 1880–1939* (New York: Viking, 1963), 324.

23. Bland, *Marshall Interviews*, 610–11; Pogue, *Marshall*, vol. 2, 22.

24. J. Garry Clifford, "Bureaucratic Politics," in *Explaining the History of American Foreign Relations,* ed. Michael J. Hogan and Thomas G. Paterson, second ed. (Cambridge: Cambridge University Press, 2004), 100.

25. George C. Dyer, *The Amphibians Came to Conquer: The Story of Admiral Richmond Kelly Turner* (Washington, DC: U.S. Government Printing Office, 1969), vol. 1, 173; Bland, *Marshall Papers*, vol. 2, 391–2, 416–18, 430–32, 613–14 ; Stoler, *Allies and Adversaries*, 44–45, 56–57; Buell, *Master of Sea Power*, 235–44; Larrabee, *Commander-in-Chief*, 171, 194–5; Pogue, *Marshall*, vol. 2, 29–32, 74–79; Mark A. Stoler, *George C. Marshall: Soldier-Statesman of the American Century* (Boston: Twayne, 1989), 69–75, 82–84.

26. Waldo H. Heinrichs, *Threshold of War: Franklin D. Roosevelt and American Entry into World War II* (New York: Oxford University Press, 1988), 107–8.

27. Roosevelt letter, July 16, 1943, in JCS 415, CCS 300 (1–25-42), sec. 2, Record Group (RG) 218, National Archives and Records Service, College Park, MD (NARA).

28. Forrest C. Pogue, "The Wartime Chiefs of Staff and the President," in *Soldiers and Statesmen: Proceedings of the 4th Military History Symposium,* ed. Monte D. Wright and Lawrence J. Paszek (Washington, DC: Office of Air Force History, Headquarters USAF and Air Force Academy, 1989), 73; Bland, *Marshall Interviews,* 623.

29. Ibid., 431–2; Press Conference #836, July 21, 1942, in *Complete Presidential Press Conferences of Franklin D. Roosevelt* (New York: Da Capo, 1972), vol. 20, 14–19; Leahy, *I Was There*, 102. Interestingly, FDR in this press conference referred to Leahy as Chief of Staff *of* the Commander in Chief who would do legwork for the president, and he asserted that the admiral was definitely *not* being appointed chief of staff of the army and navy. On MacArthur, see Richard W. Steele, *The First Offensive, 1942: Roosevelt, Marshall, and the Making of American Strategy* (Bloomington: Indiana University Press, 1973), 90; and Larrabee, *Commander-in-Chief*, 20.

30. Bland, *Marshall Interviews*, 431.

31. See page 66 and note 10 above.

32. Greenfield, *American Strategy in World War II*, 80–84. See also Emerson, "Roosevelt as Commander in Chief," 181–207.

33. Robert Sherwood, *Roosevelt and Hopkins: An Intimate History*, rev. ed. (New York: Grossett and Dunlap, 1950), 803.

34. But not when presented the way Admiral Richardson apparently did in the fall of 1940.

35. Bland, *Marshall Interviews*, 108–9; Pogue, *Marshall*, vol. 1, 330; John Gunther, *Roosevelt in Retrospect: A Profile in History* (New York: Harper & Brothers, 1950), 45, quoted approvingly in King and Whitehill, *Fleet Admiral King*, 413, n. 24.

36. Bland, *Marshall Interviews*, 418, 433–4, 604. On the cross-Channel versus North Africa debate, see page 75 and notes 39 and 40 below.

37. See, for example, Leahy's comments at the JCS 65th, 69th, 72nd and 79th mtgs., March 9, 23, April 2, and May 10, 1943, CCS 334 JCS (3–2943) (mtgs. 71–86), RG 218, NARA.

38. Watson, *Chief of Staff*, 312; David Reynolds, *From Munich to Pearl Harbor: America and the Origins of the Second World War* (Chicago: Ivan R. Dee, 2001), 81.

39. Stoler, *Allies and Adversaries*, 79–90. Quotes are on 85–88 and come from FDR handwritten messages, July 12, 1942, Map Room File, Box 7-A, Folder 2, Franklin D. Roosevelt Library, Hyde Park, NY; Henry L. Stimson Diary, July 15, 1942, Sterling Library, Yale University, New Haven, CT; and FDR memo reproduced in Sherwood, *Roosevelt and Hopkins*, 602–5.

40. Memos, Marshall to King, July 15, 1942, and Wedemeyer to Handy, July 14, 1942, OPD Exec. 5, Item 1, Tab 10, Record Group 165, NARA, quoted in Bland, *Marshall Papers*, vol. 3, 275–6; Marshall to Pogue quote in Bland, *Marshall Interviews*, 622.

41. Thomas Parrish, *Roosevelt and Marshall: Partners in Politics and War* (New York: William Morrow, 1989).

42. Dean G. Acheson, *Sketches from Life of Men I Have Known* (New York: Harper and Brothers, 1959), 163–4.

43. Bland, *Marshall Interviews*, 415; Pogue, *George C. Marshall, 3: Organizer of Victory, 1943–1945* (New York: Viking, 1973), 315.

44. See Mark M. Lowenthal, "The Stark Memorandum and American National Security Process, 1940," in *Changing Interpretations and New Sources in Naval History: Papers From the Third United States Naval Academy History Symposium*, ed. Robert William Love, Jr. (New York: Garland, 1980), 352–9; Mark M. Lowenthal, *Leadership and Indecision: American War Planning and Policy Process, 1937–1942* (New York: Garland, 1988), vol. 1, 408–14; and Stoler, *Allies and Adversaries*, 29–34. See also Louis Morton, "Germany First: The Basic Concept of Allied Strategy in World War II," in *Command Decisions,* ed. Kent Roberts Greenfield (Washington, DC: U.S. Government Printing Office, 1960), 11–47. The key documents are reproduced in Steven T. Ross, *American War Plans, 1919–1945* (New York: Garland, 1992), vol. 3, 225–300.

45. Stoler, *Allies and Adversaries*, 109–19.

46. Ibid., 123–30 and 171–5. The key documents are JCS 838/1, "Disposition of Italian Overseas Territories," May 6, 1944, ABC 092 Italy (April 27, 44), Record Group 165, NARA; and JCS 973/1, "Fundamental Factors in Relation to Discussions concerning Territorial Trusteeships and Settlements," August 4, 1944, CCS 092 (7-27-44), Record Group 218, NARA. These documents are partially reproduced in 3 volumes within the U.S. Department of State series, *Foreign Relations of the United States*

(Washington, DC: U.S. Government Printing Office), 1944, vol. 1 (1966), 699–703; *The Conferences at Malta and Yalta, 1945* (1955), 107–8; and *The Conference of Berlin, 1945,* vol. 1 (1960), 264–6.

47. The key documents are in the JCS 570 series, "U.S. Requirements for Post-War Air Bases," beginning November 6, 1943, in CCS 360 (12–9-42), Sec. 2, Record Group 218, NARA. These and related documents are analyzed in James F. Schnabel, *History of the Joint Chiefs of Staff: The Joint Chiefs of Staff and National Policy, Vol. 1, 1945–1947* (Wilmington, DE: Michael Glazier, 1979), 299–346; Stoler, *Allies and Adversaries,* 158–60; Lester J. Foltos, "The New Pacific Barrier: America's Search for Security in the Pacific, 1945–1947," *Diplomatic History,* 13 (Summer 1989): 317–42; Melvyn P. Leffler, "The American Conception of National Security and the Beginnings of the Cold War, 1945–1948," *American Historical Review* 89 (April 1984): 364–5 and *A Preponderance of Power: National Security, the Truman Administration, and the Cold War* (Stanford, CA: Stanford University Press, 1992), 55–61; and William Roger Louis, *Imperialism at Bay: The United States and the Decolonization of the British Empire* (New York: Oxford University Press, 1978), 259–61, 271–3. See also Michael S. Sherry, *Preparing for the Next War: American Plans for Postwar Defense, 1941–1945* (New Haven, CT: Yale University Press, 1977); Perry McCoy Smith, *The Air Force Plans for Peace* (Baltimore, MD: Johns Hopkins University Press, 1970); and Vincent Davis, *Postwar Defense Policy and the U.S. Navy, 1943–1946* (Chapel Hill: University of North Carolina Press, 1962).

48. See Stoler, *Allies and Adversaries,* 35–37, 58–63.

49. Ibid., 20–21.

50. See Stoler, *Allies and Adversaries,* 120, 189–90, 230–39, and *The Politics of the Second Front: American Military Planning and Diplomacy in Coalition Warfare, 1941–1943* (Westport, CT: Greenwood Press, 1977), 94–95, 112–15, 137–52; and Diane S. Clemens, "Averell Harriman, John Deane, the Joint Chiefs of Staff, and the 'Reversal of Co-Operation with the Soviet Union in April 1945,'" *International History Review* 14 (May 1992): 277–306.

51. David Stafford, *Roosevelt and Churchill: Men of Secrets* (Woodstock, NY: Overlook Press, 2000).

52. The literature on Ultra and other SIGINT, as well as the OSS and Allied intelligence in general during World War II, is enormous. For an annotated introduction to some of the most important works, see Robert L. Beisner, ed., *American Foreign Relations since 1900: A Guide to the Literature,* 2nd ed. (Santa Barbara, CA: ABC-CLIO, 2003), 999–1007.

53. Bradley F. Smith, *The Ultra-Magic Deals: And the Most Secret Special Relationship* (Novato, CA: Presidio Press), 157. See also F.H. Hinsley, *British Intelligence in the Second World War: Its Influence on Strategy and Operations* (Cambridge University Press: New York, 1979, 1981), vol. 1, 311–14; vol. 2, 41–58.

54. See Warren F. Kimball, *Forged in War: Roosevelt, Churchill, and the Second World War* (New York: William Morrow, 1997), 146–7, 215, 220–21, 279–81; and Robin Edmonds, *Setting the Mould: The United States and Britain, 1945–1950* (New York: Norton, 1986), 78–87.

55. Fred I. Greenstein, *The Hidden-Hand Presidency: Eisenhower as Leader* (New York: Basic Books, 1982).

56. Larrabee, *Commander-in-Chief,* 12.

CHAPTER 4

THE SHERIFFS: FDR'S POSTWAR WORLD[1]

WARREN F. KIMBALL[2]

WILLIAM HENRY CHAMBERLAIN, a biting and bitter critic of Franklin
Roosevelt's foreign policies, sarcastically warned in 1940 that "I am
anticipating the day when possession of Tibet and Afghanistan will be
represented as vitally necessary to the security of Kansas and Nebraska."
"Nothing short of eerie," observed one historian.[3] Whatever those eerie
echoes in today's world, FDR would have been appalled by the very concept. His vision of the postwar world order specifically excluded using
military power for political goals, and envisaged a regional approach
that would limit the direct policing and persuading role of the United
States to the Western Hemisphere. Of course, to elaborate a bit on a
commonplace—power corrupts, or is at least an irresistible temptation,
and absolute (or near-absolute) power corrupts accordingly.

FDR's legacies? There are two broad ones, although the subcatego-
ries make it a bit more complex. In reality, all these legacies are interconnected and part of what I have previously lumped under the term, FDR's
Americanism.[4] He was heir to all his nation's traditions. But World War II
created a *tabula rasa* of sorts that allowed Roosevelt to distill the mix of
what he inherited and what he foresaw into a world order or system that has
lasted for sixty years—though not everything came out as FDR intended.[5]
(As an aside: Whether or not the so-called War on Terrorism proclaimed
by President George W. Bush after the 9/11 atrocities is an indicator of a
new world order is a question for future historians. My sense is that the
world Franklin Roosevelt helped, in a major way, to create will outlast the
thugs and ideologues who believe that random killing will allow them to

impose their views. FDR would have certainly condemned the terrorists as persons operating outside of any reasonable and civilized interpretation of law and order—one of the highest priorities of both Roosevelt and the United States).[6]

So what were, and are, FDR's legacies for the world?

First: "Regionalized cooperative internationalism" or globalism, which includes the "scrapping" of so-called isolationism—A.K.A. unilateralism— the designation of the dominant role of the Great Powers (the four or so policemen), the establishment of an international organization *to facilitate Great Power collaboration*, the everlasting American crusade for economic "liberalism," the creation of an atmosphere into which "containment" could comfortably fit, and raising the issue of decolonization—although that fits also in the second great legacy, which is:

Americanism—shorthand for everything besides Roosevelt's geopolitical thinking: the internationalization of the New Deal, FDR's conviction that leadership and persuasion were the means for creating peaceful relationships, and his calm and unshakable belief in the American democratic tradition, combined with the awareness that the results were far from perfect (as Eleanor Roosevelt constantly reminded him).[7]

There are a number of mythical or non-legacies that serve as defining antonyms for Roosevelt's shadow:

- Roosevelt was a believer in and practitioner of *realpolitik*.
- Contradictorily, Roosevelt is guilty of "making Wilsonianism . . . the U.S. diplomatic tradition."[8]
- Roosevelt sought to establish the kind of international organization that emerged at the end of World War II—the United Nations Organization.
- Roosevelt planned for nation- or state-building in postwar Germany and Japan.
- Roosevelt caused the precipitate decolonization of European empires.
- Roosevelt became a "cold warrior" before his death.
- The last entry is the famous quote from British historian A.J.P. Taylor: "Of the great men at the top, Roosevelt was the only one who knew what he was doing: he made the United States the greatest power in the world at virtually no cost."[9]

All these statements are myths, or exaggerations, or distortions. (I do assume that by this time we can safely dismiss, without comment, the silly and historically unsupportable accusations that FDR was an international Socialist, or that his musings about so-called convergence meant that he wanted the United States to become more like Stalin's USSR. Similarly for exaggerated claims that his actions and policies contributed to the Holocaust).[10]

* * *

But before digging into the mind of Franklin Roosevelt, before trying to assess his international legacy in the postwar world, we need a brief reminder of the legacies that helped shape FDR's thinking.

The popular judgment, and FDR's oft-repeated claim, is that his "great crusade" was against "the isolationists." A "second chance" is what historian Robert Divine called the effort—a second chance to do what Woodrow Wilson had tried—a second chance to get America and Americans committed to internationalism. But Roosevelt did not rescue the United States from "isolationism." The very word still begs for clear definition, but FDR had no interest in clarifying the debate. For him it simply described the enemy, the political opposition (for the most part the Republicans), those who opposed his steady steps toward aiding the Allies. Thanks to Hitler and the Nazis, the label was too politically useful, too politically powerful, too much of a political tar baby to throw away by defining it. By 1944, *Life* magazine could proclaim in an editorial that "Isolationism is Dead." FDR reacted strongly, commenting that "anybody who thinks isolationism is dead in this country is crazy. As soon as this war is over, it may be stronger than ever."[11]

But what Roosevelt fought before World War II was not "isolationism," no matter how useful he found that label. The real issue was American complacency, overconfidence, and even indifference regarding Hitler's Germany. Just when FDR started that fight is debatable, but what he had to fight was the persistent American conviction that the United States was always right and that what was "right" was invincible.[12] He had to contend with the popular sentiment that the United States could "go it alone" in the world—something the founding fathers had rejected out of hand 165 years earlier. To the end of his days, FDR feared a resurgence of what he called isolationism, but he could not have foreseen that it would reemerge in its true character—unilateralism.

Of course, America and most Americans had never been isolationist, not in any dictionary meaning of the word. To isolate is to quarantine, to separate completely from outside contacts. Roosevelt's early thinking on international affairs and structure came, according to most historians, from two sources—his cousin, President Theodore Roosevelt, and Woodrow Wilson, who in 1913 became the first Democratic president in sixteen years and was the man who brought FDR onto the national political scene.[13] TR brought "realism" and Great Power politics to bear; Wilson offered, well. . . . Wilsonianism, that idealistic combining of belief in an American style political economy (though Wilson emphasized democracy more than economics) with a mission, a duty to proselytize, all wrapped neatly in a blanket labeled "international cooperation."

The mix of realism and Wilsonianism, both of them *internationalist* concepts, that FDR inherited was itself an inheritance. The founders of the American state and government were far from being isolationists. After all, they lived in a world of empires—political and economic—that linked peoples of differing ethnicity, history, and cultures. To survive in that world of empires required that the fledgling United States of America take a low profile, staying out of squabbles between the powerful empire-nations of Europe. That may have seemed to later generations as an attempt by the United States to isolate, to quarantine itself, to play the role of ostrich with its head in the sand. But the ostrich's ample rump was as visible to its enemies as was the mound of American resources and trade that had made the New World worth the fight. Thomas Paine understood just that when he recommended that the United States stand aloof and let the empire-nations of the world seek it out. Trade and commerce would bring them to America. The mercantilism of that era assumed that empires had to be closed corporations. John Adams and Paine stood mercantilism on its head and argued that the entire world was America's "empire" for commerce.[14] This was not isolationism, but a search for an appropriate combining of political caution (noninvolvement) and greatly expanded global trade. Little wonder that the autarkic economic polices of Hitler and Japan were viewed with deep suspicion and anger by Roosevelt, Hull, and the entire Administration.

No less a personage than Senator J. William Fulbright proposed that Roosevelt's public policies in the two years before American entry into World War II constituted an unfortunate legacy. "FDR's deviousness in a good cause made it much easier for [LBJ] to practice the same kind of deviousness in a bad cause." Perhaps "stealth and deception" did characterize Roosevelt's path to war.[15] But Fulbright's argument mitigates or even excuses Congressional behavior. Given the degree of American aid to Britain and the Soviet Union before the United States entered the war, FDR can be, and is, seen as the president who set the pattern followed during the Cold War and afterward for fighting undeclared wars. Although undeclared wars, perhaps, have been an American "tradition" since the Quasi-War with France in the late 1790s. In the case of both Germany and Japan, Roosevelt's vaunted skills at "educating" the American public were not so great as to be able to convince them, and Congress, that the United States should declare war on Germany in the summer and autumn of 1941, *if* that was his intention. Whatever the tactics Roosevelt used,—from disingenuousness to lies—Congress (and thus the public) had ample opportunities to say "No!" But that is not what happened. Instead, Congress questioned, carped, harped, and waffled, but ultimately concluded that FDR was on the right path. A great myth is that the American people (whatever that means), given information and the opportunity, will not choose war and violence, but rather rational discussion and negotiation, to solve confrontations. History suggests otherwise. The entry of the United States into World War II, however halting and accompanied by Roosevelt's deceptions and disingenuousness, came about because the American people—speaking through their representatives in the assembled Congress—agreed to and accepted (few ever desire) war. If lies were told, Congress had the power to question and dig into the truth. Responsibility for foreign policy lies not solely in the West Wing.[16]

In any event, the hands-down favorite for Roosevelt's most significant legacy is what one historian referred to as the "scrapping" of unilateralism—mistakenly called isolationism—in favor of embedding "conflicting unilateral priorities within a cooperative multilateral framework." In other words, cooperative globalism or, more simply, working with other nations to achieve peaceful resolution of significant clashes of national interest.[17] It was, of course, a great deal more complicated than that.

The place to start with any analysis of FDR's thinking is where he started—with the assumption that great (world) wars are generated by great (world) powers. Everything else proceeded from that premise. The grand myth held by twentieth-century American warriors has been that a peaceful world would be the happy and legitimizing outcome of a vast military conflict. Roosevelt was no exception. He dreamily mused about worldwide disarmament, once blithely stating that "the smaller powers might have rifles but nothing more dangerous." The Great Powers were exempted, of course, for he knew they would not disarm. But he decriminalized that exemption by calling the Great Powers "policemen"—an idea he broached even before the United States entered World War II. He mentioned it to Churchill at their first meeting in August 1941, and a few weeks later casually spoke during a dinner party about the need for Britain and America "to police the entire world."[18] He quickly went on to describe "police procedures": The key was "trust," not the application of "sanctions," that is, force (political, military, or, presumably, economic).

In the spring of 1942, when Soviet Foreign Minister V. M. Molotov visited Washington, Roosevelt seized the opportunity to outline his conception of a postwar "system." FDR offered his notion of three or four policemen (including the USSR) for the postwar world, and elaborated on his belief that other states should be disarmed. Stalin's private reaction, sent to Molotov, was enthusiastic. "Roosevelt's considerations about peace protection after the war are absolutely sound.... Tell Roosevelt... his position will be fully supported by the Soviet Government."[19]

Crucial to any understanding of FDR's postwar vision is his consistent emphasis on the regional role of each of the policemen, which by the time of the Teheran Conference included the Soviet Union and China. Journalist/ reporter Forrest Davis, writing with FDR's approval and assistance about that first Big Three meeting, related how Roosevelt had conducted a "seminar" for Stalin on the Good-Neighbor Policy in the Western Hemisphere. Davis concluded that Roosevelt staked "much on his good-neighbor diplomacy with Moscow."[20] "But how are regional 'policemen' to avoid the Orwellian temptation, even necessity, of creating a sphere of influence in their region? How is such a region different from a Pax Britannica, a Russian Empire, or a Monroe Doctrine? That Roosevelt perceived a difference is clear. It was one of many apparent contradictions that he never clarified."[21]

Yet the concept was not as vague as it appeared. The Good-Neighbor Policy and U.S. relations with Canada both illustrated what FDR had in mind. Leadership—which combined persuasion, power, and especially patience—would prevent local crises from morphing into global confronta-tions. Davis described the president's thinking: "This American association of nations has become a highly effective organization capable of express-ing the hemisphere's united will....Its bonds are loose....The system functions as a continuing peace conference, which mediates before, not after, hostilities."[22] The lecture to Stalin might well have been titled: "How to Run a Region."

But regionalism was not to be exclusive. In spring 1943, a time when Harry Hopkins certainly spoke for FDR, the presidential advisor warned the British against any attempt to establish a European Council (based, of course, in London) for fear it would result in American "isolationists" doing the same thing in the Western Hemisphere. FDR's regional group-ings could not exclude any of the Great Powers lest that set one region (and one policeman) against another.[23] At the start of the war, Roosevelt had viewed European power politics and colonialism as the greatest threats to postwar peace. By 1943, he recognized that the Soviet Union had become a new major player on the scene and could, if it so chose, be an even greater threat to international cooperation. The president had no intention of fighting World War II in order to get ready for the next one, so bring-ing the USSR into a cooperative relationship with the other Great Powers became *the* priority.

By mid-1943, with the Germans halted in North Africa and the tide about to turn on the Russian front, European frontiers and self-determination became a major issue. From the outset, Stalin had been unequivocal about having "friendly" governments around the Soviet periphery in Eastern Europe, and Roosevelt's (and Churchill's) dreams of persuading Stalin to be a coopera-tive participant in the postwar world required that the Soviet leader feel secure, satisfied, and sure of Anglo–American reliability. But since self-determination meant independence for the Balts and the establishment of an anti-Soviet government in Warsaw, how then to avoid the obvious? Both Roosevelt and Churchill had tried to create a good postwar relationship with the Soviet Union even before the Stalingrad victory, in February 1943, demonstrated the likelihood of Red Army occupation of the territory Stalin demanded. What recourse was left to London and Washington? Military confrontation was no option, at least not with Anglo–American forces still struggling in North Africa and fifteen months away from an invasion of Western Europe. More to the point, what long-term hope for peace if the United States and Britain chose to confront the Russians? More frightening and apparently possible, what if playing diplomatic hardball prompted Stalin to cut a deal with Hitler? The atomic bomb might change that calculation, but that weapon was still only a project, not a reality. Then there was Japan waiting in the wings. Rather than fruitlessly opposing any expansion of Soviet power in Eastern Europe, the Anglo–Americans opted to continue to promote long-term cooperation. As Roosevelt and Undersecretary of State Sumner Welles told British Foreign Secretary Anthony Eden, "the real decisions should be made by the United States, Great Britain, Russia and China, who would be the powers for many years to come that would have to police the world." Self-determination would, quite obviously, be bestowed by the Big Four, assuming they could agree on the details.[24]

A 1943 British Foreign Office memorandum, "The United Nations Plan for Organising Peace," echoed Roosevelt's thinking: "Stability" and "world order" were possible only if "the World Powers are prepared to accept the responsibilities of leadership *within* the United Nations." That would require Great Power agreement and a willingness "to take joint action to enforce it." With remarkable prescience, the memo went on to warn that the alternative would be "the World Powers, each with its circle of client States, facing each other in a rivalry which may merge imperceptibly into hostility."[25]

Roosevelt did not formally endorse the "percentages" agreement made by Churchill and Stalin at their Moscow (tolstoy) meeting in October 1944, whereby the two divided up Eastern Europe into various quite silly and unworkable degrees of influence in Bulgaria, Greece, Yugoslavia, Romania, and Hungary. The arrangement seemed to constitute a clear-cut spheres of influence deal, although neither the British nor the Russians could define what 90 percent/10 percent influence meant. Even so, FDR quietly accepted it without protest because how they cooperated to lead in their regions was their business—so long as they did not create closed, exclusive areas of influence and control (or use the dreaded phrase "spheres of influence").[26]

FDR's descriptions of how the Police would work resembled the role of an American frontier sheriff more than that of a big city police chief. In the classic American Westerns, the sheriff seems aloof, or nearly so, protecting the people but not really working for them; following his own practical set of rules; preferring persuasion and using his gun only when forced to (which was, of course, routinely the case); his authority coming from his own strength and character and principles rather than from a structured, elected town government.[27]

Fifty years after the war, former president George H. Bush told a West Point audience that "if we don't defend our interests and stand up for what we believe, no one else will,...Where we choose not to lead, no other country or institution is apt to magically appear." But he emphasized that the United States should not be the world's "policeman," but be more like a "sheriff" who would "organize the posse, but not shoulder the burden ourselves." Bush pointed to his own success in the first Persian Gulf War as an example of how the United States can lead other nations against a hostile enemy. Whether or not FDR would have agreed with the example is speculation; but he would have pulled back from the word "posse," with its implication that the use of force to achieve political goals was legitimate. And he would have been aghast at the recent suggestion of one political scientist who took a giant step beyond what G.H. Bush suggested by seizing the "sheriff" analogy to praise and promote a unilateralist global guardian's role for the United States. Somehow, Darth Vader seems a more apt image for that role than does the classic Hollywood sheriff. Unilateralism was Roosevelt's opponent, not his legacy.[28]

Roosevelt (with help from Nazi Germany and Japan) had convinced Americans that they were *in* the world, not safe from it. They had to be routinely involved rather than being involved only when it suited them. FDR's approach to globalism, however regionalized, emphasized leadership and persuasion. Nonetheless, implicit in the policemen approach was that force was available if leadership and persuasion failed. But that has been true historically for all nonviolent movements—as Gandhi in India and Martin Luther King in the United States both illustrate. Failure threatened to unleash stronger passions and purposes and thus prompt the use of less peaceful methods.[29]

By war's end five nations had qualified to join the police force—Great Britain, China, the Soviet Union, the United States, and France (at Britain's special request). The Five "Sheriffs" received their badges in mid-1945 when the United Nations Organization enshrined them as permanent members of the Security Council, each with full and equal veto power.

That international organization seems to be one of FDR's shadows, one of his legacies. His longtime secretary of state, Cordell Hull, epitomized those who believed, or at least argued, that had the United States entered Wilson's League of Nations, World War II could or would have been avoided. That was a powerful political argument, one that smoothed the path for U.S. support of what became the United Nations Organization (UNO).

But those searching for a patron saint for the UNO should quickly pass Franklin Roosevelt by. Quoting FDR is a bit like quoting the Bible or the Koran to prove an argument. Words out of context and divorced from actions tell us much less, or more, than meets the eye. Roosevelt spoke with positive optimism in public about the UNO. But more privately and inside the government he consistently expressed coolness and doubt about the utility of the United Nations as an international body, always emphasizing that what mattered, what really mattered, was Great Power cooperation. At no time did he believe that the UNO was a critical element in his conception of a workable, practical international structure. The peaceful global cooperation that FDR thought indispensable was a consultative, trusting, regionalized relationship between the major powers. If a UNO fostered that, fine. If it did not, then the UNO was marginal or even dangerous. He did persuade Stalin and Churchill to support a postwar international organization, but what mattered for FDR (as well as for Stalin and Churchill) was providing an institutional structure for that Great Power cooperation—what became the Security Council. Everything else was secondary at best. He saw the UNO as a convenient venue for Great Power negotiations, and the UN General Assembly as a "talking shop" that could threaten the practicality of the organization. As Churchill cynically put it: "The eagle should permit the small birds to sing and care not wherefore they sang."[30] Whatever the ruminations of others about a world federation, Roosevelt paid scant attention.[31] His international organization was a convenience, not a necessity.

Nonetheless, by 1944, growing public support in the United States for joining a formal international organization meant that the idea had become a vehicle for committing Americans to the regionalized cooperative internationalism (globalism) that FDR advocated.[32] He would tell reporters that "the United Nations will evolve into the best method ever devised for stopping war," but what he meant was the Great Powers. That might develop into working through the Security Council—he once mused about serving as secretary-general of the UNO. The Great Powers would be the only nations with the necessary military and economic power. Only they could "stop war."[33]

FDR played a role in creating what became today's United Nations, but he was nobody's saint. After all, the veto was Roosevelt's idea, not Stalin's. Even the debate over whether the veto could be used to prevent matters from coming before the Security Council for discussion found FDR ambivalent. He could (and did) imagine issues of U.S. conduct in the Western Hemisphere that were better kept within the Good Neighborhood he hoped to foster. Edward Stettinius recorded FDR remarking that "he was not too worried about the question of voting in the [Security] council since, if the shoe were on the other foot, the American people would be very reluctant to see the United States deprived of a vote if it were involved in a dispute with Mexico."[34]

FDR's operational principle was obvious. If the Security Council could challenge one of the Great Powers, that nation would simply refuse to obey. If pressured, it would drop out of the UNO just as had happened to the League in the 1930s. When the Republican House Minority Leader Joe Martin insisted that the "absolute veto" would allow any of the Great Powers to "create chaos," Stettinius summarized the president's thinking: If the Big Three—the United States, Britain, and Russia—had a falling out, the "world organization" could do nothing about it and would destroy itself if it tried.[35] Irrespective of whether or not FDR intended to exclude France and China from the designation "Big," that certainly characterized his thinking. As FDR once told Eden, the Great Powers would have the key responsibility for "all the more important decisions and wield police powers..." The general assembly would meet once a year to let "the smaller powers...blow off steam,"[36] but if that body tried to make policy, the organization was doomed. A month after Roosevelt's death, Stalin told Harry Hopkins that the dispute about vetoing Security Council discussions was "an insignificant matter."[37] FDR would have quickly agreed.

The great flail over the veto was, for Roosevelt, small potatoes. Not only did it threaten U.S.–Soviet cooperation, but the reality was that FDR agreed—as did his major Congressional allies. Arthur Vandenberg and Tom Connally, the Republican and Democratic godfathers of the UNO in the Senate, both insisted that the veto was "untouchable," for "it provided a shield against encroachments on national sovereignty,..." The "small nations' revolt" at the San Francisco Conference (April–May 1945), which aimed at limiting the veto held by the Big Five, only proved the point.[38]

Similarly insignificant was Stalin's request for additional votes in the UN General Assembly for ostensibly independent Soviet republics (he eventually accepted two). The president's concern was domestic public relations, not how or whether the General Assembly of the UNO could function effectively or if it adhered to the principle of one nation, one vote. When word leaked out, Roosevelt told the press that the General Assembly "is not really of any great importance. It is an investigatory body only...." To use the phrase of historian Robert Divine, FDR "let the mask fall at a critical moment to reveal his own commitment to a great power peace."[39]

But in the postwar world where the United States was a superpower and eventually *the* super(dooper)power, that commitment to a "great power peace" turned out to be a far more important legacy than did the creation of the United Nations Organization. Roosevelt did not see the UNO as an organization that could operate and succeed on a voting system. The success that would lead to an era of peace required an attitude adjustment, not a vote. Roosevelt believed that the USSR could become a reasonable member of international society, but only if it felt secure. That meant that the United States should not and would not threaten the Soviet system. It also meant that he believed that the Soviet system would change—which is exactly what happened in the Cold War, a period of time that is brief when compared to other world-shaping historical changes. And FDR and George Kennan were right—the Soviet system collapsed from within under the pressure of consumerism, modernization, and speed-of-light communications. The effect of the U.S. military buildup that began with the Carter administration and for which the Reagan faithful take credit, was only a small part of what FDR's "Americanism" predicted.[40]

What then of the legacy of Roosevelt's policies toward the Soviet Union? Some have argued that it was a horrible, unhappy legacy that "appeased" Stalin's insatiable appetite for expansion into Eastern Europe and beyond. In 2005, when President George W. Bush condemned the Yalta agreements, he implied that the legacy of the Roosevelt years was FDR's failure to be an early Cold or perhaps "Hot" Warrior:

> The agreement at Yalta followed in the unjust tradition of Munich and the Molotov-Ribbentrop Pact. Once again, when powerful governments negotiated, the freedom of small nations was somehow expendable. Yet this attempt to sacrifice freedom for the sake of stability left a continent divided and unstable. The captivity of millions in Central and Eastern Europe will be remembered as one of the greatest wrongs of history.[41]

That is, of course, appalling and distorted history, as is the holy-pretense that Bush's own foreign policy did not similarly ignore smaller nations. Roosevelt (and the British) concluded early on that Stalin was "a political descendant of Peter the Great rather than of Lenin." Eden did not think Soviet leaders actively planned for the spread of international communism, but even if they did, "if we are to win the war and to maintain the peace, we must work with Stalin and we cannot work with him unless we are successful in allaying some at least of his suspicion." But it would not be easy. The Soviet Union was "our most difficult problem," Eden warned Roosevelt.[42]

That echoed the president's sentiments. His suspicions about British intentions and hopes for cooperation with the Soviet Union did not blind him to the dangers of growing Soviet strength. During his regular meetings with State Department officials drawing up plans for the postwar world, he worried aloud that "he didn't know what to do about Russia...."[43] But the only way to avoid a third world war was to take the sharp edges off of Great Power confrontations and build confidence, not suspicions.

There is truth in what Arthur Schlesinger wrote: "It was the deployment of armies, not words on paper, that caused the division of Europe."[44] That is certainly the case for events from summer 1944 to war's end. But timing is everything. The fundamental postwar agreements (concessions if you prefer a critical phrase) between the Soviet Union and the Anglo–Americans came *before* mid-1944, largely during or in the wake of the Teheran Conference in December 1943. FDR (and Churchill) assumed/conceded/sacrificed the Baltic nations and much of Eastern Europe to Soviet "liberation" well before the great offensives in the East and the West began in June 1944. Given Stalin's (and Churchill's and Roosevelt's) axiom—"whoever occupies a territory imposes on it his own social system"—the postwar political results were a foregone conclusion. But then that was also true for places like West Germany, Italy, and Greece. Churchill's version of Stalin's axiom was more grandiloquent: "the right to guide the course of history is the noblest prize of victory."[45] FDR offered a typical sparse comment on this point: "occupying forces had the power in the area where their arms were present and each knew that the others could not force things to an issue." Better to acknowledge that reality than to wait for potential disagreements to arise. The Russians controlled or would control Eastern Europe and all we could do was use our influence "to ameliorate" the situation. The Normandy invasion, quickly followed by the massive offensive in the east that Stalin had promised, only fulfilled expectations, made Nazi Germany's demise only a matter of time, and made Soviet–Western differences more apparent and higher on everyone's agenda. In the atmosphere of the wartime and postwar roseate hue cast over the Normandy invasion, questions about the reasons for launching overlord, when the Red Army stood poised to roll across central Europe, were never asked.[46]

FDR was, of course, optimistically patient. A year later, on the day before he died, he personally drafted a message he sent to Churchill—his last substantive message to the Prime Minister:

> I would minimize the general Soviet problem as much as possible, because these problems…seem to arise every day and most of them straighten out.…We must be firm, however, and our course thus far is correct.[47]

His thinking was transparent; Great Power cooperation took precedence. Small insults and side issues must not distract America from the big picture. Nor was Roosevelt naive. He saw the Soviet Union was a challenge but not necessarily a threat. Some sort of preemptive diplomatic or even military action would only realize the danger. Even George Kennan, hardly a Roosevelt admirer, concluded that neither Churchill nor "Roosevelt either, for that matter—could have done much more than they did to prevent the Russian conquest of half of Europe. That was a function and consequence of Western weakness in the prewar period, and of our own simultaneous involvement with Japan."[48] This will, of course, change the mind of no one convinced that, before FDR's death, he became a Cold Warrior. But it surely does indicate the depth of his desire to avoid unnecessary confrontation with his wartime ally.

Which brings us to another issue of candor and honesty—the Yalta agreements. The real problem about Yalta was not the nature of the agreements, but the matter of candor and great expectations. Neither Churchill nor Roosevelt believed they could admit to their publics or their political opponents that they had consigned the Baltic States and much of the South Balkans to the tender mercies of Soviet control. Neither could admit that they had made concessions in Northeast Asia that restored Russian economic and political influence in Manchuria and northern Korea. In each case the reasons were mixed—ensuring Soviet entry into the war against Japan, shoring up Chiang's regime in China, the reality of Soviet occupation of much of East Europe—but establishing a cooperative rather than a confrontational relationship with the Soviet Union was the overriding motive. It was sometimes a case of making a silk purse out of a sow's ear, especially in places like the Baltic States, but better that than playing dog in the manger and getting suspicion and enmity in return. The Declaration on Liberated Europe, agreed to at Yalta, called for the kind of openness and political freedom enjoyed in the United States and Britain. But that was no rhetorical "victory" over the Soviet Union, nor was it intended as such. It expressed a hope not a reality, and thus served to raise expectations for the war's outcome to unrealistic levels. When those expectations were dashed, American and British frustrations and disillusionment would, as after World War I, intensify tensions. Only this time it became the Cold War.[49]

FDR did not "give away" Eastern Europe to Soviet domination, any more than his legacy was the "loss" of a China that the United States had never controlled. The sense of moral outrage that, after Roosevelt's death, came to characterize Western Cold War rhetoric may have made some Americans feel good, but it could not and did not change the realities of history, power, ideology, and economics that created the Cold War. Peaceful coexistence would take time—much more time than the "Last of the Giants" or the "Greatest Generation" could command.[50]

Roosevelt's "strategies" (which implies too much structure) for the postwar world never engaged what came into being. "Containment," Kennan's label, if not his invention,[51] became America's strategy for the tense Soviet–American confrontation that developed soon after World War II. However FDR would have reacted to that approach, he unsuspectingly helped create a climate that facilitated adoption of containment as the American policy.

But how did FDR prepare the way for containment? The early (pre-Korea) Cold War structure had aimed at war/conflict avoidance, one of FDR's goals, although the United States could bargain from the position of strength created by the atomic bomb. Perhaps in some unspoken, inchoate way, containment had echoes of FDR's quarantine speech of 1937—though that initiative hardly achieved popular recognition. There is nothing in FDR's words or actions to suggest he thought consciously in terms of containment.

Kennan (and those who agreed with some of his thinking) proposed a broad strategy aimed at outlasting the Soviet threat by both patience (sounds like FDR, doesn't it?) and pressure. Three broad concepts stand out:

1. There were five areas of strategic importance—U.S./UK/central Europe/Japan/USSR—an approach that fit neatly with FDR's four or more Policemen (even if Kennan expressed contempt for the concept).[52]
2. Use of diverse means to protect U.S. interests; that is, avoid war while containing Soviet communism. FDR likewise tried to devise a system that would avoid war, though he was not worried about communism as an ideology.
3. The need for allies that, in direct opposition to unilateralism, echo Roosevelt's commitment to globalism (regionalized internationalism).[53]

Perhaps Kennan came to sense the affinity between containment and FDR's policies. Some thirty years after writing Article X, Kennan concluded that FDR had, "in the back of his mind, his own independent purposes, which in some instances deviated quite extensively from the prevailing consensus;..." He added that the president "influenced public opinion less through the power of his own words than through the quiet shaping, in a manner conducive to his own purposes, of the... factors, in which the formulation of wartime policy had to proceed." In short, Roosevelt was not the whimsical leader Kennan had thought when they met during World War II. Kennan quickly returned to form, calling FDR "a very superficial man," but the point remained that even so harsh a critic believed that Roosevelt had a purpose, a reason, for what he did.[54]

Recognition of the need for allies, real and "listed," is most interesting. FDR's eagerness to find formal allies in World War II broke sharply with long-standing traditions and practices since the American Revolution and the French Alliance. George Washington, in his Farewell Address, had warned against "permanent alliances," but sanctioned "temporary alliances for extraordinary emergencies."[55] But the United States faced no such emergencies until World War I, and even then Woodrow Wilson refused to join the alliance against the Central powers.[56]

Certainly the over-analyzed Anglo–American Special Relationship is the most powerful example of Roosevelt's (and World War II's) shadow. Since 1945, Great Britain and the United States have almost always found that, after careful consideration, their interests and desires coincided. The most obvious exception is the Vietnam War, where Britain steadfastly refused to support American policy. But while that refusal angered President Lyndon Johnson and U.S. policymakers, it did not break the pattern.[57]

But the search for allies also often resembled the 1942 "Declaration by United Nations" (i.e., nations signing on to use their "full resources, military or economic," against the Tripartite Pact of Germany, Italy, and Japan), which eventually grew to a largely symbolic list of forty-five such governments.[58] It was the "if you're not with us, you're against us" syndrome that would become so strong during the Cold War. Neutrality was wrong, if not evil.

The commitment to an "allied" policy helped legitimize President Harry Truman's promotion of what seemed like a "real" alliance in the North Atlantic Treaty Organization. But he also worked to build a "list" during the Korean War. Yet, despite UNO support, few nations sent significant numbers of troops. Eisenhower and Dulles created their own "lists" in the form of regional security treaties (sanctioned by the UN Charter). Next came the obsessive search by Lyndon Johnson for a list of allies during the Vietnam War—his "more flags" campaign. The only reliable ones were the "mercenaries" he hired, primarily from South Korea, with much smaller contingents from Thailand and the Philippines.[59]

The 1990–1991 Gulf War generated a full-fledged response from the UNO, with even the Soviet Union and Cuba voting to condemn Saddam Hussein's "criminal" aggression against the oil-rich kingdom of Kuwait. Even so, the United States did the overwhelming bulk of the fighting. The continuation of the Gulf War, delayed for only a decade, found George W. Bush trumpeting creation of a Coalition of the Willing (carefully not an alliance) of between 46 and 50 nations, from Great Britain to Tonga. But only Britain provided significant military support—9,000 personnel in Iraq as of March 2004. Most contributions were token gestures of less than 1,000 persons. By 2007, the coalition had dwindled to meaninglessness, with the United States providing 168,000 (about 94 percent) of the troops.[60]

But the size of the contribution for any and all of these "police actions" (is the term "police" actions another FDR legacy?) did not matter, any more than it did during World War II. Truman sent U.S. forces to implement "containment" and defend South Korea *before* the United Nations condemned the North Koreans as aggressors. American presidents from Eisenhower to Nixon, fearing the falling dominoes, acted in Vietnam without UN approval. The Bushes, father and son, made clear their willingness to use military force in Iraq, first to protect U.S. oil supplies and then for reasons labeled "national security," with or without a UN sanction. The "lists" were for public consumption and to provide a cloak of respectability for action that one of the Great Powers, in these cases the Greatest Power, was going to take regardless of UN votes or the number of names on a list of ostensible supporters. The precedent of working with allies set by Franklin Roosevelt lived on, through and beyond the Cold War, but in a way fundamentally different from what he imagined. Instead of regionalized cooperative internationalism, unilateral (formerly isolationist) nationalism returned to rule the roost. What he feared the most, what he believed to be the basic cause of World War II, once again threatened the peace of the world.[61]

There are irony and legacy in President Richard Nixon's pronouncement in July 1969 of the " 'Guam Doctrine' in which he asserted that the United States would avoid future imbroglios by relying upon regional stabilizers."[62] The Shah's Iran was to play that role in the 1970s. The irony is that it was the same as Roosevelt's "regionalized cooperative internationalism" distorted into unilateralism—the new isolationism wherein the United States would isolate itself from those nations that disagreed with American policies and priorities. Either they were with us, or against us.

But there were other threats to the postwar peace FDR sought to establish, and European colonial empires were at the top of his list. His Americanism reflected historical memory in the United States, memory that warned that colonialism fomented violence and revolution. Moreover, colonies were objects of desire and competition among more powerful nations, something that had and would create confrontation between the Great Powers. Roosevelt's persistent nudging of the British, French, and Dutch to establish devolution schedules, made decolonization (a word he would not have recognized) part of American foreign policy.

But the reality of that legacy is certainly not the popular image (and not just in Great Britain) of FDR as the effective destroyer of European Empires.[63] Walter Russell Mead, when a senior fellow at the Council on Foreign Relations, offered the most grotesque exaggeration of that myth: "No reptilian brain could have dealt as unsentimentally with an old friend as Franklin Roosevelt and the Treasury Department dealt with Churchill's government.... [T]he Americans dismantled the British Empire...."[64] Whatever Mead's overdrawn theme about American policy mixing the approaches of both "serpent and dove," the historical fact is that decolonization was essentially the work of the colonized, not the United States. FDR persistently pressured Churchill, directly and indirectly, to establish schedules for self-rule in India and other major British colonies, though he never went beyond mere words. Anticolonialism was, in part, an American reflex. But for Roosevelt, colonialism promised to cause war, and that made its elimination an integral part of his postwar planning. FDR's death thwarted his most innovative scheme for decolonization—trusteeships accountable to the UNO,—for the arrangement that came into effect allowed his own military leaders and the two major colonial powers, France and Britain, to put the foxes in charge of the chicken coops. The colonial powers were given the responsibility for decolonization of their own empires, while the American military could create overseas bases under apparently permanent U.S. control.[65]

Overseas bases offer one of FDR's more ambiguous legacies. While he insisted on trusteeships accountable to the international community, places he thought strategically crucial to American security, such as Dakar on the bulge of West Africa, seemed to slip partway through a crack. Were other Sheriffs to have such strategic bases? He told Churchill that Dakar and New Caledonia, in the Pacific—presumably a key strategic point for Britain and/or Australia—would be subject to international accountability, but that was apples and oranges. How could an entire island be equated to a small, if strategically located city? Was Dakar to be rejoined with Senegal, or would it remain, forever, a "crucial strategic point" for the United States? Throughout the Cold War, overseas bases provided a means to project both American power and, particularly since 2001, an international testimony to the American way of life. Sixty years after the end of World War II, U.S. military forces would still be in Okinawa. As historian Lloyd Gardner has put it, the public relations name for the Second Gulf War, enduring freedom, might instead have been enduring bases.[66]

Whatever the disconnect between American words and actions regarding decolonization,[67] the issue provides a bridge between the two great Roosevelt legacies—"regionalized" cooperative internationalism and Americanism. Which raises the issue of Wilsonianism. Gardner subtly presents Wilson as "the pivotal figure . . . for discussing the relationship of liberalism to power."[68] The relationship and its dilemma—as old as the American republic—are a "covenant," that wonderfully rich word that, in its biblical sense, cannot be defined without either blaspheming or using the word "covenant." But whatever the definition, it is the connection between the use of force to impose the liberal ideals of democracy and freedom that characterizes so-called Wilsonian diplomacy, which suggests that FDR is not a Wilsonian, at least if that force is military.[69] Did Roosevelt unintentionally succeed in creating such a legacy? Obviously not, as history since 1945 demonstrates. The covert wars and wars-by-proxy that characterized the Cold War and the American interventions in the post-Cold War era might or might not have been prevented by effective regional leadership, limited by the existence of other "sheriffs," but somewhere along the way the United States had become the chief of police.

Roosevelt's awkward, imprecise, poorly articulated distinction between "closed" or "exclusive" spheres of influence and what might be called "open" spheres was the bridge he tried to construct between the spheres of influence proposed by Churchill and Stalin, and the collective security suggested twenty-five years earlier by Woodrow Wilson. Although the references are few and undeveloped, what FDR meant was that the passage of ideas, goods, and people between one regional sphere and another should not be restricted by any of the Sheriffs. His emphasis on persuasion and leadership and his rejection of "exclusive" regional police powers, all the while realizing that power lay available in the background, suggests that FDR was neither a Wilsonian nor a realist—he was Franklin Roosevelt, unabashed purveyor of Americanism.[70]

A connected idea that seemed curious, even silly, to contemporaries may well have been prescience if not precisely a legacy. The free flow of information was, for FDR, necessary to the liberties and freedoms needed to protect against the rebirth of fascism. Just what he meant when he spoke to Eden about "free ports of information" is not clear, though he obviously meant that governments could not censor the news. The proposal had little impact; certainly Roosevelt gets no credit for "inventing" the Internet. But he did leave a small legacy with his suggestion of a worldwide communications web.[71]

Part of FDR's Americanism and legacy is the internationalization of the New Deal. His repeated espousal of free ports for trade addressed both trade and politics; since such ports were frequently former colonial trading centers, the scheme provided a political transition from colonial empire, and at the same time massaged American liberal trade beliefs. World War II convinced Americans that global economic and political involvement were two halves of the same walnut, though that was hardly a new idea. Roosevelt's efforts to stabilize international markets in, for example, wheat, were typical of his attempts to take the New Deal—and American commerce—abroad. The notion that international economic reconstruction, specifically the establishment of the International Monetary Fund and the World Bank, was some sort of do-goodism or "global meliorism" flies in the face of reality. The "American mission to make the world a better place" was part of the legitimizing arguments for those institutions, as it was at home for the New Deal, but suffice to say that the postwar international economic institutions that FDR proposed, however global and however helpful to others, invariably served U.S. interests.[72]

The reconstruction of Germany and Japan after World War II raises a related example of "global meliorism" as a false Roosevelt legacy. Was FDR a nation- or state-builder in the sense of that popular (and quite unsuccessful) postwar impulse? One commentator on national security issues has rightly dismissed arguments that restructuring the Nazi and militarist foundations of governmental legitimacy in Germany and Japan was state-building. Both those countries were strong, powerful nation-states before World War II.

Each already had a sense of identity and viable economic and governmental institutions. Throughout the war, Roosevelt consistently spoke of "reforming" the Germans and Japanese, as even a cursory look at things like the Morgenthau Plan for Germany demonstrates. FDR repeatedly called for the dismemberment of the German nation-state—hardly a meliorist conception. The reconstruction of Germany and Japan was stimulated less by do-good instincts than by fears that, unchanged, those nations would once again cause a world war; later strengthened by the desire to make Japan and West Germany allies in the Cold War. A change in their governing concepts was a matter of international security, not state- or nation-building.[73]

Roosevelt's most ambiguous, even hubristic, geopolitical legacy came with his and Churchill's impossible dream that the Anglo–Americans could maintain an atomic monopoly. Prompted by warnings and advice from Albert Einstein and other European scientists about German research into atomic energy, the British and Americans teamed up, early in the war, to pool British and American knowledge and resources into what became the now famous Manhattan Project. Time, strategic bombing, and sabotage ensured that the Germans would not succeed before their defeat. Anglo–American scientific success came too late for the atom bomb to be used against Germany, but two were dropped on Japan, seeming to shorten the war.[74]

Yet one of the most unhappy of Roosevelt's and Churchill's legacies is the absurd, jejune dream that the Anglo–Americans could maintain monopolistic control over atomic/nuclear energy. Whatever the strategic advantages or entrepreneurial benefits, it was a dream doomed to failure; a dream that became a nightmare. After both of the Quebec Conferences (1943–1944), Churchill and Roosevelt met in Hyde Park and agreed not to share the atomic secret. Niels Bohr, the Danish physicist and atomic scientist, had pleaded with both the president and the prime minister to disclose the atomic secret to the world lest it poison postwar relationships. Although Bohr's proposal fell afoul of now discredited suspicions that he had leaked information to the Soviet Union, there were advisors in both the British and American governments (Henry Stimson and Lord Cherwell, for example) who found merit in some sort of internationalization of the bomb. But FDR and Churchill were having none of it.

In 1946, the Americans proposed the so-called Baruch Plan for international control of atomic energy through a United Nations commission—one historian called it "emasculated internationalism" as it allowed the United States to remain the only nation capable of making an atomic bomb. Moreover, the proposals eliminated the Security Council veto on atomic matters, which would allow the United States to control the very process of atomic energy research in other countries. The Soviet Union opposed the plan, Churchill argued against it in his Fulton speech, and the Attlee government was unenthusiastic. "Let's forget the Baroosh and get on with the fissle (Britain's own atomic energy project)" was Foreign Secretary Ernest Bevin's alleged quip.[75] The message was clear. Great power "equality" and status now seemed to depend on developing an atomic bomb.

When the Soviet Union refused to accept the inspection requirements of the Baruch Plan (which actually passed in the United Nations, but quickly became dormant), the U.S. Congress and President Harry Truman, either ignorant or dismissive of the Roosevelt–Churchill agreements to jointly share the atomic secret, put legislation (the McMahon Act) into effect that ended their wartime cooperation. The Anglo–American "special relationship" wobbled on its axis, though shared Cold War fears kept it alive. More significant, the extensive U.S. nuclear development and testing program quickly followed. The nuclear arms race was on.

So here we are in 2008, scrambling in vain to hold on to the atomic secret even as membership in the nuclear "club" (one of those "soft" words that seem to legitimize nuclear weapons) continues to grow. The Soviet Union joined in 1949. The British and French soon followed. China, India, Pakistan, Israel have all come on board. North Korea agreed to close down its bomb producing facilities, but only *after* it developed the ability to make one. Iran, which is knocking on the door, is likely to do the same. We are told there still are nuclear devices (bombs?) scattered around in the former Soviet empire. We are losing count of how many members of the club there are now, but what is certain is that trying to keep that genie in a bottle is just a variation on the ostrich's head-in-the-sand reaction to things it doesn't want to see. It was neither Mr. Churchill's nor Mr. Roosevelt's finest hour.

Since World War II, we have experienced a half century of meetings, conferences, back-stairs diplomacy, and back-channel parleys. Even Dwight Eisenhower, the most intense and committed Cold Warrior of all the presidents—he spoke of the Soviet Union in terms of evil long before Ronald Reagan made "the evil empire" a commonplace—ignored his own hyperbole and used back-channel diplomacy and negotiations (too slowly for Churchill) within the informal structure FDR had fostered. It was precisely what Roosevelt expected. He did not predict the Cold War dynamic; he was certainly not an early Cold Warrior.[76] But he did play a key role in establishing the unwritten "system," the informal structure, which channeled Cold War tensions into regional confrontations between proxies, not global ones between the Great Powers. That offers small consolation to those whose land and societies have been devastated as the proxies played their awful games, but it was arguably better than the Third World War.

Some would have it, or wish, that FDR was wrong and that the sixty years since his death have seen the nation-state structure begin to shift away from narrow national priorities and international sheriffs toward something more global. Change is inevitable, but when, in spring 2005, France and other European countries rejected the draft constitution for the European Union, the general consensus among analysts was that voters were uneasy about the loss of national sovereignty. One can almost hear Mark Twain muttering, "*The report of my death was an exaggeration.*"

Historians have long argued that while Roosevelt "educated" the American public about internationalism, he failed to educate those in government who would be positioned to implement his vision of how the postwar world would operate. His diplomats (such as Averell Harriman) and the career officers in the State Department (such as Dean Acheson and George Kennan) seem to have not understood or came to disagree with his nonconfrontational approach toward the Soviet Union or, for that matter, toward any of the Great Powers.[77] Within a year after Roosevelt died, the new president, Harry Truman, had taken the advice of Roosevelt's confidants and the Cold War was on. That is, perhaps, a negative legacy. FDR made no attempt to bring Truman, who was not Roosevelt's choice, into the know. But no one expects to die just when they do, and Roosevelt had little time within which to discuss grand strategy. Truman became vice president on January 20, 1945. Two days later (January 22), FDR left for meetings at Malta and Yalta, not to return to Washington until February 27 (despite rumors that he had died enroute).[78] A month later (March 29) he left for his cottage in Warm Springs, Georgia—where he went whenever he felt weak and ill—never to return. He died on April 12, a little less than three months after Truman came on board as vice president. That left Roosevelt precious little time to do with Truman what he had not done, or could not do, with many of his advisors and associates—explain his policies, which were based so much on hopes, instincts, feelings, style, and his wonderful optimism. In the turmoil of war's end, would a reassuring voice and an upturned cigarette holder have made a difference? Who knows, but it might. But world leaders can never buy enough time.

Oh yes, that leaves unexplained my dismissal of A.J.P. Taylor's quip: "Of the great men at the top, Roosevelt was the only one who knew what he was doing: he made the United States the greatest power in the world at virtually no cost." We all repeat that famously barbed and pungent comment. But it is an exaggeration, if not a myth, for Taylor implies conscious opportunism, if not planning, by Roosevelt. FDR sensed and assumed movement toward the Americanization of the world, but he saw no need to *make* it happen.[79]

NOTES

1. A cautionary note. This interpretive and speculative work does not provide a chronological summary of Franklin Roosevelt's wartime foreign policy.

All sorts of famous events, political and military, are not mentioned or downplayed; a category that also includes the Yalta Conference decisions, which were, for the most part, an anticlimax to the Teheran Conference decisions. Those who wish to fill in the gaps, or wonder to what I refer, should consult any of the many relevant surveys and monographs, including my *Forged in War: Roosevelt, Churchill, and the Second World War* (New York: William Morrow, 1997).

2. My gratitude goes to all the participants at the conference, but especially to Lloyd Gardner who will recognize a phrase or two that I have genially lifted from him without attribution. Also a thank you to Jeremi Suri and our students at a summer graduate seminar for high school teachers held at Ashland University in summer 2005. Our chasing of labels stimulated my thinking about where FDR fits in the scheme of such things.

3. Mark Stoler, "Avoiding American Entry into World War II (Feature Review)," *Diplomatic History* 27, 2 (April 2003): 286. FDR reportedly told Harry Hopkins during the drafting of the Four Freedoms speech that "the world is getting so small that even the people in Java are getting to be our neighbors now." But that fits with Roosevelt's overall views of a shrinking, open world, rather than physical/military security. Quoted in Elizabeth Borgwardt, *A New Deal for the World* (Cambridge, MA and London: Harvard University Press, 2005), 21.

4. I have fiddled a bit with this idea before. See Kimball, *The Juggler* (Princeton: Princeton University Press, 1991), chap. 9, "This Persistent Evangel of Americanism." I have been teased and chided for not providing a clear definition of "Americanism." That omission is purposeful. Labels are fluid descriptions, changing to fit the needs of policymakers, the media, historians, and the public. By FDR's Americanism I mean the combination of "isms" and actions embodied in his postwar planning—everything from Jeffersonianism to Nationalism to Idealism to Wilsonianism to Capitalism to Realism to the New Deal, and so on.

5. For a discussion of how World War II created, or did not create, such a *tabula rasa*, see "The Future of World War Two Studies: A Roundtable," *Diplomatic History* 25, 3 (summer 2001).

6. For a stimulating discussion of Roosevelt's fixation on law and order, see Anders Stephanson, "Law and Messianic Counterwar from FDR to George W. Bush," draft of August 2005, privately circulated. The pervasive American fixation on law and order needs to be painted on a larger canvas.

7. Geopolitics is my primary concern in this chapter, thus issues of economics (both "liberal" trade and opposition to autarkic economic policies), decolonization, political philosophy, historiography, and the like receive short shrift. But see the other chapters in this volume.

8. McDougall, *Promised Land, Crusader State* (Boston and New York: Houghton Mifflin, 1997), 146.

9. A.J.P. Taylor, *English History, 1914–1945* (Oxford: Oxford University Press, 1965), 577.

10. Perhaps not as safely as I would wish. The Charleston (SC) *Post & Courier* carried a letter to the editor on August 25, 2005 that referred sarcastically, and bitterly, to Roosevelt's "fine socialism." On "convergence," see my review in the *Times Literary Supplement* (London), February 20, 1998. Accusations that FDR failed to rescue Jews from Hitler's Germany and even contributed to the Holocaust touch on issues only tangential to his postwar legacy in international affairs. The latest entry into the debate is a strident argument for FDR having done all that was practical; see Robert N. Rosen, *Saving the Jews: Franklin D. Roosevelt and the Holocaust* (New York: Thunder's Mouth Press, 2006).

11. *Life*, October 30, 1944, as quoted in Jon Meacham, *Franklin and Winston* (New York: Random House, 2003), 307. Robert Sherwood, *Roosevelt and Hopkins*, rev. ed. (New York: Grossett & Dunlap/Universal Library, 1950), 827. Generally see Justus D. Doenecke, *Storm on the Horizon: The Challenge to American Intervention, 1939–1941* (Lanham: Rowman & Littlefield, 2000).

12. Manfred Jonas pointed this out decades ago, but his quite appropriate label—"unilateralism"—never took. Too bad, for if American students had become used to calling the anti-interventionists of the 1930s the unilateralists, it would have made the parallel in the post-Cold War era much more apparent; Jonas, *Isolationism in America, 1935–1941* (Ithaca: Cornell University Press, 1966). Arthur Schlesinger, Jr., called "unilateralism" the "oldest doctrine in American history; *War and the American Presidency* (New York: Norton, 2004), 4. The debate over FDR's policies in the mid-1930s is outlined above by David Reynolds

13. Conrad Black, *Franklin Delano Roosevelt: Champion of Freedom* (London: Weidenfeld and Nicolson, 2003) is a recent example of dividing FDR into his Teddy Roosevelt and Woodrow Wilson parts.

14. Nor was it any accident that, in 1775, the first task of American diplomats was, according to the instructions from the Committee on Secret Correspondence, to learn if the United States could continue foreign trade in the face of the British Prohibitory Act, which forbade all commerce with the rebellious American colonies. So we have two interesting heritages of "original intent"—priority for trade and commerce, and government secrecy (Secret Correspondence). In April 1776, the Continental Congress declared American ports open to the trade of all nations, in direct defiance of British mercantile policies. Thomas Paine's pamphlet, "Common Sense," left no place for God (or god), but drew a clear picture of a nation with a new and unique place in the world. Because all Europe and European empires were the logical and necessary partners/market for American trade, Paine argued that the nation should "steer clear of European contentions."

15. Quotations from Eric Alterman, *When Presidents Lie* (New York: Penguin Books, 2005), 17, 16.

16. This paragraph is adapted from an expanded discussion of this argument in Warren F. Kimball, "Franklin D. Roosevelt and World War II," *Presidential Studies Quarterly* 34, 1 (March 2004): "Special Issue: Going to War," 83–99.

17. John L. Gaddis, *Surprise, Security, and the American Experience* (Cambridge, MA and London: Harvard University Press, 2004), 48, 51. Gaddis is just one of those who have come to see unilateralism as an American habit before World War II and have begun to use the term.

18. This discussion of the policemen and the quotations is taken from my *Forged in War,* especially 201–5. See also Kimball, *The Juggler,* particularly chapters 5 and 6.

19. Oleg A. Rzheshevsky, ed., *War and Diplomacy: The Making of the Grand Alliance* (Amsterdam: Harwood Academic Publishers, 1996), 204 (doc. 82). See also p. 223 (doc. 97). This invaluable collection of documents, which has all too often been ignored, significantly updates and revises our knowledge of Stalin's thinking and actions, particularly his reactions to Anglo–American policies. Part III is the record of Molotov's visit to Washington in May–June 1942.

20. The approval process is clear from F. Davis to S. Early, March 23, 1944, Roosevelt papers, Official File (OF) 4287 (Franklin D. Roosevelt Library, Hyde Park, NY; hereafter FDRL). Davis, "What Really Happened at Teheran," *Saturday Evening Post* 116 (May 13 and 20, 1944). For more about Davis' articles, see Kimball, *The Juggler,* 96, 110.

21. I shamelessly quote and paraphrase myself from *The Juggler,* 96ff. But also see Lloyd C. Gardner, *Spheres of Influence* (Chicago: Ivan Dee, 1993).

22. Davis, "Roosevelt's World Blueprint," *Saturday Evening Post* 115 (April 10, 1943).

23. Kimball, *The Juggler,* 96.

24. *FRUS,* 1943, III, 39.

25. Memorandum of July 7, 1943, Llewellyn Woodward, *British Foreign Policy during the Second World War,* 5 vols. (London: HMSO, 1970–1976), vol. V, 51.

26. Ibid., 159–83.

27. To be fair, the city police chief was also a Roosevelt analogy. In February 1938, as Neville Chamberlain pushed for agreements with Mussolini and Hitler, Roosevelt privately remarked that if the police chief makes a deal with gangsters that prevents crime, he "will be called a great man." But if the gangsters break their word, "the Chief of Police will go to jail." Chamberlain seemed to be "taking very long chances." William R. Rock, *Chamberlain and Roosevelt* (Columbus: Ohio State University Press, 1988), 85–86.

28. George H.W. Bush speech of October 5, 1994, West Point, NY, as quoted by Ed Shannon, *Middletown (Times-Herald) Record* (New York), October 6, 1994, available at http://www.aog.usma.edu/AOG/AWARDS/TA/thayer94.txt. Accessed September 1, 2007 (My thanks to Mark Stoler who was an earwitness to the speech.) The political scientist is Colin S. Gray, *The Sheriff: America's Defense of the New World Order* (Lexington: University Press of Kentucky, 2004).

29. FDR famously called for the spread of liberty and freedom when he proclaimed the Four Freedoms. Fifty years later (January 21, 2005), the *Wall Street Journal* editorialized that G.W. Bush's foreign policy was fulfilling

FDR's call for "freedom from want and fear." No one noted that FDR eschewed the use of force to expand freedom, even telling the military—to its dismay—that he would not extend American sovereignty to military bases in the Pacific, and would insist that they be part of the United Nations trusteeship system. Kimball, *The Juggler*, 155.

30. Similarly, in 1935 Roosevelt claimed that "The League of Nations has become nothing more than a debating society, and a poor one at that." As quoted in Robert A. Divine, *Roosevelt and World War II* (Baltimore: Penguin Books, 1969), 57. The Churchill comment was heard by Charles Bohlen (at Yalta as a translator) and recounted in his memoir, *Witness to History, 1929–1969* (New York: Norton, 1973), 181.

31. FDR famously referred to the U.S. Articles of Confederation as the kind of trial and error learning experience that European colonies needed to have. The comparison probably came to him as a result of journalist Clarence Streit's popular study, *Union Now*, published in 1939, which was a call for a world federation of democracies. Streit saw the League of Nations as analogous to the loose and ineffective Articles, with the experience making possible a strong federal union. He modified the prerequisite of democracy once the United States entered the war so as to allow the Soviet Union and China to qualify. At one point, there were sixty chapters of his Federal Union Incorporated movement, and supporters included Robert Sherwood, one of FDR's speechwriters. Eleanor Roosevelt invited Streit to explain his ideas to the president during dinner at the White House; Joseph P. Lasch, *Eleanor: The Years Alone* (New York: W.W. Norton, 1962), 34. Nevertheless, I have found no mention of Streit or any reference to his specific ideas in FDR's various explanations of his Policemen construct. See also Townsend Hoopes and Douglas Brinkley, *FDR and the Creation of the U.N.* (New Haven and London: Yale University Press, 1997), 20, 56.

32. Without exception, the evidence in the literature about the creation of the UNO draws a similar picture of Roosevelt's attitude, though the emphasis differs from study to study. Robert Divine, succinctly (and acidly) in *Roosevelt and World War II*, and in detail in *Second Chance* (New York: Atheneum, 1967), treats FDR's support for the UNO as realistic and practical, denying that he was committed to the idea of collective security as a faithful "disciple" of Wilson. Hoopes and Brinkley, *FDR and the Creation of the U.N.*, likewise emphasize Roosevelt's practicality regarding the UNO, as well as his lack of interest in the details, 153. Black, *Roosevelt: Champion of Freedom*, gives the UNO little attention, but on p. 850 credits FDR for gradually building "the United Nations from a slogan into a concept for an updated Wilsonian organization to preserve peace and promote progressive government." Stephen Schlesinger, *Act of Creation: The Founding of the United Nations* (Boulder, CO: Westview, 2003), asserts that FDR "had fiercely steered the idea of a world association through all sorts of political hazards," but the narrative emphasizes Roosevelt's commitment to Great Power cooperation and "a continuing U.S. commitment to internationalism"—neither of which were quite the same as the United Nations Organization, 64. Robert C.

Hilderbrand's detailed and excellent monograph, *Dumbarton Oaks: The Origins of the United Nations and the Search for Postwar Security* (Chapel Hill and London: University of North Carolina Press, 1990), has a comment on p. 21 about "Roosevelt's hegemonic Four Policemen idea," and ends with a touch of weary cynicism: "the fact remains that the Great Powers, which may have begun by trying to do too much, ended by doing too little. They created an organization that would fail to fulfill Tennyson's happy dream of a parliament of man, a federation of the world, primarily because they feared the effect that such a strong body would have on their own national objectives for the postwar era," 257. Franklin Roosevelt certainly had just such fears.

33. As quoted in Divine, *Roosevelt and WWII*, 69. FDR mused to Henry Morgenthau and Daisy Suckley about being the "Chairman" or "Sec.-Gen." of the UNO, but he insisted that "The org. itself might be run with a comparatively small staff, half the year in an island,..." See *Closest Companion*, ed. Geoffrey Ward (Boston and New York: Houghton Mifflin, 1995), 207. On another occasion he painted a picture of living in Hyde Park after the war with international leaders journeying up the Hudson Valley to seek advice.

34. Thomas M. Campbell and George C. Herring, eds., *The Diaries of Edward Stettinius, Jr., 1943–1946* (New York: New Viewpoints, 1975), 221 (January 2, 1945). The reference to Mexico suggests that FDR had in mind Mexican expropriation in 1938 of U.S. owned oil properties.

35. *Stettinius Diaries*, 300.

36. British Foreign Office files, Halifax to the Foreign Office, March 28, 1943, FO 371/35366, U 1430/G (Public Record Office, Kew), reporting on the Eden–Roosevelt conversations in Washington, DC.

37. As quoted in S. Schlesinger, *Act of Creation*, 217.

38. S. Schlesinger, *Act of Creation*, 193. The "small nations' revolt," which came only a few weeks after FDR's death, is described on pp. 222–3.

39. *Stettinius Diaries*, 305–8. Divine, *Roosevelt and World War II*, 70–71, may misread the nature of Wilson's commitment to "the concept of one nation, one vote" for an international security organization, but he is spot-on when he states that "Roosevelt never subscribed to this ideal."

40. Alan P. Dobson, "The Reagan Administration, Economic Warfare, and Starting to Close down the Cold War," *Diplomatic History* 29, 3 (June 2005): 531–56.

41. Speech by George W. Bush, May 7, 2005, Riga, Latvia, http://www.whitehouse.gov/infocus/europe/2005/may/. Accessed August 1, 2006.

42. The comment about Stalin as Peter the Great is that of Anthony Eden; Eden to Halifax, January 22, 1942, FO 954/29xc/100818, Public Record Office (PRO); Woodward, *British Foreign Policy*, V, 9–10; *FRUS*, 1943, III, 13; Sherwood, *Roosevelt & Hopkins*, 708–9.

43. Roosevelt's meetings were usually with selected members of the Subcommittee on Political Problems—primarily Hull or Welles, Leo Pasvolsky, Norman Davis, Myron Taylor, and Isaiah Bowman; U.S. Dept. of State [Harley

Notter], *Postwar Foreign Policy Preparation* (Washington, USGPO, 1950), 92–93, 96–97; and U.S. Dept. Of State, *Post World War II Foreign Policy Planning: State Department Records of Harley A. Notter* (microform; Bethesda, MD, 1987) file 548–1 (a summary of contacts with the president).

44. Arthur Schlesinger, Jr., foreword to *My Dear Mr Stalin: The Complete Correspondence of Franklin D. Roosevelt and Joseph V. Stalin*, ed. Susan Butler (New Haven and London: Yale University Press, 2005), xiv.

45. As quoted in Kimball, *Forged in War*, 209–10.

46. *Stettinius Diaries*, 214. For Soviet military support of the invasion of Normandy (overlord), see David Glantz and Jonathan M. House, *When Titans Clashed: How the Red Army Stopped Hitler* (Lawrence: University Press of Kansas, 1995). There were awkward questions for Americans, raised by Gabriel Kolko nearly four decades ago and studiously ignored thereafter: To what degree was overlord a political rather than a military imperative? To what degree did Anglo–American leaders fear a Soviet move, or opportunity, to "liberate" western Europe? Kolko, *The Politics of War* (New York: Vintage, 1968). But timing is everything, and whatever the growing worries about expanded Soviet influence in Europe, failure to launch the Second Front would have doomed any hopes of postwar Soviet–Western collaboration—always FDR's primary goal.

47. Warren F. Kimball, *Churchill & Roosevelt: The Complete Correspondence*, 3 vols. (Princeton: Princeton University Press, 1984), vol. III, R-742, 630. See also, Kimball, *Forged in War*, 335.

48. George F. Kennan, "Comment on Papers by Professors Dallek, Dallin, and Dilks," delivered at the Organization of American Historians meeting, April 17, 1974 .

49. This echoes the persuasive argument of Alterman, *When Presidents Lie*, esp. 59–82, who points out that "in refusing to reveal the truth about the accords, the administration only aided and abetted the Yalta conspiracy-mongers...," 62.

50. The quotes are two self-satisfied book titles; C.L. Sulzberger, *The Last of the Giants* (New York: Macmillan, 1970), and Tom Brokaw, *The Greatest Generation* (New York: Random House, 1998). Both treat the generation of World War II as unique, special, out of the ordinary. FDR would have chuckled at the notion. The alleged "loss" of China is discussed elsewhere in this volume by Michael Schaller.

51. The starting point for discussions of Kennan's conception of "containment" strategy remains John L. Gaddis, *Strategies of Containment*, rev. ed. (Oxford: Oxford University Press, 2005, originally 1982). But see Lloyd C. Gardner's "pre"-corrective, "James V. Forrestal and George F. Kennan: Will the Real 'Mr. X' Please Stand Up?" in Gardner, *Architects of Illusion* (Chicago: Quadrangle, 1970), 270–300.

52. Kennan's dismissal of the "policemen" came from his conviction that the Soviet Union's political and ideological system made it incapable of negotiating rational agreements or of moving toward integrating with the West. Only the collapse of that system could make such civilized conduct possible.

In the apt phrasing of Anders Stephanson, Kennan characteristically took "presidential rhetoric too literally," failing "to consider the political dynamic." Stephanson, *Kennan and the Art of Foreign Policy* (Cambridge, MA and London: Harvard University Press, 1989), 118. Kennan's comment in 1974 was, "The truth is—there is no avoiding it—for all his charm, and for all his skill as a political leader, [Roosevelt] was, when it came to foreign policy, a very superficial man, ignorant, dilettantish, severely limited in intellectual horizon.... The prewar schemes...were as unrealistic as were the concepts of unconditional surrender and the 'four policemen' and the Morgenthau Plan for Germany by which his wartime policy was informed." Kennan, "Comment on Papers."

53. Gaddis, *Strategies of Containment*, 29.

54. Kennan, "Comment on Papers." See also Kimball, *The Juggler*, 18.

55. The text of Washington's Farewell Address is printed in Felix Gilbert, *To the Farewell Address* (Princeton: Princeton University Press, 1961), 144–7.

56. Perhaps the War of 1812 is an exception. In the words of Anders Stephanson, "Woodrow Wilson may have been able to imagine in 1917 that he was entering a bloody stalemate as a saviour, [but] Roosevelt had no such option. This was a military coalition, a genuine alliance. Roosevelt himself took that position early on, eschewing the Wilsonian precedent of 'association' rather than alliance." Stephanson, "Law and Messianic Counterwar."

57. I have participated in that overanalysis. See my "Dangerously Contagious? The Anglo–American Special Relationship," a debate with Alex Danchev, in *The British Journal of Politics and International Relations* 7, 3 (August 2005): 437–41 [electronically at doi:10.1111/j.1467–856X.2005.00194.x]; Accessed September 1, 2005, and "The 'Special' Anglo–American Special Relationship: 'A fatter, larger underwater cable,'" *Journal of Transatlantic Studies* 3, 1 (Spring 2005): 1–5. The Suez Crisis strained relationships at the very top, but at the next level British policymakers agreed that the invasion was ill considered.

58. For the Declaration and the original list of signatories, see United States, Dept. of State, *Foreign Relations of the United States* (Washington: USGPO, 1862–), *Conferences at Washington, 1941–42*, and *Casablanca, 1943*, 376–7.

59. See David Reynolds, *One World Divisible* (New York and London: W.W. Norton, 2000), 286–8. Australia and New Zealand added two flags by sending token contingents.

60. Statistics for 2004, taken from http://www.pwhce.org/willing.html. Accessed September 1, 2005. By 2007, the coalition had 5,000 British—dropping to 2,500 in 2008, 11 Moldavians, 120 Albanians, 40 Macedonians, 27 Kazakhs, 100 Czechs, and so on; Roger Cohen, "Coalition of the Reluctant," *The New York Times*, October 15, 2007.

61. Before the inevitable accusations of "moral equivalency" ring out, please note that I have not judged the righteousness of U.S. military actions in Korea, Vietnam, and the Gulf Wars. I am happy to make such judgments, but not in this paper. Nor does my focus on FDR and U.S. policy suggest

that I somehow absolve Stalin and the Soviet Union or other American foes of wrongdoing, or of not being unilateralist nationalists.

62. The quotation is from an October 4, 2005 draft of a speech by Lloyd C. Gardner, "Beyond Baghdad."

63. I suppose the works of John Charmley serve as one example of evidence, though I am not convinced that Charmley believes his own arguments; see his *Churchill: The End of Glory* (London: Hodder and Stoughton, 1993).

64. Mead, *Special Providence* (New York and London: Routledge, 2002), 129–30.

65. Fred Pollock and I have examined FDR and decolonization more closely in "'In Search of Monsters to Destroy': Roosevelt and Colonialism," in Kimball, *The Juggler*, 127–57. FDR agreed on the need for U.S. overseas bases in the Pacific and in the northwest coast of Africa. But he rejected American sovereignty over such bases, and insisted that they be included in the UN trusteeship system; ibid., 155. Insistence on the elimination of Imperial Preference and other neo-mercantilist British economic practices was part of a long-standing campaign, not something unique to Roosevelt and his administration.

66. Kimball, *The Juggler*, 114, 143, 190. Gardner, "Beyond Baghdad."

67. This is not the place for an academic debate over words and phrases like empire, informal empire, hegemony, and imperialism, but for a brief explication of my thinking, see my foreword to *The United States and Decolonization*, ed. David Ryan and Victor Pungong (New York: St. Martin's, 2000), xiii–xvii.

68. Lloyd C. Gardner, *A Covenant With Power* (New York and Toronto: Oxford University Press, 1984), 27.

69. The definition of Wilsonianism is a moving target. Historian Robert Divine, in his perceptive set of essays *Roosevelt and World War II*, may be correct to bemoan the false image of FDR as Wilson's disciple and to argue that "Roosevelt's collective security concepts differed radically from Wilson's." But Wilsonianism has come to mean much more than that—or perhaps much less. Traditional usage of "Wilsonianism" has made it a catchall label for anything less than untrammeled power politics, supposed dangerous daydreaming. The Atlantic Charter and FDR's subsequent scheme for bringing the Soviets into his group of world policemen have routinely been dismissed as unrealistic "Wilsonian nonsense." The label Wilsonianism became more curious and useless every day as the White House of George W. Bush rejected the label *realpolitik* and embraced both the concept and the mission of traditional Wilsonianism, while adding preemptive war and open coercion as acceptable methods (and without embracing the label Wilsonian). "I am not a Wilsonian idealist, I have problems to solve," FDR once commented (the *only* example I have found of FDR making such a connection). He was speaking to a French emissary and may have been sensitive to the contempt European leaders had for Wilson's diplomacy, but the words summed up Roosevelt's approach to international issues. But what did FDR mean by Wilsonian? One historian's description emphasized that "... the Wilsonians professed faith in human nature, the strong commitment to human rights,

and the persistent dream of a world of nation-states united by their devotion to the ideas of liberty and their detestation of war,..." On the other extreme, two other historians jointly characterized FDR "as a thoroughly disenchanted Wilsonian idealist" who "had become an advocate and exponent of realpolitik." Go figure. [Citations available on request. Footnotes within a discursive endnote are a bridge too far.]

70. I discuss "open" spheres of influence and free ports, and Americanism, more fully in *The Juggler*, 150, 159–83, and chapter 9.

71. Sherwood, *Roosevelt & Hopkins*, 708.

72. McDougall, *Promised Land*, 177. I would not make a specific challenge to this curious notion were it not that McDougall's book is commonly used in undergraduate survey courses.

73. McDougall, *Promised Land*, 177, 146; Francis Fukuyama, *State Building: Governance and World Order in the 21st Century* (Ithaca: Cornell University Press, 2004), refutes the claim that the reconstruction of Germany and Japan was "nation-building"; Warren F. Kimball, *Swords or Ploughshares?* (Philadelphia: Lippincott, 1976). On "state-building" in Germany see also Carolyn W. Eisenberg, *Drawing the Line: The American Decision to Divide Germany* (Cambridge and New York: Cambridge University Press, 1996), and James McAllister, *No Exit: American and the German Problem, 1943–54* (Ithaca and London: Cornell University Press, 2002).

74. That is, of course, the subject of an ongoing, endless debate. For references, see *American Foreign Relations since 1600: A Guide to the Literature*, ed. Robert Beisner, 2 vols. (Santa Barbara, CA: ABC Clio, 2003), II, 1068–12–22.

75. Robin Edmonds, *Setting the Mould* (New York and London: Norton, 1986), 83. Bevin's remark apparently alluded to "fissile," defined as materials that are fissionable by neutrons with zero kinetic energy. Fissile materials are necessary in some cases to sustain a chain reaction.

76. See Warren F. Kimball, "Churchill and Eisenhower: Sentiment and Politics," in *Churchill Proceedings, 1998–2000* (Washington: The Churchill Centre, 2004), 64–74. A succinct summary of the case against FDR as a Cold Warrior is in Alterman, *When Presidents Lie*, 47–55; see also Kimball *Forged in War*, 335–7. A curious example of the transmutation of FDR into a Cold Warrior (of sorts) is in John Gaddis' latest revision of himself, *The Cold War: A New History* (New York: Penguin, 2005), 6, wherein he states that the United States was "at war" with the USSR before the end of World War II. That contradicts what he wrote in *We Now Know* (Oxford: Oxford University Press, 1997), 36: "It did not automatically follow, though, that the Soviet Union would inherit the title of 'first enemy' once Germany and Japan had been defeated.... The threat, rather, appeared to arise from war itself, whoever might cause it, and the most likely candidates were thought to be resurgent enemies from World War II.... The Cold War developed when it became clear that Stalin either could not or would not accept this [multilateral] framework.... At no point prior to 1947 did the United States and its Western European allies abandon the hope that the Russians might

eventually come around...to multilateralism." In other words, the Cold War began no earlier than 1947.

77. Ibid. For an up to date study of FDR's problems with his diplomats and State Department officers over his policy regarding the Soviet Union, see Mary E. Glantz, *FDR and the Soviet Union: The President's Battles over Foreign Policy* (Lawrence: University Press of Kansas, 2005).

78. Jim Bishop, *FDR's Last Year* (New York: Pocket Books, 1975), 616. Alterman, *When President's Lie*, 47–79, presents a strong argument for Truman's supposed ignorance of the Yalta agreements (misleading shorthand for all the postwar settlements) being grossly exaggerated, particularly once he went to the Potsdam Conference in August 1945.

79. That is, perhaps, what some historians mean by "hegemony by consent," though that phrase is all too reminiscent of the notion of "imperialism by invitation." Gaddis, *Surprise*, 46–65. The other side of that coin is columnist Maureen Dowd's description of George W. Bush's foreign policy as "entirely constructed around American self-love—the idea that the United States is superior, that we are the model everyone looks up to, that everyone in the world wants what we have." *New York Times*, September 7, 2005.

CHAPTER 5

FDR AND THE "COLONIAL QUESTION"

LLOYD GARDNER

THERE WAS SOMETHING APPROACHING UNANIMITY in the American public's attitude about the "colonial question" during World War II. One would have to look very hard to find anything favorable to "empires" in newspapers or magazines, whatever their point of view on Roosevelt and the New Deal. Restoring colonialism was not considered a worthy war aim. The only place where that might not have been true was inside the State Department, and even there the only real dissent came from the heads of the Western European "desks." Secretary of State Cordell Hull acknowledged in his memoirs the difficulty of trying to work with the Europeans in the war against Hitler, while opposing their imperial policies in Asia. Hull had spent his career in Congress and at State preaching the gospel of "free trade" against the sins of high tariffs and colonial restrictions and looked upon the war as the best chance in a lifetime to knock down the walls of autarchy and imperial trade preferences. He had even told the Japanese ambassador in the last days before Pearl Harbor that after the war many of their supposed grievances against the West would disappear as the world returned to economic sanity behind American leadership. It was a most remarkable thing to say to a presumed enemy. But it does capture the depth of feeling American leaders had about the connection between "selfish" colonial trade policies and the causes of war.

For Hull, then, colonialism's greatest sin was that it choked the life out of the world economy and brought on the Great Depression and the war. For many others, however, it might be racial discrimination and destruction of indigenous cultures. For still others, it was a political concern that colonialism was inherently unstable, especially given the rise of nationalist movements in Asia and Africa. Underneath it all there were the history books that reminded every generation of school children how the American republic was born in a war against a colonial empire.

These powerful currents did not prescribe specific policies, however, and therein, as FDR liked to quip about his difficulties, was the rub. Wartime exigencies and postwar planning for economic and political recovery required more than moral indignation or anodyne prescriptions. Compared to the work that went into the Bretton Woods system to restore the mechanics of international trade and reconstruction aid, the colonial "question" received much less attention. Partly that was because, as Hull had said, how did one work with allies whose attitudes were quite different? After the Yalta Conference Roosevelt had remarked almost in passing that his closest ally, Prime Minister Winston Churchill, had a mid-Victorian attitude about the empire, so it was necessary to go slow.

Roosevelt had no intention, for example, of pushing his ally to the brink over immediate independence for India. He knew it would do no good to do so—and might harm the war effort in the Pacific. When Harold Ickes pressed him on one occasion to take a stronger position, he replied that he could not indulge in pointless rhetoric. "You are right about India," he wrote his secretary of the interior, a fiery progressive, "but it would be playing with fire if the British Empire were to tell me to mind my own business."[1] Nevertheless, FDR did speak out publicly in general terms, as for example when he claimed there were no differences—not a controversy in a carload— between his views and those of the Republican leader Wendell Willkie, who had become the scourge of British imperialism on a 1942 world tour.

The "colonial question" worried just about everyone in policy positions, whether they feared Roosevelt's sometimes rambling, off-the-cuff pronouncements, or the shortsightedness of America's wartime allies. As soon as "the lid is taken off" in Europe, mused the old New Dealer, now assistant secretary of state, Adolf Berle, there will be a "European revolution," either along Stalinist lines or "liberal and individualist lines." Plans would have to be made so that it did not become the former by default, as the result of a general upheaval and chaos. A general security system "on a global basis" needed to be in place as soon as the war ended. "The territories of Indo-China, Thailand, the Indies, and so forth, have to be worked into some sort of a cooperative system."[2]

Roosevelt did give some thought to a cooperative system—even inviting Russian participation in solving the colonial question as part of the postwar Big Four. At one point he shocked State Department professionals with a sudden notion he had at Tehran about encouraging Stalin to participate in a kind of trusteeship over postwar Iran. Largely forgotten after Roosevelt's death and the onset of Russian–American tensions, the "plan" grew out of a casual remark about trusteeships for immature nations the president had made at the time of the first Big Three conference to the Soviet delegate to the Allied advisory council on the Mediterranean, Andrei Vishinsky. Without much further thought, Roosevelt elevated it to a full-blown overture for Russian cooperation by channeling age-old Tsarist desires for a warm water port on the Persian Gulf into a three-power consortium. The State Department was aghast at the notion of inviting the Soviet Union to bask in the sun all along the coast of Iran and to come ashore and help run the railroads! Acting Secretary of State Joseph Grew sent Roosevelt a two-page memo before Yalta that began by giving Roosevelt credit for thinking creatively about a way to damp down inter-Allied rivalries and push matters toward three-power cooperation. But it was really a terrible idea in practice. Hitting a sensitive point, Grew suggested that it smacked of the worst of Old World imperialism. The Iranians would never let foreign powers take over the railroads without a fight. The Russians, on the other hand, would suspect it was just another way to gain control of the northern regions, where they were particularly sensitive. And the British would have fits. Their whole policy was to prevent any other power, especially Russia, from gaining a foothold in the Persian Gulf. The episode reminded everyone that reconciling Big Four leadership with other goals was not going to be easy to accomplish, as Warren Kimball reminds us, not in terms of political structures or in dealing with the colonial question.[3]

The president did not bring up his Iranian scheme again. But America watchers in the British Foreign Office noted on more than one occasion that it really did not matter which "Henry" ultimately prevailed in policy, Henry Luce of the American Century or Henry Wallace of the Century of the Common Man, the United States would inevitably pursue an anti-colonial policy—at least rhetorically—and always without much thought to European objections. Henry Luce's *Fortune* magazine summed up the projected American role in the new Asia, envisioning the first altruistic "imperialism" to finish what the Europeans had started in phrases that could just as easily have come from Vice President Henry A. Wallace:

> American imperialism can afford to complete the work the British started; instead of salesmen and planters, its representatives can be brains and bull-dozers, technicians and machine tools. American imperialism does not need extraterritoriality; it can get along better in Asia if the tuans and sahibs stay home....
>
> So long as Asia does not try to foist an economic feudalism of the Jap type on its neighbors, the U.S. can believe in Asia-for-the-Asiatics too.[4]

Wendell Willkie almost gave Churchill apoplexy in 1942 when he dropped by London on his 1942 world trip seemingly for no other purpose than to scold the British for their colonial policies. Three years later the prime minister had not forgotten Willkie's performance. At the Yalta Conference he apparently mistook an American proposal for a United Nations trusteeship plan for a general assault on the British Empire. He had told Willkie, Churchill burst out, that he would never tolerate sixty or seventy fingers interfering in the affairs of the empire. Roosevelt could not resist a puckish comment. Was that what killed Willkie? he asked.

It took a short recess to get Churchill calmed down so they could continue the discussion about former enemy territories. But he was not alone. For London, the "colonial question" was not Willkie or the two Henry's, it was essentially the Roosevelt question. Certainly that was true in the short term, and it would be FDR who set the jumps for the postwar steeple chase. He seemed to love talking about the new day for colonial peoples. Roosevelt talked all the time about the colonial question and his conversations, even the most private ones, inevitably wound up being heard a considerable distance away from the White House—probably by design. It is important to keep in mind that FDR always regarded his statements as having policy ends in themselves. On one occasion after the Casablanca Conference, referring to conditions in Africa, he said that many wrongs could be righted by using "pitiless publicity." He frequently spoke about the colonial question to various foreign leaders, and, improbably enough, specifically about Indochina to the Turkish prime minister, of all people, as well as the Egyptian "heir apparent," one afternoon in his villa during the First Cairo Conference in late November 1943. Was this seeming casualness and randomness about such serious matters evidence that Roosevelt operated from a "second rate intellect," as Justice Holmes once quipped? Why discuss Indochina in such a non-consequential setting? Roosevelt had in mind the need not to allow the initiative on the colonial question to remain with his European allies. If he discussed it with improbable as well as skeptical listeners, it was to remind everyone that the United States now had a stake in its allies' postwar plans—just as he had intervened with Churchill over Lend-Lease issues to insure that attention was given to the American position that the imperial preference system was not to be tolerated.[5]

"What am I to believe when the British tell me that my future is with them and not with America?" asked King Ib'n Saud when Roosevelt met with him after Yalta. America's political interest in his country was just a transitory war interest, the British told him, and once the wartime Lend-Lease aid ended, the Americans would return to the Western Hemisphere—leaving Saudi Arabia within the area bounded by pound sterling controls, connected by British communications, and defended by the Royal Navy and British army. "On the strength of this argument they seek a priority for Britain in Saudi Arabia. What am I to believe?" Roosevelt assured the king the postwar world would see a "decline in spheres of influence in favor of the Open Door." The door of Saudi Arabia should be open to all nations, he promised, with no monopoly for anyone.[6]

Ever since the turn of the twentieth-century diplomacy in regard to China, the United States had championed the Open Door against spheres of influence and colonialism, but World War II suggested a much wider geographic and political scope to conflicts between metropolitan powers and semicolonial as well as colonial dependencies. Six months after Pearl Harbor, the Battle of Midway foretold the ultimate defeat of Japan's effort to establish its Asian Coprosperity Sphere as a bulwark against the West's dominance of the world economy; the White House brimmed with confidence that military success could be translated into political success. "Our victory at Midway," Roosevelt's aide, Harry Hopkins, declared, "may turn out to have been a great one. So much so that it may change the whole strategy of the Pacific. The days of the policy of the 'white man's burden are over." Asia's "vast masses of people" were simply not going to tolerate it any longer.[7]

Roosevelt's grand design for facilitating the transition began (as did many other plans) with the idea of the Big Four, which he hoped to sell to Churchill, Russia's Josef Stalin, and Chinese leader, Chiang Kai-shek. He seldom linked the colonial issue publicly to postwar security matters quite so definitely as he did musing about what would come after the war to an intimate friend at the end of 1942. He hoped to go to Khartoum, Egypt, he told Margaret Suckley, and there meet with the other world leaders. The discovery of Ms. Suckley's diaries has been one of the most important "archival" finds in recent years. Among other reasons, it is important because it confirms many of the things Roosevelt supposedly told his son Elliott, and which were considered doubtful or distorted during the Cold War. He thought Stalin might understand his plan better than Churchill. She paraphrased his idea in her diary:

> In general it consists of an international police force run by the four countries—All nations to disarm completely, so that no nation will have the chance to start out to conquer any other—
>
>   Self determination to be worked out for colonies over a period of years, in the way it was done for the Philippines.[8]

Roosevelt's friend gently suggested that perhaps the "Empire owners" might not take to the idea so easily. What would Queen Wilhelmina think, for example, she asked? " F.[ranklin] said he [already] gave [the queen] a hint about it!" His companion was still skeptical. "Perhaps she [the queen] didn't realize what he really meant."[9]

As matters developed, Roosevelt hoped to play the "Dutch" card to further his plans for speeding the transition, but in a circuitous fashion. The president's impatience with Winston Churchill's view of colonial matters was famous. But he hoped to divide and conquer, so as to avoid driving the lesser colonial powers into an alliance with the fading but still powerful British raj. Roosevelt would claim on occasion that he had spoken to Churchill at least twenty-five times about Indochina's future, singling that colony out as the most eligible place to impose a trusteeship "solution." Churchill for his part suspected, rightly, that the president did not expect to halt his interference in the decolonization process at Indochina's borders with Burma. But the president feared pushing things too fast. "When we've won the war," he told his son Elliott, he intended to work with "all my might and main" to prevent the imperial powers from maneuvering the United States into supporting their ambitions.[10]

Meanwhile, he would keep the Big Four idea in play and see where that led. Because of their common ancestry, perhaps, Roosevelt believed he had a special relationship with "Minnie," Queen Wilhelmina, enough so, apparently, that he thought he could drop hints and give little nudges that she should begin the process of granting self-government to the Netherlands East Indies. He no doubt believed that winning her over would be very useful with the tougher cases when it came to dealing with the French and the British. The queen was not particularly responsive to these "friendly" suggestions, however, telling the president that while Java might, perhaps, become independent in something between fifteen and fifty years, anything for the more backward areas was "sheer speculation."[11]

Roosevelt backed off from a direct confrontation. His main worry, all along, was that he would scare the lesser European powers into placing their faith in British leadership. At war's end, both Churchill and Roosevelt knew American demands for change could hardly be ignored by a largely bankrupt world in debt both to the United States and to the colonies. Certainly that was the case with the British in India. There were mechanisms already being put in place to insure that the British Empire was not shut up, as Secretary of State Cordell Hull had once complained, like an "oyster shell" against world trade.[12]

Churchill would never think of choosing Paris over Washington, of course, but he had no compunctions about turning the tables on FDR, employing Holland and France as counterbalances to an overweening America. Roosevelt could afford to wait him out, but he would never allow Britain to sink out of simple self-interest. But the British as well as the continental Europeans were going to have to learn to adjust to an empire-less existence, though exactly how that was going to happen he really did not know, either in terms of mechanisms or time frame. "Don't think for a moment," Roosevelt admonished his son Elliott during a private moment at the Casablanca Conference, "that Americans would be dying in the Pacific tonight, if it had not been for the shortsighted greed of the French and the British and the Dutch."[13]

When it suited his purposes, he could play the gallant rescuer of European fortunes with blithe disregard for any inconsistencies. Thus his response when he heard from one of his diplomatic representatives and old friends that Queen Wilhelmina felt a sense of anxiety for "her people in Holland...as a result of the fall of the Indies," and had been "deeply touched" by Mr. Churchill's vow at a meeting of the Pacific War Council that the restoration of the East Indies was a "sacred trust." The Dutch foreign minister had conveyed this information, along with a request that President Roosevelt offer similar assurances, even though "he was well aware of the delicacy of the situation." And so FDR did. "You have been much in my thoughts," he wrote the queen, and he wanted her to know that he was well aware of the "gallantry of the Netherlands' forces in the Netherlands Indies." When Germany was defeated, it would not take long to drive the Japanese back into their own islands. "The Netherlands Indies must be restored— and something within me tells me that they will be."[14]

FDR was gratified when Wilhelmina then broadcast promises of future reform for the Indies, as that seemed to demonstrate the wisdom of his policy of nudges and hints; but he also informed a British diplomat that the Dutch, "the poor dears," were very unlikely to get the East Indies back as they liked to imagine.[15] Observing these ploys, Free French leader Charles deGaulle deplored Roosevelt's scheming forays into colonial questions, claiming that the president had somehow forced the Dutch to "renounce their sovereignty over Java."[16] That accusation gave the president too much blame or credit. Roosevelt and deGaulle never got along—not from the start. He was determined not to recognize deGaulle's Free French regime as the government of France in exile. It would take twenty years or more for France to return to Great Power status, he had declared, and, as if to make the prophecy self-fulfilling, he had once listed France among those countries to be completely disarmed after the war.[17]

Roosevelt's much put upon secretary of state, Cordell Hull, excluded not only from many wartime conferences but often also from the president's inner thoughts on postwar matters, was well-versed, nevertheless, on Roosevelt's attitude toward French colonial possessions. "He could not but remember," Hull recalled of Roosevelt's outbursts, "the devious conduct of the Vichy Government in granting Japan the right to station troops there [Indochina], without any consultation with us but with an effort to make the world believe we approved."[18] Because Roosevelt wished to maintain some sort of relationship with that same Vichy regime, however, he had had

Under Secretary Sumner Welles offer assurances in April 1942, that the United States recognized the "sovereign jurisdiction of the people of France over the territory of France and over French possessions overseas."[19]

In a 1942 conversation with Russian Foreign Minister V.M. Molotov, Roosevelt broached the idea of international trusteeships, passing it off as Generalissimo Chiang Kai-shek's idea. "There were," he suggested to the Russian, "all over the world, many islands and colonial possessions which ought, for our own safety, to be taken away from weak nations." Besides Indochina, he said, Siam and the Malay States ought to be put under interim trusteeships until they were ready for self-government. And Russia should have a role in all this.[20]

Molotov promised the Soviet Union would give the matter serious attention, noting it was premised upon Allied cooperation to make sure Germany and Japan did not again threaten the peace. "Starting from this principle, Mr. Molotov expressed his conviction that the president's proposals could be effectively worked out."[21] Encouraged that he was moving steadily toward his long-range goals, the president scarcely worried about the letters he had sent to the Dutch and French. With Churchill seated nearby at a session with the Sultan of Morocco during the Casablanca Conference several months later, the president suddenly launched into a discussion of his sympathy with all colonial aspirations for independence, suggesting that he would like to see postwar economic cooperation between the United States and the sultan's country.[22]

Alone with his advisers, Roosevelt openly discussed with his military leaders the transfer of Dakar, Indochina, and other French possessions to some postwar international authority. He congratulated diplomat Robert Murphy on his diplomatic dealings with the Vichy French rulers of North Africa before the landings. "But you overdid things a bit in one of the letters you wrote," he reproached Murphy, "pledging the United States Government to guarantee the return to France of every part of her empire. Your letter may make trouble for me after the war."[23] But perhaps not, because Vichy would not survive, and he thought he could handle de Gaulle. France was "in the position of a little child unable to look out and fend for itself," Roosevelt said, "and that in such a case a court would appoint a trustee to do the necessary." Including, it would seem, concludes historian Christopher Thorne, taking away some of the child's possessions.[24]

At Cairo and Tehran, Roosevelt approached Chiang Kai-shek first, and then Stalin, trying to line them up for his trusteeship plan. Inviting the former to be an active member of the Big Four, Roosevelt proposed that China and the United States consult together before any decisions were reached on matters concerning Asia. They should, for example, reach "a mutual understanding" on the future status of Korea, Indochina, and other colonial areas.[25] At his very first meeting with Stalin at Tehran on November 28, 1943, the two immediately plunged into a discussion of postwar France. To Stalin's opening statement that the French ruling classes were corrupt and "should not be entitled to share in any of the benefits of the peace," Roosevelt replied Churchill thought the country would recover quickly. But that was not his view. "Many years of honest labor would be necessary before France would be re-established. He said the first necessity for the French, not only the Government but the people as well, was to become honest citizens." By its manifest weaknesses, they agreed, France had forfeited the right to reclaim Indochina.[26]

Stalin then declared that he "did not propose to have the Allies shed blood to restore Indochina...to the old French colonial rule." It was necessary to fight Japan in the political sphere as well as the military, "particularly in view of the fact that the Japanese had granted at least nominal independence to certain colonial areas." Roosevelt was delighted with Stalin's forthright declaration. "He was in 100 percent agreement," the president said, "and remarked that after 100 years of French rule in Indochina, the inhabitants were worse off than they had been before." What did the Soviet leader think about a system of trusteeship to prepare the people for independence within a definite time period, perhaps twenty to thirty years? Stalin said he "completely agreed with that view."[27]

Things seemed to be shaping up nicely. Chiang sent word to Roosevelt after the Cairo Conferences that he regarded the president not only as his friend, but as an older brother, to whom he would speak frankly. Roosevelt took this to mean that Chiang's government would follow his lead, a dangerous conclusion. "I think that Stalin, Chiang and I can bring brother Churchill around," he boasted at tea on the White House porch to friends. Later, at dinner, he rambled on about the stakes in the colonial question:

> In regard to the Far East in general, which means the yellow race, which is far more numerous than the white, it will be to the advantage of the white race to be friends with them & work in cooperation with them, rather than make enemies of them & have them eventually use all the machines of western civilization to overrun & conquer the white race.[28]

Over the summer of 1944, however, the military and political situation in China worsened. His closest adviser, Harry Hopkins, confided that the president now had much less hope for China than he had had at Cairo. Roosevelt was still interested in a trusteeship solution, Hopkins went on, but was now absorbed in European questions. As these factors loomed more important in the immediate future, senior State Department officials called for a change of emphasis in postwar planning for Indochina.

American influence, wrote Joseph Grew and James Clement Dunn, could be better directed toward securing French promises to end their commercial monopolies and to integrate Indochina into the world market. "These areas [of Southeast Asia] are sources of products essential to both our wartime and peacetime economy. They are potentially important markets for American exports.... Their economy and political stability will be an important factor in the maintenance of peace in Asia."[29]

Cairo and Tehran proved to be the high points for dreaming dreams about what could be accomplished through Big Four cooperation. The descent to reality began before the end of the war, therefore, and while the internal French political situation soon became a cause for concern, its importance was in reinforcing prior decisions. A few days before the 1944 presidential election, Harry Hopkins had asked a friend from the British Embassy around for drinks and a chat. Looking past the election, Roosevelt's adviser mused about the president's plans. "You will find him right in on all these questions with his own views," he told his guest, "and you will have to pay attention to them." "Take Indo-China," he said. "I know what French rule has meant in Indo-China. It is going to be American and British boys who will die to take it back from the Japanese. Why should we let the French walk in again on their own terms when it is we and not they who will have made the sacrifices?"

Around this time Roosevelt had become wary of British maneuvers to allow Free French forces to participate in the "liberation" of Southeast Asia from the Japanese. Hence Hopkins's warning that soon the United States would be "right in batting all over the world." When he finished the lecture, his guest had a question. Did he not agree, he protested mildly, that their common interest was to see France restored as a Great Power? Hopkins said "yes," even if, the diplomat reported, rather "perfunctorily."[30]

No matter how "perfunctorily" they regarded the French, Lord Halifax wrote in a final report, they would find they needed Paris to restore the world economy, to recreate a trading system under liberal capitalist rules. "To some extent," added a Foreign Office commentator, "they are influenced by the desire to perpetuate the sort of world in which American individualism, almost isolated, can hold its own against State trading policies of other countries; but they do desire world trading arrangements for their own sake as means of knitting the world together into an orderly whole."[31]

French recovery (psychological as well as material) soon came to dominate the agenda. The lectures to the British and French about the evils of colonialism stopped—though concerns about Paris' failure to "get it" had many shaking their heads and scribbling out notes back and forth between the West European and Southeast Asian Desks in the State Department. Unlike the British, who had more in common with American ideas on the whole postwar agenda, and who badly needed American financial support, the French seemed to think they could do very well without American "guidance" on colonial matters. "The economic interests of the United States, a non-imperialist nation," read a memo from Asian desk officers skeptical of French plans, "demand not only free access and trade in Southeast Asia, but also a rising standard of living there. This would increase the market for our products in the area, and markets are one of our primary interests in the postwar world." But markets were not America's only interest, or not only America's interest. If the French continued to deny nationalist aspirations, the only result would be increased Russian influence. "We are the 'last best hope' of democracy in the colonial areas," the memo argued. "If we do not act to fulfill this hope, the Russian system and Russia may well become the 'new hope.'"[32]

The United States, in other words, had been forced into this ambiguous position by French mistakes. Hence the connection policymakers made with World War II objectives, and the logic that followed from the unfinished business of the Pacific campaign, in part also the result of the abrupt ending to the war against Japan, which did not allow for a smooth transition from war to peace. Explaining Roosevelt's wartime policies and the bewildering switchbacks from expediency to efforts to force a solution to the colonial "problem" became difficult terrain for his successors.

His notion that he could manage Brother Churchill by manipulating Chiang and Stalin was replaced by an almost desperate effort to secure Russian cooperation in propping up the Nationalist regime by becoming China's (uninvited, perhaps) intercessor with Stalin. In a private conversation with Stalin near the end of the conference, Roosevelt admitted that "for some time we had been trying to keep China alive." Stalin shrugged off the implications of this statement and posed as a disinterested observer, wondering why the Nationalists and Communists could not form a united front against Japan. On the matter of trusteeships, Roosevelt gave a rambling account of his troubles with Churchill, who feared that a trusteeship for Indochina would lead to pressure to create one for Burma. Stalin pointed out that the British were being shortsighted. They had already lost Burma once by relying on Indochina. And then he put a point that must have triggered some ideas in FDR's mind. "It was not his opinion," he said, "that Britain was a sure country to protect this area." Perhaps it would be possible to work on something that would hold France up to a standard that would "protect this area," and would disengage the colonial powers from one another.[33]

From the beginning of the war, Roosevelt had seen Indochina as an area needing protection. His statements about the Indochinese at Yalta indicated that he had never really given much thought to them as independent actors—nor had his advisers, for that matter. Speaking with Stalin, he asserted that the Indochinese "were people of small stature, like the Javanese and Burmese, and were not warlike." France had done nothing "to improve the natives since she had the colony." And now de Gaulle wanted ships to transport French forces to Indochina. Where was he going to get the troops? asked Stalin. "The President replied that de Gaulle was going to find the troops when the President could find the ships, but the President added that up to the present he had been unable to find the ships."[34]

In the weeks after Yalta, Indochina's fate came up in various ways. An aide recorded what turned out to be Roosevelt's last words on the question on March 15, 1945:

> I asked the President if he had changed his ideas on French Indochina....He said no....The President hesitated a moment and then said—well if we can get the proper pledge from France to assume for herself the obligations of a trustee, then I would agree to France retaining these colonies with the proviso that independence was the ultimate goal.[35]

President Truman did make some attempts to secure the "proper pledge" from France, but he mostly just wanted the problem to go away. OSS (Office of Strategic Service) agents who had been in contact with Ho Chi Minh expressed disappointment that nobody paid much attention to their reports of Ho's keen interest in an American presence in Vietnam. The United States, Ho told one of these agents, Frank White, was in the best position to come to Vietnam's aid, but Washington could not be counted on because it "would find more urgent things to do."[36] Ho was right that Truman was preoccupied. He had to worry about civil war in China, and the danger that Russia might lodge itself in Manchuria and then claim a role in the postwar occupation of Japan. The atomic bomb, which was supposed to simplify at least some of his problems, actually made matters worse by speeding up the pace of events.

Frank Capra's imaginings in the *Why we Fight Series* and Normal Rockwell's *Four Freedoms* posters seemed to grow less distinct off the movie screen as the mushroom clouds of reality rose over Hiroshima and Nagasaki. No one could have foreseen just how fast the war would end, with temporary arrangements for disarming the Japanese merging into French reoccupation plans—while American military personnel simply stood by and watched. The British landed first, and behind them the French, who immediately set about "restoring order" using typically colonial methods of beatings and intimidation to demonstrate who was boss. The Japanese had already succeeded, however, in undermining the raison d'etre of Western imperialism, that Westerners had come as both exploiters *and* protectors.

The head of the OSS mission in what was then French Indochina, the improbably named Archimedes L. Patti, knew all about the debates inside the government over the fate of that colony. He believed Roosevelt's successors gave up the fight and the Vietnam War resulted. Interestingly, at the time of the 1954 Geneva Conference, Secretary of State John Foster Dulles, who, one could argue, was the real founder of the Vietnam War, felt the same way. If Roosevelt's plan had been followed, he told congressional leaders at a White House conference, the communists would not have had a chance to steal the nationalist flag from true patriots. The problem with all this ruminating about Roosevelt's supposed plans, of course, is that we do not know how he would have moved to implement any of his ideas, or, which ideas he would have pursued.

Ho Chi Minh suggested to the American OSS agents that he welcomed American involvement in his country's quest for independence, and would more than welcome capitalist investment. He wrote Truman several letters encouraging him to see the Vietnamese Revolution as fulfillment of the promises of the Atlantic Charter and the San Francisco Charter of the United Nations. None of these were ever answered. French officials, meanwhile, made their own offers. Even if France went socialist, an official of the Colonial Ministry told a State Department official, even if the Metropole nationalized mines, utilities, and heavy industries, all this would have no bearing on freedom of enterprise in Indochina. "It is apparently the purpose," his American listener wryly noted, "to make Indo-China a haven for private enterprise."[37]

The prospect of a Communist victory in the first Vietnam War forced a temporary reconsideration of Roosevelt's determination to challenge French prerogatives in Indochina. "Following relaxation [of] European controls," read a private State Department policy statement in May, 1947,

> internal racial, religious and national differences could plunge new nations into violent discord, or already apparent anti-Western Pan Asiatic tendencies could become dominant political force, or Communists could capture control. We consider as best safeguard against these eventualities a continued close association between newly-autonomous peoples and powers which have long been responsible [for] their welfare.[38]

But simply saying that we were in the same boat as the colonial powers in this situation, as this paper argued, quickly proved to be an untenable position. Benign neglect was no answer to the deepening crisis. French inability to resolve the crisis either on the battlefield or at the conference table had wide ramifications that began with its role in European recovery and rearmament but extended outward to East Asia. Instability in Southeast Asia would tempt the Chinese Communists—filled with revolutionary zeal after their momentous victory—to intervene. Surveying danger areas of

Southeast Asia in the wake of the Chinese Communist triumph, Secretary of State Dean Acheson told a Canadian diplomat that the United States felt the French had recently taken the right steps in establishing a government under the Emperor Bao Dai. In actuality everyone knew that Bao Dai was really just another makeshift solution, but Acheson had to hope for the best. "The American Government," he informed Ambassador Hume Wrong, "in distinction from its earlier views would be ready to recognize and help Indo-China as soon as the French had acted."[39]

"Whether the French like it or not," one State Department official protested the drift toward Paris, "independence is coming to Indochina. Why, therefore, do we tie ourselves to the tail of their battered kite?"[40] The outlook continued to look foreboding, as the kite was buffeted about in the storms set off in the Korean War. In the midst of their conversations on the progress of the Korean War at Wake Island, Truman and his aides took turns with General MacArthur in denouncing French policy in Indochina. MacArthur set things going by saying he was "puzzled" as to why the French with their numerical superiority couldn't win. "They are opposed by half of what the North Koreans had. I cannot understand why they do not clean it up." Admiral Radford said the reason was the French had no support among the local Vietnamese. "The rest of Southeast Asia—Burma, Siam—is wide open if the Chinese Communists pursue a policy of aggression." The place to stand was in Indochina. But the French were making a mess of things. The admiral added that recently some French ships stopped at Hawaii, but they were not anxious to go to Indochina and were dragging their feet. "They would have stayed in Pearl Harbor for six months if I had invited them." All this seemed to rev up the president:

> This is the most discouraging thing we face. [We] have worked on the French tooth and nail to try and persuade them to do what the Dutch had done in Indonesia but the French have not been willing to listen. If the French Prime Minister comes to see me, he is going to hear some very plain talk. I am going to talk cold turkey to him. If you don't want him to hear that kind of talk, you had better keep him away from me.[41]

Roosevelt had predicted the situation would evolve in this fashion. He had tried to find avenues around the impending crisis. Now Truman could find no solution to the dilemma, complaining that American policy had been "contained" by French "stubbornness" in Indochina. By the end of the Korean War, the United States was paying about 80 percent of the cost of the war. Eisenhower and Dulles thus inherited the situation, a truly vexed legacy. Eisenhower's secretary of state expressed considerable dismay that Roosevelt had backed away from his avowed goal of replacing the French with an international trusteeship. By allowing the colony to be reoccupied, Dulles complained privately, FDR and Truman put the United States in a false position. "Originally," he wrote in an unused response to critics of the "compromise" at the 1954 Geneva Conference, "President Roosevelt was against this on the ground that France did not have a good record as a colonial power and its return would not be accepted by the people." He was right. The French could only maintain their position by the "bloody massacres which started the colonial war," and that allowed the Communists an opportunity to lead the nationalist movement.[42]

At the outset of the Eisenhower Administration, John Foster Dulles talked boldly about liberating American foreign policy from the debilitating and morally unsatisfactory tenets of Containment. The American response to the Soviet challenge had been too passive, he charged, and too concerned with protecting the interests of those whose time had passed. The European colonial powers were "old, tired, worn out, and almost willing to buy peace in order to have a few years more of rest." The Free World "will only be saved if it gets out of us what is lacking in the rest of the world."[43]

There must be a revival of America's anticolonial tradition, lost since FDR's time, to discover an alternative to Ho Chi Minh's deception. In a pointed address to French National Political Science Institute in May 1952, even before he knew he would be the next secretary of state, Dulles lectured his audience on the modern "White Man's Burden" in Indochina:

> You are there paying a heavy cost, in lives and money. I am glad that the United States is now helping substantially. I should personally be glad to see us do more, for you have really been left too much alone to discharge a task which is vital to us all.[44]

Dulles sought new initiatives for "Liberation" policies not only in Southeast Asia but also in the Middle East and Africa. It soon became clear, indeed, that what liberation in fact meant was release from the constraints of following the standpat policies of America's allies in what was now being called the Third World. Southeast Asia was of particular concern, however, because an actual war was being waged there between the forces of revolution (Communist style) and the forces of reaction (nineteenth-Century style), or so, at least, Dulles believed.

Dulles was deeply disappointed by the Korean truce in June 1953, though he understood it was politically necessary if the Administration were to clear the slate for taking new initiatives. But the prospect of a permanently divided country, as the Korean "settlement" appeared to endorse, was hardly the image that one could use to entice former colonial peoples to align themselves with the West. Dulles's boasts about the threat of the atomic bomb to break open the stalemate in the truce talks should be seen from this perspective—as a replacement for the now discredited boasts of the original colonial masters that they could protect their "native" allies against outside forces and restless underclasses. The French, meanwhile, staked everything on one last roll of the dice at Dienbienphu. Eisenhower briefly considered using the atomic bomb to relieve the besieged French garrison in the spring of 1954, but he realized that his old army companions were right, military intervention in Vietnam would mean another ground war on the continent of Asia, too soon after Korea, and, despite Dulles's best diplomatic efforts, with little support in Congress or from the Allies. In the most recent book on "Why Vietnam?" Gareth Porter argues that Eisenhower never had any intention of sending ground forces to Indochina. He was bitterly opposed, Porter quotes Eisenhower as saying, because it would make the United States look just like the colonial powers.[45]

Without doubt, Eisenhower's most famous utterance on the tangle of issues surrounding the Vietnam crisis, the falling domino image, would provide cover for later presidents, who would all harken back to this pronouncement as American involvement deepened into tragedy, elevating it to the status of proven theory to be ignored only at great peril to the "national security." In fact, it was no more than an abstraction, constructed without regard to Vietnamese history. From Roosevelt to Truman, and then to Eisenhower, the Vietnam riddle was how to get the French out of the way without "losing" the contest for the hearts and minds of the people—and the resources of the land. Just as the French had sought to make Vietnam part of their history, so, too, the Americans. To all those who charge that we are seeking to take France's place in Vietnam, said National Security Adviser McGeorge Bundy in 1965, he would give this answer: "We simply are not there as colonialists." Any fair minded observer understood that fundamental point. "Our innate lack of imperial zeal is visible to any observer in Vietnam and to the Vietnamese people." The French never had such a reputation, and, therefore, became an easy target for Communist and noncommunist nationalists alike.[46]

In the profoundest sense, beyond limitations of the definition of "colonialism," Bundy was wrong: We *were* seeking to replace the French. After Geneva ended the French war in Vietnam, with an apparent agreement that elections would be held in all Vietnam within two years to determine the political future of the country and its reunification, American policymakers still believed that the central issue was how to get rid of the French, and not to deal with Vietnamese nationalism. At a National Security Council meeting in October 1954, President Eisenhower made that clear. "It is true that we have to cajole the French with regard to the European area," he said, "but we certainly didn't have to in Indochina."[47]

Was Ike also thinking of Roosevelt's legacy? John Kennedy inherited a Vietnamese situation no less complicated than what each of his predecessors had faced. In the wake of the Bay of Pigs fiasco, and the Vienna summit conference with Nikita Khrushchev, the young president lamented his fate. "I've got a terrible problem," he told *New York Times* reporter James Reston. Khrushchev acted like he believed JFK had "no guts." To disabuse the Russians, he would increase the military budget and send reinforcements to Germany. But that was still not enough. The only place in the world where there was a real challenge at the moment was in Vietnam. "...We have a problem in trying to make our power credible, and Vietnam looks like the place."[48]

The two advisers who influenced Kennedy and Lyndon Johnson the most were McGeorge Bundy and Robert McNamara. As the fateful 1965 step was taken to send the first 100,000 soldiers to Vietnam, both men offered a variation on the theme that *Fortune* magazine's editors had developed after Pearl Harbor to clarify America's purposes in reimaging the world. Bundy's memo stressed the role America had to play in the world—or see Western influence recede from Asia with the profoundest consequences. He began his comments with a blunt statement that historians of the future might designate the 1960s as the decade when "our civilization fashioned so painfully since the Reformation could be said to have reached its end." If that happened, it would likely not be because of nuclear cataclysm, but as a result of a new polarization of the world between the poor, the restless, and the nonwhite peoples, led or pushed by China, as opposed to Europe and North America. If that happened, "we will find ourselves in a virtual state of siege."

> The West, of course, still can survive as a political grouping and even as a culture. We will still maintain overwhelming military power in the sense that we could at any time reduce the land mass of Asia and of Africa to ashes. But this would provide us with slim comfort....
>
> In the last analysis, the West must preserve (or at least not willingly and voluntarily default) its access to, communications with, and benign influence on the peoples of Asia and Africa. We have much that is worthwhile to offer and much to gain. Our society and theirs can be enriched and nourished by the two-way flow of ideas and goods and peoples. China has chosen to slam its doors, at least for the present. We and the other peoples of the world cannot afford to see any more doors close, for every door that closes quickens the pace of rich–poor, colored–white, North–South division of the world.[49]

In similar fashion, Defense Secretary Robert McNamara told a reporter in an interview why Lyndon Johnson's decision was necessary.

> If the U.S. withdrew from SVN, there would be a complete shift in the world balance of power. Asia goes Red, our prestige and integrity damaged, allies

everywhere shaken (even those who publicly ask us to quit bombing, etc.) At home, he foresees as a result of these calamities, a bad effect on economy and a disastrous political fight that could further freeze American political debate and even affect political freedom.

On the other hand: If the U.S. achieved in SVN the objectives stated by LBJ in Baltimore, there would then be substantial political and economic and security gains. Way then open to combine birth control and economic expansion techniques in gigantic arc from SVN to Iran and Middle East, bringing unimaginable developments to this region, proving worth of moderate, democratic way of growth for societies.[50]

In May of 1972 the Senate Foreign Relations Committee held yet another set of hearings on the seemingly endless Vietnam War. The committee was still seeking to understand the "origin and evolution of American involvement in Vietnam."[51] The invited witnesses included academics with widely different viewpoints on the American war in Vietnam, who all agreed, however, that the problem began when President Roosevelt—or his immediate successor, President Truman—abandoned a supposed commitment to postwar independence for the French colony. They did not concur on why the reversal took place. The reason why policymakers made that fateful decision, the Roosevelt expert Arthur M. Schlesinger maintained, was the precarious and chancy situation in Europe immediately after the war. "The real reason," he told the committee, "why we acquiesced in the British–French imperial determination . . . to put the French back . . . was because of our concern with the French situation in Europe. . . . In other words, our policy in Vietnam was based, in that period, essentially on European reasons rather than on Asian reasons."[52]

Yet despite all that has been said and written on Vietnam, we are even today still uncertain about how and why America became involved in its longest war. Some continue to argue the case for "European reasons," some put forward "Asian reasons," while others take up the argument for "American reasons." In a sense, it is a matter of where the writer chooses to put his or her emphasis, for all three considerations were present as decision makers reached their conclusions. To settle on one, however, and particularly the argument for "European reasons," risks creating an impression of a passive United States, with few direct interests of its own and worried only about the internal situation in France as the Cold War began. Because American leaders from Roosevelt to Johnson expressed criticism of the French at every point, from blaming appeasement and World War II on "colonialist" obsessions to recriminations that there was no way to overcome the Communist lead in the nationalist movement, it is easy to avoid looking closely at how FDR and his successors might have converted rhetoric to policy. As historians Christopher Thorne and Walter LaFeber have demonstrated, the shift to a less ambitious goal began before Roosevelt died. Another way of looking at the origins of the Vietnam War is to locate it in the struggles of the decolonization process, during which the United States pursued a consistent policy of attempting to replace the weakened colonial powers's outdated visions of empire with a liberal world order that would reintegrate the economies of Southeast Asia with those of the industrial nations to reestablish world prosperity—and, not incidentally, prevent nationalist fervor from being directed against the West. The quest in Asia was for *interdependence*—overseen by the United States.[53]

Had he lived, Roosevelt might have acted differently than his successors on many issues. Lincoln and Reconstruction, Wilson and the League, Roosevelt and the Cold War, Kennedy and Vietnam—we are left to speculate. Roosevelt took a chance with the "Dixie Mission" to Yenan; he might have answered Ho Chi Minh's letters. Whether that would have made a difference, perhaps only Robert Frost could have told us.

NOTES

1. Roosevelt to Ickes, August 12, 1942, *The Papers of Franklin D. Roosevelt*, PPF 3650, Franklin D. Roosevelt Library, Hyde Park, New York.

2. Diary Entry, October 27, 1942, in Beatrice Bishop Berle and Travis Beal Jacobs, eds., *Navigating the Rapids, 1918–1971: From the Papers of Adolf A. Berle* (New York: Harcourt, Brace, 1973), 421–2.

3. See Mark Lytle, *The Origins of the Iranian–American Alliance, 1941–1953* (New York: Holmes & Meier, 1987), 55–57.

4. Quoted in Lloyd C. Gardner, *Economic Aspects of New Deal Diplomacy* (Madison, WI: University of Wisconsin Press, 1964), 176.

5. See Editorial Note, "Roosevelt's Conversations with Various Callers," November 24, 1943, in Department of State, *Foreign Relations of the United States: The Conferences at Cairo and Tehran* (Washington, DC: G.P.O., 1961), 345, and Editorial Note, "Memorandum of Conversation," January 3, 1944, in Department of State, *Foreign Relations of the United States: The Conferences at Cairo and Tehran* (Washington, DC: G.P.O., 1961), 864. (Hereafter: *FRUS.*).

6. FRUS, 1945, VIII, 9.

7. Robert E. Sherwood, *Roosevelt and Hopkins: An Intimate History* (New York: Harper & Brothers, 1950), 578. I have transposed sentences here.

8. Diary Entry, November 27, 1942, in Geoffrey C. Ward, ed., *Closest Companion: The Unknown Story of the Intimate Friendship between Franklin Roosevelt and Margaret Suckley* (Boston: Houghton Mifflin, 1995), 187. Warren F. Kimball, *Forged in War: Roosevelt, Churchill and the Second World War* (New York: Morrow, 1997), concludes: "Roosevelt was convinced that the pressure of nationalism in the European empires was the most serious threat to postwar peace." 301.

9. Ward, *Closest Companion*, 187.

10. Elliott Roosevelt, *As He Saw It* (New York: Duell, Sloan and Pearce, 1946), 116. From the time it was published, Elliott Roosevelt's account of his father's deep dislike of European imperialism, and especially FDR's supposed suspicion about British machinations to hold onto every part of every empire lest their own be threatened, has been denounced as inaccurate in detail and exaggerated in conclusions. Subsequent documentary evidence from various archives and memoirs has, however, strengthened confidence in Elliott's reportage of his father's attitudes.

11. Kimball, *Forged in War*, 300. See also, Albert E. Kersten, "Wilhelmina and Franklin D. Roosevelt: A Wartime Relationship," in *FDR and His Contemporaries: Foreign Perceptions of an American President*, ed. Cornelius A. van Minnen and John F. Sears (New York: St. Martin's, 1992), 85–96.

12. See Lloyd C. Gardner, *Economic Aspects of New Deal Diplomacy* (Madison: University of Wisconsin Press, 1964), 275–80, for a brief discussion of the debates at the Atlantic Charter Conference in 1941 and the debates over Article VII of the Lend-Lease Agreement that committed London to wartime negotiations over postwar trade and the removal of empire preferences. For a recent account that deals with the British predicament, see John Charmley, *Churchill's Grand Alliance* (New York: Harcourt Brace, 1995), 89–101.

13. Roosevelt, *As He Saw It*, 115.

14. Anthony D. Biddle to Roosevelt, March 27, 1942, and Roosevelt to Queen Wilhelmina, April 6, 1942, both in, *The Papers of Franklin D. Roosevelt*, Franklin D. Roosevelt Library, Hyde Park, New York, PSF, The Netherlands, 1942. The Dutch prime minister, Dr. Gerbrandy, who conveyed this delicate request, was at the same time expressing his hope to British officials that the center of gravity in the Pacific War not shift to Washington from London, out of concern for the future of the East Indies. See Christopher Thorne, *Allies of a Kind: The United States, Britain, and the War Against Japan, 1941–1945* (New York: Oxford University Press, 1978), 219.

15. Thorne, *Allies of a Kind*, 218.

16. See Warren F. Kimball, "A Victorian Tory: Churchill, the Americans, and Self-Determination," in *More Adventures with Britannia*, ed. William Roger Louis (New York: Oxford University Press, 1998).

17. Robert Dallek, *Franklin D. Roosevelt and American Foreign Policy, 1932–1945* (New York: Oxford University Press, 1979), 377–8.

18. Cordell Hull, *Memoirs*, 2 vols. (London: Hodder & Stoughton, 1948), vol. 2, 1595.

19. Thorne, *Allies of a Kind*, 217.

20. Notes of Roosevelt–Molotov Meeting, June 1, 1942, in Robert E. Sherwood, *Roosevelt and Hopkins: An Intimate History* (New York: Harper, 1950), 573. This remarkable book, published so soon after the war, would provide the most complete history of American policy for years to come, and still bears rereading, no longer for documents once unavailable elsewhere, but for a feel of the atmosphere.

21. Ibid., 573–4.
22. See Lloyd C. Gardner, *Approaching Vietnam: From World War II through Dienbienphu* (New York: W.W. Norton, 1988), 35.
23. Robert Murphy, *Diplomat Among Warriors* (New York: Doubleday, 1964), 192.
24. Thorne, *Allies of a Kind*, 218.
25. *FRUS, Cairo and Tehran*, 323–5. Elliott Roosevelt, *As He Saw It*, has his father suggesting to Chiang, however, that the French might be allowed to serve as the trustee for Indochina responsible to a United Nations organization. 165. This interesting piece of evidence certainly predicts where FDR came out in the final months of his life, and suggests that his mind was never at rest on how to manage the transition.
26. *FRUS, Cairo and Tehran*, 484–5.
27. Ibid.
28. Diary Entry, June 28, 1944, Ward, *Closest Companion*, 314. Sumner Welles, who issued many of the official statements on colonial questions during the war, wrote in 1951 that by the end of 1943 Roosevelt had become convinced that the United States had to work with China in years to come to prevent a cleavage between the Eastern and Western worlds, for our "own safety's sake." Welles, "Roosevelt and the Far East," vol. 2, *Harper's Magazine* 202 (March, 1951): 70–80.
29. Gardner, *Approaching Vietnam*, 45.
30. M.R. Wright to P.M. Broadmead, November 14, 1944, PREM 4 / 27/7 (Churchill Papers), Public Record Office, London, England.
31. Neville Butler, Minute, January 13, 1946, FO US/46/13, Public Record Office, London, England.
32. Quoted in, Lloyd C. Gardner, *Approaching Vietnam: From World War II Through Dienbienphu, 1941–1954* (New York: W.W. Norton & Co., 1988), 69.
33. *FRUS, The Conferences at Malta and Yalta, 1945*, 770–1.
34. Ibid.
35. Quoted in Gardner, *Approaching Vietnam*, 46. Warren Kimball argues that FDR's conditions for French reinvolvement in Indochina "were a trap designed to get them to dissolve their entire empire, not just in Southeast Asia." A sole trusteeship under the United Nations would force the French to accept international accountability. "Sole trusteeship and international trusteeship would achieve the same result, independence." *The Juggler: Franklin Roosevelt as Wartime Statesman* (Princeton: Princeton University Press, 1991), 153.
36. Senate Committee on Foreign Relations, *Hearings: Causes, Origins and Lessons of the Vietnam War*, 156–7. See also Archimedes L.A. Patti, *Why Vietnam? Prelude to America's Albatross* (Berkeley: University of California Press, 1980) for another account by a former OSS officer stationed in Vietnam.
37. Gardner, *Approaching Vietnam*, 70.
38. Quoted in the Senator Gravel Edition, *The Pentagon Papers*, 4 vols. (Boston: The Beacon Press, 1971), vol. 1, 31.

39. Williams, et al., *America in Vietnam*, 97–8.

40. Ibid., 91.

41. Substance of Statements Made at Wake Island Conference on October 15, 1950, in U.S. Department of State, *Foreign Relations of the United States, 1950: Korea* (Washington: G.P.O., 1976), 957–8.

42. Draft Memorandum, July 9, 1954, reprinted in William Appleman Williams, Thomas McCormick, Lloyd Gardner, and Walter LaFeber, eds., *America in Vietnam: A Documentary History* (New York: Anchor Press,1985), 166–8.

43. *Executive Sessions of the Senate Foreign Relations Committee (Historical Series)*, vol. 5, 83rd Cong., lst sess. (Washington: G.P.O., 1977), 142.

44. Gardner, *Approaching Vietnam*, 135. Emphasis added.

45. See Gareth Porter, *Perils of Dominance: Imbalance of Power and the Road to Vietnam* (Berkely: University of California Press, 2005), 80–87.

46. Bundy to Donald Graham, editor of the Harvard *Crimson*, April 20, 1965, *The Papers of Lyndon B. Johnson,* Lyndon Baines Johnson Library, Austin, Texas, Files of McGeorge Bundy, Boxes 18–19.

47. David Anderson, "Dwight D. Eisenhower and Wholehearted Support of Ngo Dinh Diem," in Anderson, ed., *Shadow on the White House*, 49.

48. Gardner, *Pay Any Price*, 47.

49. Unsigned Memorandum, February, 1965, Johnson Papers, National Security Files, International Travel, Boxes 28–29. The memo has notes in McGeorge Bundy's handwriting, but the basic themes were common enough in Bundy's day and in the days of his successors, Walt Rostow and Henry Kissinger.

50. Quoted in William Appleman Williams, et al., eds., *America in Vietnam* (New York, 1985), 247.

51. U.S. Senate, Committee on Foreign Relations, *Hearings: Causes, Origins and Lessons of the Vietnam War*, 92nd cong., 2nd sess. (Washington: G.P.O., 1973), v.

52. Testimony of Arthur M. Schlesinger, Jr., ibid., 116.

53. Steven Hugh Lee, *Outposts of Empire: Korea, Vietnam, and the Origins of the Cold War in Asia* (Montreal: McGill-Queens University Press, 1995). This outstanding monograph provides a well-argued case for an activist American policy, and a consistent one.

CHAPTER 6

FDR AND THE "CHINA QUESTION"

MICHAEL SCHALLER

PRESIDENT FRANKLIN D. ROOSEVELT'S WARTIME POLICIES toward China encompassed both the generosity of his vision and the limitations of his ability to fully comprehend and influence regional events. Between 1938 and 1941, he overrode the misgivings of State Department officials to initiate economic, then military, aid to the hard-pressed Chinese Nationalist Party (KMT) led by Chiang Kai-shek (Jiang Jieshi). For most of the next decade, this silver thread linked the two nations together during war and civil war more closely than ever before. Initially, Roosevelt merely hoped that keeping Chinese troops in the field would impede Japan's expansion and perhaps deter its future aggression. By the time of the Pearl Harbor attack, the president's horizon had grown more expansive. Not only could a democratic, united, and pro-American China hasten Japan's defeat, but it might also become a pillar of postwar stability and American influence as the Japanese and European empires in Asia receded. For better or worse, Roosevelt convinced himself, and much of the American public, that China was a vital ally whose support would hasten victory and shape the peace.

Unfortunately, the complexities of Chinese domestic politics, divisions among American civilian and military planners, and the competing military and diplomatic priorities of coalition warfare frustrated many of the president's goals. China failed to play an active role in Japan's defeat and the American-backed Nationalist regime barely survived the Allied victory. Yet, the "negative achievement" of merely keeping China in the war tied down several million Japanese troops who otherwise might have overrun much more of Asia and the Pacific.

Nevertheless, Roosevelt's opponents, especially among postwar Republicans, seized upon China's wartime internal conflict and post-1945 descent into civil war as an object lesson that proved FDR's failure as a strategist and visionary. Ironically, the wartime overselling of China as a great power convinced many Americans in the Cold War era that its eventual "loss" to communism marked a grave set back for U.S. security. This allegation haunted Democrats throughout the 1950s and 1960s. Not until twenty-five years after Roosevelt's death, with the tragic milestones of the wars in Korea and Vietnam in between, did something resembling FDR's vision of U.S.–China relations finally emerge.

Examining what the first serious historian of FDR's China Policy, Herbert Feis, aptly labeled "the China Tangle," conservative and left-liberal historians formed an uneasy consensus that, in effect, blamed Roosevelt for the "loss of China." Out of ignorance or malice, the two camps assert, the president bet on the "wrong horse," with dire consequences for both China and the United States. Critics on the right ascribed failure to FDR naïvete and his alleged manipulation by pro-communist advisers. The distorted advice provided to him by Red-tinged "China hands" and a vengeful General Joseph Stilwell supposedly led Roosevelt—like Truman after him—to treat Chiang shabbily and pave the way for the victory of Mao Zedong's Chinese Communist Party (CCP) in 1949.

Writing from a post-Vietnam War perspective, left-leaning historians saw reality through the opposite end of the telescope. This Roosevelt suffered from an inordinate fear of communism and stubbornly backed Chiang long after commitment to him had ceased paying military or political returns. By rejecting cooperation with the Chinese Communists (or even neutrality), FDR encouraged Chiang's worst tendencies and drove a reluctant Mao firmly into Stalin's embrace.

In this odd convergence, historians of the right and left perceive Roosevelt's China policy as a perfect failure. Denying Chiang greater backing against both Japan and his Communist rivals, like the failure to shift support to the CCP, led to a muddled war against Japan, betrayal of a flawed but pro-American ally, and, ultimately, the "loss of China" in 1949. Conservative scholars and political leaders saw in all this justification for McCarthyism the purge of the State Department's "China Hands" and the seeds of communist aggression in Korea and Vietnam. Those on the left believed that Roosevelt's rejection of advice that he shift support from the KMT to the CCP betrayed the real American civilian and military China experts, opening the door to the Red Scare and needless wars in Korea and Vietnam.[1]

In the initial months following the outbreak of the Sino–Japanese war, popular and presidential views of China's plight under Japanese attack could be summarized by a headline appearing in the Hearst press: "We sympathize.

But it is not our concern."[2] Official U.S. policy toward China followed the same lines. Stanley Hornbeck, the "Far Eastern Adviser to the Secretary of State" and, in effect, the State Department's senior "China Hand," made this clear in a message to the British Foreign Office in April 1938. Washington, he explained, deplored Japanese aggression in China; the United States continued to honor the principles of nonaggression and territorial integrity embodied in the Nine Power Treaty of 1922. Hopefully, Japan would see and mend the error of its ways. But no justification existed for Anglo-American mediation or intervention since neither the risk nor cost of a war with Japan was acceptable.[3]

Certainly Roosevelt concurred with this view, but by the autumn of 1938 events in Europe and Asia had begun to move the president away from a policy of sympathetic indifference. The impending Nazi destruction of Czech independence had raised serious concerns that a major war in Europe was imminent, and with a recent Japanese offensive having swept the Nationalists out of Canton, Hankow and further into the interior, it looked as if the Chinese might share a fate similar to the Czech's. To make matters worse, a peace faction, led by Chiang's KMT rival, Wang Ching-wei, had begun negotiating with the Japanese. Fearful that a Chinese collapse would accelerate Axis aggression, senior officials in the Roosevelt Administration—including Secretary of State Cordell Hull and Treasury Secretary Henry Morgenthau—broached the idea of extending a "political loan" to the Nationalists.

Ultimately, it was Morgenthau who took the initiative to devise a plan to provide China with Export–Import Bank trade credits secured by future shipments of Chinese commodities. The Treasury Secretary negotiated with several Chinese representatives, each of whom had ties to rival factions in the KMT coalition. Partly to mute Japanese protests, the credits were not actually granted to the Chinese government but to a nominally private front organization, the "Universal Trading Corporation," or UTC, which was succeeded by China Defense Supplies, or CDS. Various Chiang family factions, including those led by Finance Minister H.H. Kung and Foreign Minister T.V. Soong controlled these companies. Soong hired several former federal officials, including Thomas Corcoran, on the CDS payroll so they could lobby their old departments. The result was a tangled web of overlapping and conflicting agencies and personnel whose precise loyalties—to China or the United States—was unclear.[4]

The initial loan amounted to $25 million. It was intended to deter Chiang from accepting Japanese peace overtures. But it also created another problem, as the Nationalist leader quickly recognized that threats of surrender often elicited additional aid. From this point on, Chinese representatives often leaked stories about an impending collapse or secret peace talks with the Japanese as a way to leverage additional loans or other assistance from Washington.[5]

The U.S. aid program also had an impact on the uneasy anti-Japanese United Front truce that had been established between the Chinese Nationalists and Communists early in the war. It lessened the KMT's dependence on the Soviet Union (which to this point had been granting the nationalists more aid than the United States) and encouraged Chiang to take a harder line with the Communists. In November 1940, for example, Chiang confided to Ambassador Nelson Johnson that if the United States expanded its economic aid and began providing him with military equipment, especially aircrafts and pilots, he would move swiftly against China's "real" enemy.

In the wake of a new $100 million loan that was issued to Chiang a month later, another KMT official echoed this sentiment when he informed a U.S. diplomat in Chungking that the Nationalist leader now felt the need to "appease the Communists." In January 1941, KMT forces attacked and destroyed the CCP's New Fourth Army, which had entered territory claimed by the Nationalists. From then until the outbreak of full-scale civil war following Japan's surrender, the United Front existed only in name.[6]

With the fighting between the Nationalists and Communists on the rise, a number of American officials and informed citizens grew increasingly concerned—and divided—about the potential for civil war. Some, such as Edgar Snow, Evans Carlson, and a junior officer in the State Department's Division of Far Eastern Affairs, John Patton Davies, warned that giving aid exclusively to Chiang would do more to encourage internal warfare than to resist the Japanese. They proposed a more flexible policy of assisting any Chinese troops in the field—including Communists—prepared to fight. Outgoing Ambassador Johnson and Naval attaché James McHugh countered that any assistance to CCP forces would cripple the KMT and undermine resistance to Japan. Either because he did not fully grasp the intensity of KMT–CCP hostility or because he saw no way to impose an outside solution, Roosevelt continued along the initial path he had chosen of providing aid exclusively to the KMT.[7]

In the yearlong run up to the Pearl Harbor attack, aid to China increased substantially, especially after the passage of Lend-Lease. With the prospect of much more aid in the pipeline, Roosevelt dispatched White House economic adviser Dr. Lauchlin Currie as his personal emissary to China. An influential Keynesian economist, Currie hoped to carve out China as his special area of responsibility. During an extended visit to Chungking in February and March 1941, he drafted a report for Roosevelt that called for ameliorating conflict within China. The envoy informed FDR that Chiang's natural instinct was to fight the Communists and he would use American aid to implement a campaign. To prevent this, he urged Roosevelt to send a high level economic, military, and political advisory team to China to supervise the distribution and use of aid while pushing Chiang along the path of democratic reform. (Currie also met with Zhou Enlai to reassure him that Washington opposed any KMT attacks on the CCP.) As Currie put it, Roosevelt could encourage Chiang's better angels by publicly promoting the notion that he was a key ally and leader of a "great power." The United States should simultaneously expand aid and supervise its distribution.

Currie oversimplified the rifts in Chinese politics and misgauged American ability or Roosevelt's willingness to heal them. Nevertheless, Currie's recommendations influenced Roosevelt's approach for the next several years. Impressed by Currie's analysis, FDR designated him in the summer of 1941 as the White House "point man" to expedite Lend-Lease aid for China.[8]

Currie largely displaced Morgenthau as the president's China expert, working with the Treasury Secretary T.V. Soon and retired Army flier Claire Cennault to create an informal American air force in China, the American Volunteer Group (AVG) or "Flying Tigers." In addition to the goal of providing fighter aircraft and eventually equipment for up to thirty army divisions, Currie pushed a closely held secret plan, approved by Roosevelt in July 1941, for American-piloted planes based in China to fire bomb Japanese cities. Although Currie and Morgenthau envisioned this as a way to deter future Japanese aggression, regular military planners such as Army Chief of Staff George C. Marshall considered it a foolhardy provocation and tried to delay implementation. Still, with Roosevelt's blessing, the air war plan moved forward and was nearly operational when Japan struck Pearl Harbor on December 7.[9]

The outbreak of the Pacific War not only brought the United States fully into China's corner, but also changed the larger political equation in Asia. The humiliating rout of European and American forces in Southeast Asia foretold the demise of colonialism and begged the question of who or what would replace it.[10] In China, despite growing levels of American economic aid, Lend-Lease supplies, and a military advisory mission, Chiang proved reluctant to fight the Japanese effectively. His refusal to fight or reform eventually squandered both American support and the loyalty of most Chinese. The Chinese Communists, in contrast, began the war as a small political and military movement isolated in northwest China. Yet, the CCP emerged from the war in control of nearly a fourth of China, fielded a multimillion-man army, and enjoyed tremendous stature for their defense of the country. Four years later, all China would be theirs.

At home, influenced by the ceaseless promotional efforts of Henry Luce's publishing empire, Americans generally perceived China as a devoted ally making great sacrifices on behalf of the Grand Alliance. Most official Americans in China, save for those personally allied to the Nationalist leadership, shared a darker vision. General John Magruder, who preceded Joseph Stilwell as the Army's representative in Chungking, predicted that with America in the war, Chiang would reach a de facto truce with the Japanese and hoard military aid "largely with the idea of post-war military action" against the Communists.[11] Even Navy attaché James McHugh, normally one of Chiang's boosters, doubted that Nationalist troops could help much. Aid to Chiang was warranted, he argued, because it would permit him to sustain a large pro-American army that would be useful in the future. To fight the Japanese, he favored creating an air force under Chiang's American protégé, Claire Chennault.[12]

Ambassador Clarence Gauss, a grouchy State Department veteran but recent arrival in China, voiced the gloomiest assessment. Chiang, he informed Washington, suffered from a "touch of unreality derived from a somewhat grandiose or ivory tower conception of his and China's role." Far from reforming his regime, since December 7 he had bolstered the power of the most reactionary elements in the KMT. Gauss cautioned against giving Chiang blank check approval. Instead, the United States should identify moderate and liberal elements within the KMT and among other parties and cultivate their friendship as future leaders.[13]

Roosevelt, ever the optimist, paid little head to these warnings before 1944. Until his death in April 1945, the president struggled both to win the war and assure the peace by harnessing the nationalist forces unleashed by Japan's rampage through Asia. Assuming Japan's defeat, what political movements would replace the Dutch, British, and French colonial order? What force would be strong enough to restrain Soviet expansion? How would China, with a fourth of the world's population, influence postwar events? Would it be pro-American, antiforeign, pro-Soviet, chaotic, or some combination of it all? As with his approach to the Depression at home, Roosevelt followed eclectic paths, often improvising, in the hope that *something* would be found to keep China unified, in the war, moving toward greater democracy, and prepared to play the role of one of the "Four Policeman" in the postwar world.

From the inception of the Grand Alliance, Roosevelt groped for a China policy that would do several, sometimes contradictory, things at once. Minimally, he hoped to sustain China as an active ally, tying down several million Japanese troops. To accomplish this and pave the way for China's acceptance into the ranks of the "great powers," FDR offered economic aid, military assistance and advisers, and rhetorical support for Chiang as a leader on a par with Winston Churchill and Josef Stalin. Roosevelt's longer view encompassed a China that would help assure stability in postwar Asia, balancing power in the region after the defeat of Japan, the end of European colonialism, and the likely expansion of Soviet influence. Until the end of 1944, Roosevelt believed that the agent of China's transformation would be Chiang Kai-shek and his Nationalist government. He supported and indulged Chiang with a view toward this future.

Neither Stalin nor especially Churchill had much patience for what they saw as FDR's romantic infatuation with China. Churchill complained that Roosevelt expected to use China as a "faggot vote on the side of the United States in an attempt to liquidate the British Overseas Empire."[14] But, in a discussion with Lord Louis Mountbatten in 1943, the president insisted that treating China as a "great power" would inhibit aggression "during the immediate postwar period." Having a half billion Chinese allies would be "very useful twenty-five or fifty years hence, even though China cannot contribute much military or naval support for the moment."[15]

Although Roosevelt had generous and farsighted impulses, the method he relied upon for implementing his vision contained deep flaws. Hoping to hold China together as a force against Japan, he tended to ignore or misconstrue advice from the best informed American diplomats and military officers in China. Many of these men shared the president's aspirations but grew increasingly frustrated with Chiang's performance and, by extension, with Roosevelt's support for him. It often seemed as if American policy existed on two parallel and nonintersecting planes, the ideal and the real. Deep fissures opened between the president and his aides in Washington, who took a broad, top-down, long-term view of events, and military officers and diplomats stationed in China, who faced the grim frustrations of political and military decay. While Roosevelt spoke of promoting China as a "great power," General Stilwell and his staff dealt with a crumbling army, corrupt leaders, and incipient civil war. Most American military and civilian officials with what we call today "boots on the ground" agreed that China could play an important wartime and postwar role. But they doubted that Chiang and the Nationalists could or should be the force to shape that future. They especially worried that exclusive American aid to the KMT would hasten civil war and also poison U.S. relations with the Communists whom they believed were likely to inherit the "mandate of heaven." The tensions between Roosevelt's grand strategy and the military–diplomatic realities of China contributed to eventual disaster.

In many ways, the disappointments of the spring 1942 campaign in Burma set the pattern of later failures. Due in large part to Chiang's interference with Stilwell's command, as well as British indifference to the enterprise, allied forces failed to hold the Burma Road lifeline that linked western China to India. This left the arduous air route over the Himalayan "hump" as the only way to bring fuel, equipment, and other Lend-Lease supplies into China. Stilwell spent the next two years ceaselessly seeking authority to launch a Burma offensive that would reopen a land route from India to China that would bring in enough supplies to equip thirty rearmed, retrained, and American-supervised Chinese army divisions. Stilwell then intended to lead "his" Chinese army in a broad offensive against the Japanese in China.

Chiang agreed to take the aid, but *not* at the price of losing control over Nationalist troops. Like other aspects of the Nationalist regime, the army represented many factions whose loyalty to Chiang depended upon his ability to punish and reward commanders through the distribution of military supplies. If Stillwell became their quartermaster, they would owe him, not Chiang, their loyalty. As a result, Chiang devoted himself to blocking all Stilwell's reform efforts.

Still, China had to do something to warrant American aid and this made the prospect of an air campaign under General Claire Chennault attractive to Chiang. Chennault had worked as an adviser to Chiang since the late-1930s. Between 1942 and 1944 he lobbied Roosevelt to support the build up of a large American air force in China. This would involve committing most of the tonnage flown in over the Hump to the air force and the remainder to Chiang. Little would be left for Stilwell's army reform plan or Burma campaign. With Chennault's projected air force attacking Japanese troops and shipping, China would appear to be carrying its weight in the alliance. Meanwhile, Nationalist troops would accumulate weapons for the coming conflict with the Communists. Although nearly all experienced American military personnel and diplomats in China faulted this strategy, it caught Roosevelt's attention because Chiang pushed for it and it won endorsement from several formal and informal boosters whom Roosevelt admired, including Lauchlin Currie and Joseph Alsop. Alsop, Roosevelt's distant cousin, served as an aide to Chennault and had access to FDR via dispatches routed through Currie and Harry Hopkins.

Stilwell, who spoke dismissively of Chiang as "the Peanut," fumed in his diary that "something must be done to clean out this stinking gang and put some real people at the head of things." He meant, of course, the Chinese Communists who had told American diplomats in 1942 they would willingly serve under Stilwell.[16]

Chiang and his inner circle began pressing for Stillwell's recall as early as the summer of 1942. In July, T.V. Soong queried Army Chief of Staff General George C. Marshall whether Roosevelt would replace Stilwell and perhaps relinquish to the Chinese full control over Lend-Lease supplies. Marshall replied, in a message signed by the president, with so forceful a dissent that Soong watered down the response before sending it to Chiang.[17]

Anxious to preserve the semblance of unity in China, Roosevelt in July 1942 sent Lauchlin Currie to China. The White House envoy hoped to restore the patina of good will that surrounded his earlier visit. Snubbing Stilwell and Ambassador Gauss, Currie spent most of his time conferring with Chiang and reassuring him of the high esteem in which Roosevelt held him. Currie told Roosevelt that most of the difficulties in China stemmed from "personality" disputes between Chiang, Soong, Chennault, and Stilwell. These would eventually work themselves out. More important, in his judgment, was the fact, as he put it:

> We have a unique opportunity to exert a profound influence on the devel-opment of China and hence Asia. It appears to me to be profoundly in our national interest to give full support to the Generalissimo, both military and diplomatic. I do not think we need to lay down any conditions nor tie any strings to this support...we can rely on him so far as lies within his power to go in the direction of our wishes in prosecuting a vigorous war policy and in creating a modern, democratic and powerful state.[18]

Currie went on to link the survival of a pro-American Nationalist China to postcolonial nationalism elsewhere in Asia. Commenting on Ghandi's rift with the British, Currie wrote to FDR from New Delhi that moderate Indian nationalists deeply resented what they saw as American–British collusion to preserve colonialism. This misconception, Currie warned the president, "endangers your moral leadership in Asia and therefore America's ability to exert its influence for acceptable and just settlement in postwar Asia." Currie (who suggested himself as a possible replacement for Stilwell *and* Ambassador Gauss) had articulated nearly perfectly Roosevelt's policy and his dream of a postcolonial Asia under moderate nationalist leadership.[19]

Partly because Currie's views melded so closely with his own, Roosevelt rejected all efforts by Stilwell to force Chiang to place Nationalist troops under American command and to stop the flow of aid unless the Generalissimo complied. General Marshall, who enjoyed the confidence of both Stilwell and Roosevelt, played the unhappy role of buffer between them. The Army Chief of Staff (who sympathized with Stilwell but never undercut the president) believed that Roosevelt's postwar vision drew him ineluctably toward supporting Chiang and with it Chennault's almost mys-tical belief in air power. (In eerie ways, this foreshadowed President Lyndon Johnson's notion of holding South Vietnam by relying on air power.) No one in the War Department or perhaps even the White House, Marshall noted, necessarily believed that air power would defeat the Japanese or save China. But Chiang desperately sought a commitment to an air strategy to preserve his own political supremacy. "Since the Chinese wanted what Chennault wanted, and Roosevelt wanted to give the Chinese what they wanted, all these things fit[ted] together very neatly and required no further presidential effort or analysis."[20]

During 1942 and 1943, dissenting voices from the embassy in Chungking supported Stilwell's case, but to little avail. Embassy Counselor John Carter Vincent depicted the Nationalists as a gaggle of selfish cliques "whose only common denominator and common objective is a desire to maintain the Kuomintang in control of the government." China might still be saved, but only if the present leadership was swept aside by "liberal reformers."[21] According to John S. Service, a Foreign Service officer detailed to Stilwell's staff, the United Front was "a thing of the past." There was no longer a question of whether civil war could be avoided, but only "whether it can be delayed at least until a victory over Japan." The certainty of U.S. support, Service warned, encouraged reactionary terror by the KMT and might swing the CCP to the left, "beyond the moderate democracy... the Communists now claim to be seeking" and "toward friendship with Russia."[22] Service's colleague, John P. Davies, reached similar conclusions. He urged the Roosevelt administration to accept the invitation extended by Zhou Enlai "for a small group of American officers to set up observer posts" in Communist base areas.[23]

Nevertheless, during most of 1943, continued British reluctance to support a ground offensive in Burma and Chiang's mounting demands for an air offensive led by Chennault continued to sway Roosevelt. In passing along Chiang's demands to the president, Marshall appended his own thoughts. A strategy premised on giving Chennault the planes and fuel to mount an air campaign against the Japanese in China, the army chief of staff wrote, made no military or political sense. It would have little effect on the Japanese but would give Chiang an exalted sense of his ability to manipulate American policy. Since Nationalist forces were unreliable, Chennault's air bases could not be protected against an inevitable Japanese counterattack. If China were to make a real contribution to the war, a Burmese land supply route must be opened. The only way to do this was to follow Stilwell's advice: put Chiang on a short tether, making all aid contingent on his giving Stilwell real control over a small Chinese force that would fight in Burma and authority to train and reform both Nationalist and possible Communist troops.

Roosevelt responded in March 1943, explaining his reluctance to adopt a "quid pro quo" approach to dealing with the Generalissimo. Using language that resembled that of Lauchlin Currie and Henry Luce, the president declared that the United States and China were allies and both "great powers." (Along these lines, in 1943 Roosevelt pushed Congress to abrogate America's "unequal treaties" imposed on China in the nineteenth century and to revise the "Chinese Exclusion Act" to permit token immigration.) It would be counterproductive to attempt to command Chiang, a man who had struggled to become the "undisputed leader of 400,000,000 people" and who had created in China "what it took us a couple of centuries to attain." Roosevelt would not "speak sternly to a man like that or exact commitments from him as we might do from the Sultan of Morocco." Instead, FDR decided to back creation of an independent 14th Air Force of 500 planes under Chennault. To the relief of both Chiang and the British, and the consternation of Stilwell, a Burma campaign would stay on the back burner.[24]

Formal presidential commitment to backing the air strategy of Chiang and Chennault came in the wake of the Washington "Trident" Conference in May 1943. There, Roosevelt had interviewed both Stilwell and Chennault, seeking their take on Chinese politics and military strategy. Stilwell had prepared a sheaf of papers arguing that "China was on the verge of collapse." But, he discovered, "nobody was interested in the humdrum work of building a ground force but me. Chennault promised to drive the Japs right out of China in six months, so why not give him the stuff to do it? It was the short cut to victory."[25]

By the end of 1943, Roosevelt's China policy faced additional challenges. The accelerating pace of the naval and ground war in the Pacific meant that long-range bombers operating from island airfields might soon be able to attack Japan proper. This, along with the likely prospect of Soviet assistance following Germany's defeat, would reduce the need to rely upon China's help against Japan. These issues, coupled with the still stalled Burma offensive, were taken up at the Cairo and Teheran conferences held between November 22 and December 7, 1943. When, at Teheran, Stalin agreed to his ally's request that the Soviet Union eventually fight Japan in return for certain "privileges" in Manchuria, Roosevelt recognized that the final stages of the Pacific War might simply pass China by.

At the bifurcated Cairo meetings attended by Chiang and Stilwell, those close to Roosevelt detected in him a changed attitude toward Chiang. At this stage, Churchill's chronic opposition to a Burma offensive resurfaced. Although Chiang seemed more willing than before to fight, he again demanded huge amounts of money and equipment before moving. The Generalissimo's grandiose sense of himself, Lord Mountbatten recalled, drove the other allied political and military leaders at Cairo "absolutely mad."[26] This frustration became manifest when, in early 1944, Roosevelt and Morgenthau turned down flat Chiang's demand for another $1 billion loan as the price for his continued cooperation. The president tacitly agreed with the Treasury Secretary's description of Chiang as a "crook" who could "go jump in the Yangtze." Ultimately, rather than call Chiang's bluff about dropping out of the war, a smaller deal was made to provide additional financial aid.[27]

In a conversation with his son Elliott, the president said he had told Chiang to cooperate more closely with Stilwell and had broached the idea of arming Communist troops and forming a "unity government" with the CCP. Elliott quoted his father as saying that Chiang might agree to these suggestions, if Stalin promised to "protect the frontier in Manchuria." Of course, at the Teheran conference and the subsequent February 1945 Yalta summit, Roosevelt did just the opposite, accepting Soviet demands for special privileges in northeast China in return for the Red Army fighting Japan.[28]

When Roosevelt and Hopkins met with Stillwell and John P. Davies at Cairo on December 6, the administration's changed tone became evident. In response to Stilwell's report about several plots in Chungking to topple Chiang, Hopkins ridiculed the Generalissimo's grandiose pretensions. The United States, Hopkins asserted, would soon decide on China's postwar role and frontiers, with little input from the Chiang. When Roosevelt joined the discussion, he hinted at an impending deal with Stalin over Manchuria and described his reluctance to give China much more aid.

Roosevelt responded to Davies warning about a coup by assuring the diplomat that Washington would support whoever stood "next in line" and was prepared to fight Japan. But before Stilwell and Davies had a chance to plumb the meaning of this remark, the president launched into a soliloquy about the impact of Christian missionaries and his grandfather's role in the old China trade.[29]

Nevertheless, Stilwell found some measure of relief in Roosevelt's apparent coolness toward the strategies promoted by Chiang and Chennault. In fact, Colonel Frank Dorn, Stilwell's deputy, reported that the general had a final, private and unrecorded talk with the president at Cairo in which FDR reportedly said he was "fed up with Chiang and his tantrums." Stilwell, Dorn recalled, quoted Roosevelt as saying "in that Olympian manner of his, 'if you can't get along with Chiang, and can't replace him, get rid of him once and for all. You know what I mean, put in someone you can manage.'"

Dorn actually devised a scheme to sabotage Chiang's aircraft while he flew on an inspection tour. However, authorization for the assassination never came. But the mere fact that FDR may have broached the idea, when combined with his other complaints at Cairo over Chiang's poor performance, and the efforts to bring the Soviets into the war, suggests that the president had begun to retreat from his twin notions of China as a vital wartime and postwar ally.[30]

By the summer of 1944, the military balance in China had turned dramatically worse. As Stilwell and Marshall predicted, the Japanese army responded to Chennault's air offensive by over running his airfields in a massive offensive codenamed ICHIGO. In the process, the Japanese occupied huge swaths of interior China they had previously bypassed. Several administration officials who had championed aid to China, including Morgenthau and Currie, now disparaged Chiang's prospects. More than before, George

Marshall had Roosevelt's ear on China policy. Roosevelt had little choice but to place more pressure on Chiang. He began by sending Vice President Henry Wallace to China, with a demand that the Generalissimo permit a group of U.S. military and diplomatic observers—the so-called Dixie Mission—to visit Yenan. FDR also insisted that Stilwell be given command of additional Chinese troops fighting in the small-scale Burma offensive that had recently begun.

In July, Marshall prevailed on Roosevelt to send Chiang a message berating him and Chennault for committing a chain of blunders. FDR signed the cable drafted by Marshall that spoke of China facing a "critical situation." He demanded that Stilwell be given command of *all* American and Chinese forces in the theater. The "future of all Asia is at stake," Roosevelt warned, and the time had come for Chiang to face reality.[31]

Chiang responded with a well-worn ploy: he promised to accept these stern demands once Roosevelt sent yet one more personal emissary to buffer relations between himself and Stilwell. Chiang, of course, hoped to play the emissary off against Stilwell and buy time. Roosevelt inadvertently made the Generalissimo's task simpler by delegating the task to Patrick J. Hurley, a flamboyant Republican who had served as Hoover's Secretary of War. Hurley, a handsome buffoon, had undertaken an earlier brief presidential mission to China and had gotten on relatively smoothly with Stilwell. Perhaps, as Roosevelt told an aide, Hurley's blunt, undiplomatic style was tailored to this situation. To reassure Stilwell, Hopkins told John P. Davies that Roosevelt was completely fed up with Chiang and wanted Stilwell to assume command over "both the central government's and the Communists' troops."[32] Once again, the president seemed to send mixed messages about his goals in China and the ways he hoped to accomplish them.

Roosevelt's selection of Hurley, a Republican, as his China emissary may have been intended as smart domestic politics, but it had awful ramifications at home and abroad. Hurley received minimal instructions from the president. He began his trip to China by conferring with Soviet Foreign Minister Molotov in Moscow and extracting from him a promise not to aid the Chinese Communists. This, Hurley explained later, gave him leverage against the CCP.

By the time Hurley reached Chungking, the Burma offensive had stalled, the Japanese offensive in East China had gathered steam, and Chiang still balked at giving Stilwell command power. At the Quebec summit conference in mid-September 1944, Roosevelt and Churchill bickered over colonial issues. The British leader demanded that the president "leave his Indians alone." In return, Britain would "leave the President's Chinese alone." At dinner Franklin and Eleanor Roosevelt spoke of their growing doubt over

China's stability and complained about the "pretensions and extravagances" of Chiang's entourage.[33]

Amidst these tensions, on September 16, FDR received Stilwell's plea that the president deliver an ultimatum to Chiang. Marshall's staff drafted a message, approved by Roosevelt, stating that unless Stilwell received immediate command over Chinese forces, all U.S. aid would cease. Blaming Chiang for courting "catastrophic consequences," the ultimatum declared that it was "evident to all of us here...that all your and our efforts to save China are to be lost by further delays." Stilwell delivered this ultimatum to Chiang in person on September 19, interrupting a private meeting between the Generalissimo and Hurley. Believing he now had Roosevelt's full support, Stilwell wrote in his diary how the "harpoon had hit the little bugger right in the solar plexus and went right through him." Finally, Stilwell could "play the avenging angel."[34]

For all his joy in having "wrecked the Peanut's face," and even as he made plans to visit Communist forces in Yenan, Stilwell had achieved a Pyrrhic victory. During September and October, Hurley colluded with Chiang to engineer the general's recall. The emissary endorsed and forwarded to Roosevelt on September 24 Chiang's refusal to turn over command of Chinese forces. Hurley supported Chiang's contention that Stilwell had become the major impediment to the war effort in China. Therefore, only his replacement could set things right. By October 10, Hurley had informed the president that Chiang and Stilwell were "fundamentally incompatible." Roosevelt had to choose between the two. There is, Hurley claimed, "no other issue between you and Chiang Kai-shek." If "you sustain Stilwell," the special emissary warned, "you will loose Chiang Kai-shek and possibly you will lose China with him..."[35]

Stilwell countered this assertion in a September 26 message to Marshall that argued "it is not a choice between throwing me out or losing CKS [Chiang] and possibly China." Rather, Chiang believed he could get away with throwing onto American shoulders the entire burden of fighting Japan while still collecting military and financial aid. The only hope for winning China's military assistance in the current war and for assuring its stability and friendship in the future was to be "very firm."[36]

Despite this plea to the president, Hurley had raised the insidious term "the loss of China," a phrase that would haunt Democrats from the late-1940s through the 1960s. Roosevelt shuddered over the prospect of a military–political collapse in China. Facing an unprecedented fourth term election in less than a month, he recoiled from appearing to break apart the Grand Alliance and abandon a "great power." For FDR, the choice between a quarrelsome general and the "indispensable" leader of 400,000,000 allies seemed obvious. If nothing else, dispensing with Stilwell and appeasing Chiang might buy some time—time for the Soviets to commit to fighting Japan, time to gauge the effects of the massive bombing of Japan from Pacific bases that was about to begin, time, perhaps, for the yet-to-be tested atomic bomb to come into play.

On October 18, 1944, FDR made the expedient decision to pull Stilwell out of China. Roosevelt divided and downgraded the China–Burma–India Theater and placed General Albert Wedemeyer (a man Stilwell derided as "the world's most pompous prick") in charge solely of American forces within China, dropping any demand for U.S. control over Chinese troops. Thoroughly disillusioned by the president's actions, Ambassador Gauss resigned in sympathy with Stilwell. Roosevelt soon appointed Hurley as ambassador, placing him in a position to further control the flow of information between Chungking and Washington.

When Stilwell reached Washington late in October, Marshall and Stimson made clear he was to be kept "out of the way and muzzled until after the elections." Stimson, who complained that Roosevelt could not discuss the situation rationally, believed that Stilwell had been treated shabbily and America ill-served by his recall. Nevertheless, the priority now had become "to keep him out of the reach of all newsmen and not give them an opportunity to catch and distort any unwary word just before [the] election."[37]

In the wake of the command crisis, U.S. policy in China appeared to veer in two contrary directions. On one hand, the American Foreign Service officers and military personnel associated with the Dixie Mission became even more certain that U.S. interests in China and East Asia required closer political and military cooperation with the Chinese Communists. Yet the two ranking American officials in China, Hurley and Wedemeyer, moved to back Chiang more forcefully. They barred any talk of military cooperation with the CCP, endorsed KMT efforts to force the Communists to submit to Chiang's authority, and presided over a purge of nearly all embassy and military staff who questioned these efforts.

At the same time, however, China's military significance diminished appreciably. The accelerating advance by naval and army forces in the Pacific brought Japan within easy range of American air and naval attack. At the Yalta Conference in February 1945, Roosevelt secured Stalin's promise to enter the Pacific War within three months of Germany's impending defeat. Finally, the progress made in Los Alamos, New Mexico, in developing the atomic bomb provided an "ace in the hole" that Roosevelt and, eventually, Harry Truman, could utilize to press Japan's surrender while limiting the need for Soviet assistance in the final stages of the war. These developments, along with the growing chaos in China, rendered China a diminishing factor in the war.

By early 1945, the Chinese Communists recognized that diminished American interest in China bode ill for them as well as the Nationalists.

Roosevelt had replaced a sympathetic American military commander and ambassador with two completely hostile officials. Soviet officials showed little interest in assisting the CCP and had assured inquiring Americans that they supported Chiang. Meanwhile, it was clear that the KMT intended to force the CCP to effectively disband or face civil war. Mao responded to domestic and foreign pressure by launching a purge of both liberal and pro-Soviet elements within the CCP. Determined to bolster his own authority, the CCP leader also recognized the importance of seeking some measure of U.S. support, if only to forestall a Nationalist attack and hedge his ties to the Soviet Union.

Americans attached to the Dixie Mission in Yenan recognized Mao's revolutionary and nationalist fervor, as well as his determination to restore China's place as a "great power." By and large, these diplomats and intelligence officers believed that adroit diplomacy could steer the CCP at least partly away from Stalin's embrace. If, as seemed possible, the Communists eventually took power, their interests and those of the United States might be more parallel than contradictory. John S. Service, John P. Davies, Raymond Ludden, and other Foreign Service officers urged interim U.S. support for a true coalition government that would at least postpone civil war and demonstrate to Mao American evenhandedness. In all likelihood, the United States could not save the Nationalist regime. It might, however, mitigate conflict with a Communist successor government.[38]

On November 7, 1944, shortly after Stilwell's recall, now Ambassador Hurley paid an unannounced visit to Yenan. In a hastily arranged meeting with Mao and Chou (who Hurley privately ridiculed as "Moose Dung" and "Joe N. Lie"; they returned the insult, calling him "Big Wind" and "the Clown."), the ambassador signed a "Five Point Agreement" to create a coalition government and army that recognized the equality of both parties and would distribute American aid to both the CCP and KMT. The terms pleased the Communist leaders and their American sympathizers. But when Chou accompanied Hurley to Chungking, he discovered that the ambassador had engaged in a "bait-and-switch" deception. Instead of a coalition of equals, Chiang and Hurley rewrote the terms, insisting that the CCP submit itself, militarily and politically, to KMT control. In return, the Communists would receive token representation in government. By early December the talks collapsed, and Mao and Hurley accused each other of betrayal. Hurley, who naively expected the CCP to capitulate, blamed the impasse on pro-communist elements among the embassy staff. He then began a purge that eventually forced out of China nearly all the foreign service officers with real expertise.[39]

As they lost contact with the Americans most sympathetic to them, the Chinese Communist leadership made a bold but futile effort to break Hurley's grip. On January 9, 1945, Mao and Chou asked OSS officers serving with the Dixie Mission to forward a secret message to Washington. The two party leaders proposed to fly to Washington, if Roosevelt would receive them, as a delegation from a "primary Chinese party." They hoped to persuade Roosevelt of their desire to cooperate with American goals and to explain the muddle Hurley had made.[40]

The secret offer set in motion a disastrous train of events for the communists and their American sympathizers. Hurley learned of the message, probably from an anticommunist communications officer on the Dixie team, who made sure that Wedemeyer and Hurley saw it. The ambassador promptly warned Roosevelt against responding to the Communist message. He repeated his contention that all problems in China stemmed from collusion between the CCP and disloyal Americans. China, Hurley insisted, could only be saved by forcing Mao to submit to Nationalist rule and by purging disloyal Americans. Then he, Hurley, would easily mediate a settlement. In a sense, this was a replay of the crisis between Stilwell and Chiang, with Hurley presenting himself as the solution.[41]

Weighed down by a thousand problems and hopeful that a deal with Stalin at Yalta might assure Japan's defeat, Roosevelt accepted Hurley's advice. He even considered sending Chiang a formal apology for the action of the OSS officers in Yenan who had agreed to convey the Communist proposal. Roosevelt instructed Marshall and Stimson to bar any future unauthorized contact between Army, OSS, and Communist officials in China. In effect, he implicitly sanctioned moves by Hurley and General Wedemeyer to impose a gag order on all critical reporting.[42]

In Chungking, Wedemeyer ordered all American military personnel to "support the existing Chinese government." No aid, support, or encouragement was to be given to any "elements" without Chiang's approval, "whether or not the decision seemed wise." Hurley imposed a similar orthodoxy on embassy personnel, demanding that he be given all political cables for review before they were dispatched. Solomon Adler, a Treasury Department representative in Chungking, continued to send critical reports to Morgenthau. But the Treasury Secretary's interest in China had waned as he devoted his energy to influencing German Occupation policy.

By February 1945, Roosevelt must have realized that his dream of fostering a "powerful, united and pro-American China" had turned into a nightmare. Not only would China play little role in defeating Japan, but it seemed likely to become a postwar disaster. Rather than serving as a stabilizing "fourth policeman" in Asia, it seemed about to descend into a civil war that might well draw both the Soviets and Americans into conflict. The only real alternative to this scenario was making a deal with Stalin at Yalta.

Unlike their tense negotiations over the fate of Germany and Eastern Europe, Roosevelt, Stalin, and even Churchill found common ground on

Asian issues. To the relief of U.S. military planners, Stalin confirmed his intention of invading Manchuria three months after Germany's defeat. He also pledged to support the Chinese Nationalist regime and not to aid or encourage CCP rebellion. In return, the Soviet dictator demanded control over two major ports and two railroad lines in Manchuria, as well as continued control over Outer Mongolia. Roosevelt and most of his aides considered this a reasonable price to pay for Soviet assistance in the war against Japan.

The so-called Yalta Far Eastern Agreement, concluded on February 11, 1945, remained secret until the following summer, although many details leaked out quickly. Both Chiang and Mao resented its terms, deeming it one more "unequal treaty" that sacrificed Chinese sovereignty on behalf of foreign powers. The Communists were stunned by Stalin's willingness to sign a friendship treaty with Chiang that cut them adrift. Roosevelt's actions at Yalta demonstrated how little faith he retained in *either* Chinese faction. He hoped, instead, to stabilize East Asia through a Soviet–American deal in China and an American-dominated occupation of Japan. FDR, like Stalin, probably saw the Yalta strategy as a way to buy time. The deal might push the Communists into reaching a compromise with the Nationalists, since they could turn neither to Moscow nor Washington for support. Chiang would also be constrained by the fact that he survived in large part on tacit support from the United States and Soviet Union. In spite of these assumptions, Chiang's rigidity and Mao's independent streak played havoc with great power diplomacy.[43]

In the wake of the Yalta meeting, Hurley and Wedemeyer returned to Washington for consultations. While the ambassador was en route, the embassy staff rose in revolt, sending a collective warning to the Department of State. On February 28, 1945, every political officer signed onto a cable sent to the State Department over the signature of charge George Atcheson. The message condemned Hurley for compromising any chance of peace and unity in China. The only hope for averting civil war, they collectively declared, was for the United States to compel Chiang to share power with the CCP. This, they warned, might be a last chance to influence the Communists who would otherwise "seek Russian aid or intervention." Treasury attaché Adler concurred in a separate message. America's future in China, he cautioned, "should not be left in the hands of a bungler like Hurley."[44]

Mao fell back upon one of his few remaining American contacts in an effort to persuade the Roosevelt administration to change course. In March 1945, John S. Service had returned to Yenan with the Dixie Mission after a lengthy visit to Washington. Mao described American policy as an "enigma." He still hoped it was not "fixed and unchangeable." Why had Roosevelt wavered after his "good start?" Unless Washington was willing to force Chiang into creating a true coalition, "all that America has been working for will be lost," Mao warned. There was "no such thing as America *not* interfering in China," the Communist leader declared. "You are here, as China's greatest ally. The fact of your presence is tremendous."[45] Not surprisingly, on March 30, Hurley—still in Washington—ordered Service out of Yenan and, on April 4, out of China. The ambassador had decided that Service was the true author of the embassy staff's February 28 dispatch. Upon reading it he yelled: "I know who drafted that telegram: Service! I'll get that son of a bitch if it's the last thing I do!"[46]

During March and April, Hurley and Wedemeyer conferred with the joint chiefs of staff, the president, the state department leadership, and other high officials. They insisted that things were fine in China, except for the subversive activities of certain embassy staff and OSS personnel. They dismissed the Communists as a waning force whose "rebellion" would be quashed by "comparatively small [U.S.] assistance to Chiang's central government." Wedemeyer predicted a quick KMT victory in case of civil war.[47]

It is uncertain what Roosevelt knew or understood of these activities. Although he met privately with both Hurley and Wedemeyer, no substantive account of their discussions has surfaced. Wedemeyer recalled that Roosevelt spoke to him mostly about problems with the French in Indochina and said little about the political situation in China. Hurley's two meetings with FDR in March remain shrouded in mystery. Admiral Leahy, in a second hand account, reported that Hurley complained to Roosevelt about the disloyalty of his subordinates who "ganged up on the new ambassador" because he came from "outside the foreign service." Given the president's impatience with many professional diplomats, and his past praise for Hurley's irreverence, he may have been taken in by this claim. In any case, Roosevelt expressed confidence in his envoy and instructed him to return to China via London and Moscow where he was to seek renewed British and Soviet support for backing Chiang.[48]

The only suggestion that Roosevelt may have still thought in terms of a more nuanced policy appears in an account by Edgar Snow of a conversation he had with the president about six weeks before Roosevelt's death. FDR expressed frustration with Chiang over his refusal to share power with the Communists. If the Generalissimo did not compromise, then he (FDR) was prepared to work through what he called "two governments" and might even cooperate militarily with Red forces in North China. However, Roosevelt then added he greatly looked forward to Hurley's impending visit because he highly valued the ambassador's viewpoint. This account hardly helps to ascertain Roosevelt's deeper thoughts and understandings.[49]

Whatever hope remained for a change in policy evaporated on April 2. In a Washington press conference that followed a meeting with FDR, Hurley put on a virtuoso performance. He denied the Communists had ever requested American aid or political recognition. He insisted that only minor differences separated the CCP and KMT. No justification existed for the Communists not to enter a KMT dominated coalition. Hurley concluded by lumping Mao together with various Chinese warlords. Less than two weeks later, Roosevelt died, leaving Hurley's angry soliloquy as Roosevelt's indirect but apparent last word on China.[50]

Hurley departed Washington shortly before Roosevelt's death. He traveled to China by way of London and Moscow, eager to secure British and Soviet backing for his tough approach. Churchill, as usual, seemed miffed by anything any American had to say on the subject of China. He told Hurley that he had no respect for the "great American illusion" about China, or FDR's intent to decolonize Asia. Hong Kong, he stressed, would be "eliminated from the British Empire only over my dead body." Stalin proved more sympathetic, telling Hurley that he still favored a KMT led coalition and considered Chiang a "selfless patriot." Based on these words, Hurley cabled FDR that "Stalin agreed unqualifiedly to American policy in China."[51]

AFTERMATH AND LEGACIES

Roosevelt's passing on April 12 left the United States' China policy in a state of limbo. Japan's imminent defeat seemed likely to trigger the full scale civil war Americans had long dreaded. In his first months as president, Harry Truman evinced little interest in Chinese politics as he focused on the questions of Soviet behavior in Eastern Europe and how to compel Japan's surrender. Early in August, as Roosevelt had anticipated, the combined impact of the atomic bombs and the Soviet entry into the war compelled the emperor and the military hardliners around him to capitulate.[52] Militarily, China had become yesterday's news.

Japan's surrender on August 15, however, brought no peace to China or respite for American policymakers. Almost immediately, Kuomintang, Chinese Communists, Soviet troops, and American Marines raced to seize vital ports, airfields, and rail lines in north China and Manchuria. Washington's General Order # 1 instructed the two million or more Japanese troops in China-proper to surrender *only* to Chiang. (Those in Manchuria surrendered to the Soviet Red Army.) Truman and the Joint Chiefs of Staff approved plans devised by Hurley and Wedemeyer for American ships and planes to transport hundreds of thousands of Nationalist troops to coastal and north China so that they, rather than Communist forces, would take Japanese-held territory and weapons. But when these poorly led KMT forces faltered, almost 60,000 American marines were dispatched to north China to prevent CCP seizure of rail lines and ports.

Despite substantial American efforts on his behalf, things went badly for Chiang in the autumn of 1945. As the fighting between Nationalist and Communist troops escalated, Truman and his advisers feared the worst: the Soviets might become entrenched in Manchuria and assist the CCP and then the Communists might seize the initiative over the Nationalists, drawing U.S. forces into the middle of the civil war, with Soviet armies nearby. To make matters even more complicated, all sides considered using some of the two million Japanese troops located in China in their competing effort to assert control. Truman initially expanded the American military commitment to Chiang, hoping to block the CCP. But by November 1945, this had only succeeded in putting over 50,000 Marines in harms way with little likelihood they could stem the Communist tide in north China. Truman then resolved to cut his losses by reducing involvement. Turning back to Roosevelt's game plan, Truman called on the warring Chinese factions to accept American mediation as a way of heading off civil war and limiting Soviet penetration.

Ambassador Hurley, then in Washington, feared once again he was about to be blamed for the chaos engulfing China. At a November 27 news conference, he condemned the "hydra-headed direction" of China policy, which he again attributed to State Department officers who "sided with the Communist armed party...against American policy." His wild charges prompted a brief Senate investigation that, in retrospect, resembled a dry run of Senator Joseph McCarthy's later accusations of "who lost China?"[53]

The same day that Hurley resigned, Truman asked retired Army Chief of Staff George C. Marshall to go to China as his personal representative in an effort to avert civil war. The appointment of Marshall, who enjoyed immense respect, muted Hurley's reckless allegations. During 1946, Marshall arranged the mutual withdrawal of Soviet forces from Manchuria and American marines from north China. But he had no more success than previous American emissaries in resolving China's underlying crisis.[54]

Around the time Marshall left for China at the end of 1945, Henry Luce placed Chiang's portrait for a record sixth time on the cover of *Time* magazine. An accompanying editorial in *Life* argued that "the safest thing" for America was to "rededicate our wartime alliance with China and its government." Luce dismissed those who questioned the integrity and leadership of America's wartime ally. The Generalissimo and those around him, Luce argued, were "man for man" as "able and as liberal as Truman's cabinet."[55]

Truman had, in fact, instructed Marshall that no matter what happened, the United States would provide "at least indirect support of Chiang Kai-shek's activities against dissident forces in China." If the Communists balked at making "reasonable concessions," Marshall could assist Chiang's efforts to move and equip his forces. But even if the Communists behaved reasonably and Chiang blocked a compromise, the United States would not abandon him because America could no accept a "divided China" or the "resumption of Russian power in Manchuria." As Marshall rued, no matter what the Nationalist regime did, Washington "would have to swallow its pride and much of its policy" and continue to support the Kuomintang.[56]

By early 1947, when a despondent Marshall abandoned his peace effort and came home to become secretary of state, full scale civil war had erupted. Yet, despite earlier intentions of standing by Chiang, the Truman administration avoided direct intervention. Instead, it shifted priorities to rebuilding Germany and Japan, the "two great workshops of Europe and Asia," in Dean Acheson's phrase, as barriers to Soviet expansion.

For a decade before the Chinese Communist victory in 1949, the American public had heard political and cultural leaders from Franklin Roosevelt to Henry Luce describe China as a "great power" whose fate was linked to both control of Asia and America's global security. After 1949, many Republicans and some conservative Democrats condemned Roosevelt and Truman for engineering this dire "loss." Like the State Department's "China Hands" who were punished for accurately reporting what they saw and predicting the course of China's revolution, FDR, Truman, and the professional foreign service officers who served them, paid a heavy price for their exertions on China's behalf. Throughout the 1950s and well into the 1960s, echoes of the "who lost China" debate weighed heavily on the minds of Americans concerned with foreign affairs. Both Presidents John F. Kennedy and, especially, Lyndon B. Johnson referred frequently to the political consequences suffered by Democrats for the "loss of China" and explained their decisions to defend South Vietnam largely in these terms.[57]

Yet, in spite of the bitter recriminations and fear of Maoist China from 1949 to 1969, Roosevelt's long-term vision of China as a Great Power and a potential buffer against Soviet expansion retained an underlying salience. Ironically, it would be Richard Nixon, an early cheerleader and beneficiary of the "Who Lost China" campaign, who eventually implemented an updated version of Roosevelt's China policy. Shortly after taking office as president in 1969, Nixon, along with his National Security adviser Henry Kissinger, envisioned Mao's China as a new pivot to American policy in Asia. By cultivating a relationship with China, the United States could develop a counterbalance to an expansionist Soviet Union and an increasingly economically competitive Japan. Improved ties with China might also put pressure on Hanoi to negotiate a face-saving American exit from Vietnam. Ultimately, in the wake of an impending American exit from Southeast Asia, an alliance with the People's Republic of China would stabilize the region and encourage China to act as an American surrogate.

The Maoist leadership, weakened by ideological excesses, wary of an increasingly assertive Japan, and terrified that border skirmishes with the Soviet Union in August 1969 might trigger a major war, looked upon cooperation with the United States as its only path to security. Nixon, who saw himself as the consummate strategic realist, was prepared to abandon his old friend on Taiwan, Chiang Kai-shek, in a heartbeat in order to seal a deal with Mao.

Whether Nixon and Kissinger realized it or not, the evolving relationship they forged with China between 1969 and 1974 resembled in some ways the one Roosevelt had hoped would emerge after World War II. Kissinger, hardly a New Deal acolyte, conveyed his belief to President Nixon that the People's Republic of China (PRC), though communist, had become America's "tacit ally" in the Cold War. It was "extraordinary," Kissinger reported following secret talks with Mao Zedong and Zhou Enlai, that amongst all nations "with the possible exception of the United Kingdom, the PRC might well be closest to us in its global perceptions." As Roosevelt had remarked a quarter century earlier to skeptical British officials, China, with its vast population and potential, would be "very useful twenty-five years hence," even if it "cannot contribute much military or naval support for the moment." In a belated affirmation of Harry Hopkins' prediction that "in any serious conflict of policy with Russia," China "would line up on our side," the Chinese Communist leader Mao eventually did just that, confirming, whether or not he recognized it, part of Roosevelt's strategic vision for a new world balance of power.[58]

NOTES

1. This chapter draws heavily on my study of American policy in China during World War II, Michael Schaller, *The U.S. Crusade in China, 1938–45* (New York: Columbia University Press, 1979). See also, Herbert Feis, *The China Tangle* (Princeton: Princeton University Press, 1953); Robert Dallek, *Franklin D. Roosevelt and American Foreign Policy, 1932–45* (New York: Oxford University Press, 1979); Christopher Thorne, *Allies of a Kind: The United States, Great Britain and the War Against Japan, 1941–1945* (New York: Oxford University Press, 1978); Barbara Tuchman, *Stilwell and the American Experience in China, 1941–1945* (New York: Bantam Books, 1972); Charles Romanus and Riley Sunderland, *Stilwell's Mission to China* (Washington: Office of the Chief of Military History, Dept. of the Army, 1953), *Stilwell's Command Problems* (Washington: Office of the Chief of Military History, Dept. of the Army, 1956), *Time Runs out in CBI* (Washington: Office of the Chief of Military History, Dept. of the Army, 1959); Tang Tsou, *America's Failure in China* (Chicago: University of Chicago Press 1963); E.J. Kahan, *The China Hands: America's Foreign Service Officers and What Befell Them* (New York: Viking, 1975); Theodore White and Annalee Jacoby, *Thunder out of China* (New York: William Sloane Associates, 1946); John Patton Davies, *Dragon by the Tail* (New York: Norton, 1972); Joseph Esherick, ed., *Lost Chance in China: The World War II Dispatches of John S. Service* (New York: Random House, 1974); Gary May, *China Scapegoat: The Diplomatic*

Ordeal of John Carter Vincent (Prospect Heights, IL: Waveland Press, 1982); James Reardon-Anderson, *Yenan and the Great Powers* (New York: Columbia University Press, 1980); T. Christopher Jespersen, *American Images of China, 1931–1949* (Stanford, CA: Stanford University Press, 1996); John W. Garver, *The Diplomacy of Chinese Nationalism* (New York: Oxford University Press, 1988); Xiaoyuan Liu, *A Partnership for Disorder: China, the United States, and their Policies for the Postwar Disposition of the Japanese Empire* (New York: Cambridge University Press, 1996); Russell Buhite, *Patrick J. Hurley and American Foreign Policy* (Ithaca, NY: Cornell University Press, 1973); Marc Galicchio, *The Cold War Begins: American East Asia Policy and the Fall of the Japanese Empire* (New York: Columbia University Press, 1988); Odd Arne Westad, *Cold War and Revolution: Soviet–American Rivalry and the Origins of the Chinese Civil War, 1944–1946* (New York: Columbia University Press, 1993); Stephen MacKinnon and Oris Friesen, *China Reporting: An Oral History of American Journalism in the 1930s and 1940s* (Berkeley: University of California Press, 1987); For the extreme conservative interpretation of Roosevelt's China policy, see: Don Lohbeck, *Patrick J. Hurley* (Chicago: H. Regnery Co., 1956) and Anthony Kubek, *How the Far East Was Lost: American Policy and the Creation of Communist China, 1941–1949* (Chicago: H. Regnery Co., 1963).

2. Gallup surveys from 1937 on showed large and growing majorities of Americans sympathizing with Japan over Japan. In September 1937, for example, 43 percent of the public saw China as a victim and Japan an aggressor. Only 2 percent of the public sided with Japan in its war with China. In 1938, the spread grew to 59 percent pro-China to 1 percent pro-Japan, with 40 percent undecided. By 1939, the numbers were 74 percent pro-China, 2 percent pro-Japan, and 24 percent undecided. Nevertheless, in mid-1939, only 6 percent of Americans favored fighting Japan on China's behalf. About half supported imposing strict trade sanctions on Tokyo. On this, see T. Christopher Jespersen, *American Images of China, 1931–1949* (Stanford, CA: Stanford University Press, 1996).

3. Hornbeck to Alexander Cadogan, April 13, 1938, FRUS 1938, III, 141–3; John Carter Vincent to Hornbeck, July 23, 1938, ibid., 234–7.

4. Transcript of discussion, April 18, 1940, *Morgenthau Diaries I,* 100–108; Memorandum of conversation with K.P. Li, ibid., 112–18; See "Comment on Draft History of First Burma Campaign," box 2, Boatner Papers; Transcript of Treasury Department Group Meeting, April 21, 1941, *Morgenthau Diaries I,* 385–94; McHugh to Currie, April 27, 1941, McHugh Papers; Transcript of Treasury Dept. Group Meeting, May 12, 1941, *Morgenthau Diaries I,* 408–18; Transcript of telephone conv. with Currie, July 10, 1941, ibid., 339–42.

5. Ibid.; Romanus and Sunderland, *Stilwell's Mission to China,* 14–17.

6. Johnson to Hull, October 24, 1940, *FRUS 1940,* IV, 429; Johnson to Hull, October 18, 1940, ibid., 672–4; Johnson to Hull, December 23, 1940, ibid., 472; Hull to Johnson, December 28, 1940, ibid., 476; Johnson to Hull, November 29, 1940, DOS, Decimal File, China, 893.00/14599, RG 59; Johnson to Hornbeck, December 12, 1940, Hornbeck Papers.

7. Johnson to Hornbeck, April 11, 1941, Hornbeck Papers; Johnson to Hull, January 23, 1941, DOS, Decimal File, China, 893.00/14630, RG 59; McHugh quoted in a memorandum by George Atcheson, April 24, 1941, *FRUS 1941*, V, 494; Report of December 27, 1941, Far Eastern Section, G-2, Regional File; memorandum by John P. Davies, January 24, 1941, DOS, Decimal File, China, 893.00/14621, RG 59; memorandum of a conversation by Davies, January 29, 1941, ibid., 893.00/14656; memorandum by Davies, April 12, 1941, ibid., 893.00/14680.

8. Report by Currie to Roosevelt, March 15, 1941, box 427 Roosevelt Papers; Visit to China of Lauchlin Currie file, March 3, 1941, DOS, Decimal File, 003.1193, RG 59; Currie to Roosevelt, ibid. Following up on Currie's recommendation, the United States sent both a military and a civilian advisory mission to China to address transportation, currency, and military supply issues. The State Department also dispatched Owen Lattimore, an academic specialist on Asia, as a political advisor to Chiang. As with later American emissaries, they were largely ignored. By the late-1940s, Currie was accused of being a Soviet sympathizer or even spy. Although never charged, he left the United States. At least through early 1944, Currie was among Chiang's most ardent supporters in Roosevelt's inner circle, not an advocate for the Communists.

9. For a detailed discussion of the "secret air war plan," see Schaller, *U.S. Crusade in China*, 65–85.

10. William Rogers Louis, *Imperialism at Bay: The United States and the Decolonization of the British Empire, 1941–45* (Oxford, UK: Clarendon Press, 1977); New Harvard University Press book on defeat of British and other colonial armies in SEA.

11. Report of AMMISCA to War Department, December 10, 1941, box 3, Magruder Mission Material, Dept. of the Army, Supporting Documents, CBI Theater History, Office of the Chief of Military History; Magruder to War Dept., January 5, 1942, *FRUS 1941*, IV, 769–71; Magruder to War Dept., February 10, 1942, *FRUS 1942 China*, 13–16.

12. McHugh to Secretary of the Navy, December 19, 1941, PSF, box 2, Roosevelt Papers; Currie to Roosevelt, December 27, 1941, ibid.; McHugh to Currie, January 10, 1942, McHugh Papers, Cornell University.

13. Gauss to Roosevelt, November 19, 1941, DOS Decimal File, China, 893.00/14827; Gauss to Hull, December 29, 1941, ibid., 893.00/14834; Gauss to Hull, December 14, 1941, *FRUS 1941*, IV, 753–4.

14. Memorandum by Hopkins of Eden visit, March 27, 1943, box 138, book 7, Hopkins Papers, cited in Walter LaFeber, "Roosevelt, Churchill and Indo-China, 1942–1945," *American Historical Review* 80 (December 1975): 1277–95; Churchill quoted in *the Diaries of Sir Alexander Cadogan, 1938–1945*, David Dilks, ed., 488; While Churchill and Eden were notorious for their condescending attitude toward China and what they saw as Roosevelt's childish fascination with it, Christopher Thorne, in *Allies of a Kind*, argues that many other British officials took a more measured and sympathetic view of both China and American policy in East Asia.

15. Roosevelt to Lord Louis Mountbatten, November 8, 1943, PSF, box 38, Roosevelt Papers; J.W. Pickersgill and D.W. Forster, *The Mackenzie King Record,* I, 553.

16. Entry of July 25, 1942, Black and White Books, Stilwell Papers, Hoover Institution. For a vivid record of the Stilwell–Chiang rivalry, see the published selections in Theodore White, ed., *The Stilwell Papers* (New York: W. Sloane Associates, 1948). See also Tuchman, *Stilwell and the American Experience in China.*

17. Roosevelt to Chiang, July 14, 1942, Map Room, box 10, Roosevelt Papers.

18. Report by Currie to Roosevelt, August 24, 1942, Dept of the Army, Operations Division 336, RG 165, National Archives.

19. Ibid.; Currie to Roosevelt, August 11, 1942, *FRUS 1942* I, 712–14.

20. Record of Interview with Gen. George C. Marshall, July 6, 13, 1949, box 3, supporting documents, CBI Theater History.

21. Memorandum by Vincent, July 30, 1942, DOS, Decimal File, China, 893.00/14876, RG 59. On Vincent and the other China specialists in the Foreign Service, see, May, *China Scapegoat* and Kahn, *China Hands.*

22. Report by John S. Service, January 23, 1943, DOS, Decimal File, China, 893.00/14969, RG 59. For an overview of Service's dispatches, see, Esherick, *Lost Chance in China.*

23. Report by John P. Davies, March 23, 1943, ibid., 893.00/14989; Davies to Gauss, *FRUS 1943 China,* 25–29; See also Davies' memoir, *Dragon by the Tail.*

24. Romanus and Sunderland, *Stilwell's Mission to China,* 271; Roosevelt to Marshall, March 8, 1943, ibid., 279–82; Dept. of State, Washington and Casablanca, Casablanca Conference folders, Map Room, box 26, Roosevelt Papers; Chiang to Roosevelt, February 7, 1943, Stilwell CBI Correspondence, Dept of the Army, CBI Theater Records; for a selection of Joseph Alsop's spirited and extensive messages to the White House on Chennault's behalf, see, Chennault to Roosevelt and Hopkins, December 27, 1942, box 138, "Chinese Affairs," Hopkins Papers, Roosevelt Library; Alsop to Hopkins, December 10, 22, 28, 1942 and March 1, 3, 5, 26, 1943, ibid.; Soong to Hopkins, September 25, 1943, ibid.; Memorandum of conversation with Joseph Alsop, January 9, 1953, Herbert Feis Papers, Library of Congress; entry of March 7, 1943, Black and White Books, Stilwell Papers. Characteristically, Stilwell referred to Alsop as "Allslop." Perhaps to balance the information coming from Alsop, Hopkins also encouraged correspondence from John P. Davies, Stilwell's political advisor. See, for example, Davies to Hopkins, December 31, 1943, *FRUS 1943 China,* 397–9; For a useful discussion of popular and press opinion of China and Chiang, see, Jespersen, *American Images of China.*

25. Notes of May 1943, Washington Conference, fold. 61, Stilwell Papers; See also *The Stilwell Papers,* 204–7.

26. Tuchman, *Stilwell,* 400–406.

27. Morgenthau to Roosevelt, December 18, 1943, *Morgenthau Diaries* II, 944–6; record of Treasury Dept. group meetings, December 21, 1943, ibid.,

947–67; record of conversation between Morgenthau and White, January 18, 1944, ibid., 1022–4; memorandum by Hornbeck, December 27, 1943, DOS Decimal File, China, 893.51/7725, RG 59; Roosevelt to Chiang, January 5, 1944, ibid., 893.51/7727A; Chiang to Roosevelt, January 16, 1944, ibid., 893.51/7731; memorandum of group discussion on Chinese loan request, January 19, 1944, ibid., 893.51/7732; record of meeting of representatives of the State, War, and Treasury Departments, February 14, 1944, *Morgenthau Diaries*, II, 1054–6.

28. Elliott Roosevelt, *As He Saw It*, 152–64.

29. Ibid.; Dorn to Stilwell, November 28, 1943, Stilwell CBI Correspondence; Solomon Adler to Treasury Dept, December 30, 1943, *Morgenthau Diaries*, II, 970; Report by John Service, February 3, 1944, Dept of the Army, G-2 Regional File, 1933–44, also in *FRUS 1944*, IV, 319; Davies, *Dragon by the Tail*, 279–81; daily diary entry of December 6, 1943, and memorandum of December 6, 1943, box 33, Stilwell Papers; *The Stilwell Papers*, 251.

30. Frank Dorn, *Walkout with Stilwll in Burma*, 75–79.

31. Marshall to Stilwell, July 2, 1944, box 13, Stilwell Papers; Stilwell to Marshall, July 3, 1944, ibid.; Roosevelt to Chiang, July 6, 1944, ibid.; diary entry of June 1, 1944, vol. 47, Henry Stimson Papers, Yale University.

32. Chiang to Roosevelt, July 8, 1944, quoted in Romanus and Sunderland, *Stilwell's Command Problems*, 385–6; Chiang to Roosevelt, July 23, 1944, ibid.; Gauss to Hull, July 12, 1944, *FRUS VI*, 124; Marshall to Stilwell August (n.d.) 1944, box 17, Stilwell Papers; entry of August 3, 1944 diary vol. 48, Stimson Papers; Buhite, *Patrick J. Hurley*, 150–2; Harriman to Hull, September 5, 1944, *FRUS 1944*, VI, 253–6; memorandum by Davies of conversation with Hopkins, September 4, 1944, box 15, Stilwell Papers; a story circulated in Washington that after FDR appointed Hurley the president quipped, "well, the next thing we hear from Pat will be his memoirs. The title will be 'Alone in China.'" Owen Lattimore quoted in Thorne, *Allies of a Kind*, 426.

33. Pickersgill and Forster, *Mackenzie King Record*, II, 67, 71.

34. See the discussion on the proposed text of letter to Chiang, *FRUS Quebec*, 374, 464; *The Stilwell Papers, 334*; Schaller, *U.S. Crusade in China*, 169–70.

35. Memorandum from Stilwell to Hurley, September 23, 1944, box 89, folder 1, Patrick Hurley Papers, University of Oklahoma; memorandum by Stilwell for Ho Ying-chin, September 28, 1944, box 27, Stilwell Papers; Hopkins to Hurley, October 7, 1944, box 88, folder 10, Hurley Papers; daily diary entry of October 1, 1944, Stilwell Papers; Gauss to Hull, October 5, 1944, *FRUS 1944*, VI, 264–6; Henry Wallace, *Price of Vision*, entry of October 4, 1944, 386–7; entries of October 3, 4, 1944, diary vol. 48, Stimson Papers; Roosevelt to Chiang, October 5, 1944, quoted in Romanus and Sunderland, *Stilwell's Command Problems*, 459; Chiang to Roosevelt, via Hurley, October 10, 1944, box 89, folder 2, Hurley Papers; Hurley to Roosevelt, October 10, 1944 and Stilwell to Marshall, October 10, 1944, both cited in "The President and U.S. Aid to China," November 15, 1944, George Elsey

Papers, Harry S. Truman Library; Roosevelt instructed Elsey to prepare this 59 page account of American aid to and involvement in China shortly after Stilwell's recall. The tone of the report and the documents quoted clearly suggest that most of China's problems were self-inflicted by Chiang and not caused by U.S. actions. Roosevelt may have wanted this document available should, as many thought possible, the KMT regime collapse. In many ways it foreshadowed the so-called China White Paper of 1949 that Dean Acheson had prepared in response to the Chinese Communist victory.

36. Dallek, *Franklin D. Roosevelt,* 497.

37. Daily diary entry of November 4, 1944, Stilwell Papers; Roosevelt to Hurley, October 14, 1944, box 88, folder 8, Hurley Papers; Hurley to Roosevelt, October 15, 1944, ibid.; Roosevelt to Chiang, via Hurley, October 18, 1944, ibid.; entry of November 3, 1944, vol. 48, Stimson Papers. Hurley was a flamboyant egotist and later a raving reactionary. Many Amerians who met him in China in 1944–1945 also thought he was mentally unstable. See the discussion in MacKinnon, et Al., *China Reporting.*

38. For two somewhat different assessments of CCP policy toward the United States, see, Reardon-Anderson, *Yenan and the Great Powers* and Westad, *Cold War and Revolution*; A good sample of John Service's reports from Yenan are found in Esherick, ed., *Lost Chance in China;* For the "flavor" of CCP–U.S. interaction among the members of the Dixie Mission, also see, David Barrett, *Dixie Mission: The U.S. Army Observer Group in Yenan, 1944* (Berkeley: Center for Chinese Studies, University of California, 1970); Davies, *Dragon by the Tail*; John S. Service, *The Amerasia Papers: Some Problems in the History of U.S. China Relations* (Berkeley: Center for Chinese Studies, University of California, 1971); Carolle J. Carter, *Mission to Yenan* (Lexington, KY: University Press of Kentucky, 1997); Mackinnon, *China Reporting;* Schaller, *U.S. Crusade in China,* 184–94.

39. Barrett, *Dixie Mission,* 56–59, 75–76; Davies, *Dragon by the Tai,* 366, 383; Kahn, *The China Hands,* 122–4, 135; notes of conference in Yenan, November 8, 1944, box 97, folder 12, Hurley Papers; copy of five point proposal, ibid.; memorandum by Davies for Hurley, "American–Chinese Relations During the Next Six Months," November 15, 1944, box 89, folder 13, Hurley Papers; Stelle to Col. John G. Coughlin, November 22, 1944, OSS-Yenan Documents, Modern Military Records Branch, National Archives; Chou to Morgenthau, December 8, 1944, *Morgenthau Diaries,* II, 1379–86; Chou to Hurley, December 8, 1944, box 97, folder 13, Hurley Papers; Barrett to Wedemeyer, December 10, 1944, ibid.; Hurley to Chou, December 11, 1944, box 97, folder 13, ibid.; Hurley to Roosevelt, December 12, 1944, box 93, folder 1, ibid.

40. Dixie Mission to Wedemeyer, January 10, 1945, box 98, folder 1, Hurley Papers; for more discussion of this proposal, see, "Wires Re: Communists," Modern Military Records Branch, National Archives; Barbara Tuchman, *Notes from China,* 78.

41. Wedemeyer to JCS, December 28, 1944, box 87, folder 21, Hurley Papers; Mao to Hurley, January 11, 1945, box 98, folder 1, ibid.; Memorandum

by Gen. Robert McClure, January 24, 1945, in "Wires Re: Communists"; Romanus and Sunderland, *Time Runs out on CBI,* 251–2; Hurley to Roosevelt, January 14, 1945, *FRUS 1945,* VII, 172–7.

42. Marshall to Wedemeyer, January 15, 1945, quoted in Romanus and Sunderland, *Time Runs out on CBI,* 252; Marshall to Wedemeyer, January 23, 1945, box 98, folder 1, Hurley Papers; Wedemeyer to Marshall, January 27, 1945, ibid.; Grew to Hurley, January 23, 1945, *FRUS 1945,* VII, 181; Hurley to Mao, January 20, 1945, box 98, folder 1, Hurley Papers; Mao to Hurley, January 22, 1945, ibid.

43. For a comprehensive assessment of the agreements reached at Yalta, see, Dallek, *Franklin D. Roosevelt,* 506–28.

44. Atcheson to Secretary of State, February 28, 1945, *FRUS 1945,* VII, 242–6; Service, *The Amerasia Papers,* 188–91; Adler to White, February 25, 1945, *Morgenthau Diaries,* II, 1419–23.

45. Memorandum by Service of conversation with Mao, March 13, 1945, *Amerasia Papers,* II, 1400–4; reports by Service, March 14–23, 1945, ibid., 1405–46.

46. Schaller, *U.S. Crusade in China,* 215–17.

47. Wedemeyer to War Department, March 9, 1945, box 1, Wedemeyer Files; entries of March 8, 9, 1945, diary vol. 49, Stimson Papers; Leahy, *I Was There,* 337; Wedemeyer, *Wedemeyer Reports!,* 342; Romanus and Sunderland, *Time Runs Out on CBI,* 338.

48. Wedemeyer, *Wedemeyer Reports!,* 340–1; Leahy, *I Was There,* 337.

49. Edgar Snow, *Journey to the Beginning,* 347–8.

50. Transcript of Hurley Press Conference, April 2, 1945, *FRUS 1945,* VII, 317–22.

51. Buhite, *Hurley,* 204–9; Memorandum of Hurley conversation with Stalin, April 17, 1945, *FRUS 1945,* VII, 338–40; Hurley to Secretary of State, April 14, 1945, ibid., 329–32.

52. On the end of the war in China and East Asia, see, Galicchio, *The Cold War Begins*; and Tsuyoshi Hasegawa, *Racing the Enemy: Stalin, Truman, and the Surrender of Japan* (Cambridge, MA: Belknap, 2005).

53. Hurley's dramatic resignation and the debate it set off are discussed in Kenneth Chern, *Dilemma in China: America's Policy Debate, 1945* (Hamden, CT: Archon Books, 1980).

54. The role of Marshall as mediator and the contest over control of Manchuria is analyzed in Steven I. Levine, *Anvil of Victory: The Communist Revolution in Manchuria, 1945–48* (New York: Columbia University Press, 1987).

55. See Jespersen, *American Images of China.*

56. Notes by Marshall of Meetings with Truman, December 11, 14, 1945, *FRUS 1945,* VII, 767–70.

57. The purge of State Department China experts is discussed in E.J. Kahn, *The China Hands: America's Foreign Service Officers and What Befell Them* (New York: Viking, 1975); The debate within the Truman administration over whether to recognize the PRC is analyzed in Nancy B. Tucker, *Patterns in the Dust: Chinese–American Relations and the Recognition Controversy,*

1949–50 (New York: Columbia University Press, 1983). The impact of McCarthyism on the decisions of Kennedy and Johnson are discussed in Robert Dean, *Imperial Brotherhood: Gender and the Making of Cold War Foreign Policy* (Amherst: University of Massachusetts Press, 2001).

58. For the "flavor" of the Nixon administration's approach to China, see William Burr, ed., *The Kissinger Transcripts: The Top Secret Talks with Beijing and Moscow* (New York: New Press; Distributed by W.W. Norton, 1999); the emerging strategic partnership with China in the 1970s, is discussed in James Mann, *About Face: A History of America's Curious Relationship with China from Nixon to Clinton* (New York: Alfred Knopf, 1999); and Michael Schaller, *Altered States: The U.S. and Japan Since the Occupation* (New York: Oxford University Press, 1997).

CHAPTER 7

FDR AND THE NEW ECONOMIC ORDER

RANDALL B. WOODS

ALTHOUGH PLANNING FOR THE POSTWAR WORLD BEGAN even before the United States officially entered the conflict, the Roosevelt administration's thinking on security matters remained in flux throughout World War II. In matters of international economics, however, FDR and his advisers were more consistent. Following his brief flirtation with economic nationalism at the World Economic Conference in London, the president began gravitating toward an international trade regime characterized by cooperation and reciprocity. In supporting the Reciprocal Trade Agreements Act of 1934 (RTAA), FDR endorsed a mechanism that had the potential for lowering trade barriers by shifting responsibility for setting the foreign trade agenda from Congress to the executive and authorizing negotiations for reciprocal tariff reductions. Strong political opposition to the trade agreements program and the need for congressional renewal every three years led the administration to act cautiously in reducing duties on goods that competed seriously with domestic products.[1] Yet RTAA was a significant innovation. During the nineteenth century tariff rates had been a matter for domestic interest groups to resolve. In passing the trade agreements act, Congress and the administration recognized that tariffs against American goods were related to tariffs against foreign goods. More important, out of the RTAA kernel would develop a comprehensive program for creating a truly interdependent world economy.

Ever sensitive to the mood of the American people, a mood that grew increasingly conservative during the course of the war, FDR searched for a mechanism that would prevent widespread unemployment in the United States, promote international understanding and prosperity, and deflect charges from conservatives that he was taking the United States further down the road toward state socialism. The economic policymakers in the State Department, some of whom had cut their teeth on the reciprocal trade agreement legislation, stepped forward with an answer—multilateralism.[2]

The concept was rooted in the free trade ideas of Cordell Hull. The secretary of state, seventy years old in 1941, was the embodiment of old fashioned southern progressivism. As congressman and then senator from Tennessee, Hull had railed against the malfeasances of Wall Street financiers and industrialists who had fashioned monopolies and erected tariff barriers designed to enrich themselves and exploit farmers and workers. Hull and Roosevelt had met during the Wilson years, and FDR cultivated the Tennessean throughout the 1920s. Because Hull supported him at Chicago in 1932, and because he represented two great constituencies—Congress and the South—FDR asked him in 1933 to be his secretary of state, a post Hull would retain until his retirement in 1944.[3] Hull's stock-in-trade as America's chief diplomat was, of course, commercial liberalism. Trade barriers—particularly the tariff—retarded production, raised prices, created inefficiency, held down living standards, and thus bred hostility among nations. "Economic Wars," he told the House of Representatives in September 1918, "are but the germs of real wars." He would certainly have agreed with Richard Cobden, the spiritual leader of the nineteenth-century British free traders, who claimed to see "in the Free Trade principle that which shall act on the moral world as the principle of gravitation in the universe—drawing men together, thrusting aside the antagonisms of race and creed, and language, and uniting us in the eternal bonds of peace."[4]

Hull himself was something of a simpleminded visionary. Like his Populist forebears, the secretary of state chose to believe rather than understand, to put his faith in a few simple truths rather than to clutter his mind with price structures, demand curves, and demographic trends. It remained to Hull's subordinates—Francis Sayre, Harry Hawkins, Henry Grady, Clair Wilcox, and Herbert Feis—to translate his simple obsession into reality.[5] The program advocated by the economic internationalists in the State Department rested on two cornerstones: nondiscrimination and a simultaneous lowering of all trade barriers. In their trade, tariff, and currency exchange policies, nations should not favor one member of the international community over another. Moreover, no exporter or importer, no matter what the person's nationality, should have to contend with "artificial impediments." That is, trade should be conducted purely on economic and not political grounds.

The multilateralists were reacting in part to contemporary developments in international economics. Bilateralism, the signing of exclusive trade agreements between two nations, was the norm in international commerce in the 1930s. The competition to build arsenals and control strategic minerals precluded any chance of a simultaneous reduction of trade barriers.

All of the great European powers signed bilateral pacts with their smaller neighbors and with developing nations in Latin America and East Asia, in which the trading partner was granted increased import quotas and a special low tariff rate in return for allowing the larger power to monopolize the imported product. In a fit of neo-mercantilism, each country, by raising tariffs, imposing quota restrictions, negotiating preferential arrangements, utilizing restrictive and discriminatory exchange controls, and subsidizing its exports, tried to take care of its own exporters and producers at the expense of those in other countries.[6]

Multilateralists maintained that competition among countries for the wealth of the world restricted trade, wasted resources, and bred war; competition between individuals and corporations based on price, product quality, and market demand bred efficiency and economic expansion, and raised living standards. As long as nations tried to protect infant industries and inefficient agricultural operations with artificial, "uneconomic" trade barriers, the world would continue to be made up of relatively inefficient national economies or clusters of national economies.[7] The multilateralists looked forward to the creation of a world market in which citizens of each region concentrated on producing the commodity that they could produce most cheaply and efficiently. This specialization, coupled with the elimination of trade barriers, would mean production and distribution of the greatest number of goods at the cheapest possible price.[8]

Domestic economic and political considerations aside, the Roosevelt administration recognized the importance to America of a stable, democratic, noncommunist, and non-fascist Europe. Because V-E Day would find America in possession of a large portion of the world's industrial capacity, and because much of Europe and Asia, ravaged by war, would be in desperate need of finished and semifinished products, multilateralism held out the promise not only of banishing unemployment from America but rehabilitating war-torn areas abroad and protecting liberal capitalism from a revived fascism on one hand and Soviet-style communism on the other.[9]

The Roosevelt White House was circumscribed in its policymaking and decision making, however, by the forces of nationalism, fiscal conservatism, and isolationism within Congress and the federal bureaucracy, and among the American people as a whole. As a result, multilateralists were forced to modify their programs and mechanisms until, at least in the short run, they threatened to become counterproductive.

For multilateralism to work, that is, for members of the trading community to lower their barriers and end their controls over foreign exchange and still achieve a balance of payments and an ever-rising volume of trade, the United States would have to meet two conditions. First, Washington would have to provide adequate liquidity to its trading partners in the form of gold or dollars; second, it would have to agree to a horizontal tariff reduction tied to simultaneous reductions made by other countries.[10] Because Great Britain was the second largest noncommunist trading nation in the world and operated a relatively closed empire trading bloc, it was the key, at least in foreign policy, to the realization of the Roosevelt administration's multilateral dreams.

In 1932, at the Ottawa Conference, the United Kingdom and other members of the Commonwealth and Empire had formed a trading bloc within which member nations awarded each other's exports preferential treatment. The drain on Britain's financial and material resources caused by World War II compelled the Exchequer and Board of Trade to strengthen this bloc and generally to accelerate the trend toward governmental control of international finance and foreign commerce. The War Cabinet authorized long-term bulk purchasing agreements with exporters of primary products, strictly limited imports from non-sterling area nations, and blocked sterling payments to members of the sterling area. In the latter mechanism, Britain acquired huge amounts of raw materials from India, Egypt, and other nations with which Britain traded regularly (and which, generally speaking, Britain had dominated politically and militarily). But it refused to make its sterling freely convertible into other currencies, like dollars, so that sterling bloc members might buy from third parties such as the United States. American policymakers perceived that if Britain used the leverage of these blocked sterling balances to maintain and strengthen its trading and monetary union into the postwar period, multilateralism would never come to pass.[11]

World War II and the deterioration of Britain's overseas financial position presented American multilateralists with a unique opportunity to bring down the walls of imperial preference and destroy the sterling area.[12] During the two-year period from 1939 through 1941 when it stood virtually alone against the forces of international fascism, the United Kingdom exhausted its gold and dollar resources as it acquired the material and munitions with which to fight. Passage of the Lend-Lease Act in 1941 helped end the strain on British finances, but the Exchequer was never able to recover. By 1944 British overseas indebtedness was increasing at a rate of $650 million a year, and as of July 1945 British gold and dollar resources stood at $1.8 billion, less than half the 1939 figure. (At this point the United States had accumulated more than $21 billion in gold bullion at Fort Knox.) Britain's external liabilities amounted to $13 billion, most of it in sterling owed to sterling area creditors but held in London in blocked balances. If the United Kingdom lowered its trade barriers without restoring a balance of trade and if it made sterling freely convertible, as multilateralism required, it would be drained of gold and dollars within the blinking of an eye. In order for His Majesty's Government, whatever the party in control, to achieve a balance of trade and payments, compete for overseas markets, and provide food, homes, and work to the common man, it would need massive economic assistance from the United States. American multilateralists recognized the urgency of Britain's predicament and were determined to take full advantage of it.[13]

Meanwhile, Roosevelt and the multilateralists struggled to keep their own house in order. During World War II a battle raged within the administration between those who wanted to provide Britain with adequate liquidity in the form of lend-lease, loans, or credits, and those who did not. Presidential aide Harry Hopkins and his circle of advisors, a group of professional economists in the federal bureaucracy, and liberal internationalists such as Secretary of Commerce Henry Wallace, advocated a generous foreign aid program for Great Britain on political, strategic, economic, and ideological grounds.[14] In opposition was a coalition of conservative nationalists in Congress, bureaucratic imperialists in the United States Treasury, and, of course, special interests who believed that the object of foreign trade was to enrich America at the expense of the rest of the world, those who saw foreign aid as a first step to United States entanglement in European affairs, and after July 1945, those opposed to subsidizing a collectivist state.

Passage of the Lend-Lease Act in March 1941 marked the culmination of an effort by the federal executive to reassert itself in the area of foreign affairs. Isolationism, defined both as nonintervention into European affairs and preservation of congressional prerogatives in the area of formulating foreign policy, was driven into temporary eclipse. But the isolationists had no intention of allowing the Roosevelt administration and internationalism, which they equated with surrender of national sovereignty, executive control of foreign policy, and increasingly, distribution of the nation's wealth among the less fortunate nations of the world, to go unchallenged. Republican leaders such as Arthur Vandenberg, Robert Taft, and Gerald Nye had opposed lend-lease in 1941 because they believed that passage would lead directly to United States involvement in war. They could hardly take that position in 1943 when the measure came up for renewal; public opinion was overwhelmingly in favor of passage and Vandenberg made it clear that he and his colleagues would vote yea. It soon became apparent, however, that Republicans in Congress, in line with Vandenberg's stated objective of holding the administration to "strict accountability" for implementation of lend-lease, intended to scrutinize and seek justification for every provision. Their hope, of course, was to weaken the executive's power over administration of the program while strengthening that of Congress. Led by Hugh A. Butler of Nebraska, the Republicans began their drive in the Senate in January when they demanded a complete congressional investigation of the aid program. Butler criticized it for being based on the "dole" and compared lend-lease to a global WPA (Works Progress Administration). He argued that it would eventually wreck the American

Treasury and contribute to the spread of communism.[15] In the fall of 1943 five members of the Senate Military Affairs Committee went to Europe to investigate lend-lease. Back from the battlefront, they reported to Congress that charges of widespread waste and mismanagement in the delivery of aid to the Allies, particularly the British, were true. The Senators accused Britain of using lend-lease supplies to win friends and influence people at the expense of the United States in such strategic areas as the oil-rich Middle East.[16]

In other ways and in other areas, Congress gave notice of the intention in 1943–1944 to guard the nation's sovereignty and to prevent the establishment of any kind of "international New Deal." In July 1943 Vandenberg took to the floor of the Senate to demand that the proposed interallied agreement on a United Nations Relief and Rehabilitation Administration be submitted to Congress as a treaty rather than consummated as an executive agreement as the White House intended. The president seemed "hell-bent," declared Ohio Republican Robert Taft, on implementing a foreign economic policy through executive action without even consulting Congress.[17] Earlier in the year Congress had gotten wind of the fact that British gold and dollar balances were rising. If London could accumulate reserves, asked congressman Frederick Smith of Ohio, why was lend-lease necessary? Could it be that the United Kingdom was once again exploiting its gullible cousins and converting wartime aid into cash?[18]

Thomas E. Dewey, the Republican presidential nominee, and his foreign policy advisor, John Foster Dulles, promised the Roosevelt administration that their party would keep foreign affairs out of the 1944 election, but apparently economics and finance were not included. After warning a Lincoln's Day banquet that the Democrats were in danger of being taken over by a group of "Nazi New Dealers" headed by "Vice-President Wallace and his fellow travelers," GOP standard-bearer Alf Landon charged that the administration intended to use lend-lease for postwar relief and reconstruction. Roosevelt and his minions, he charged, were indulging in "mystical dreams" of raising the living standards of all the "heterogeneous" peoples of the world and at the expense of the American taxpayer.[19]

The parsimony so apparent among the nation's politicians was an accurate reflection of popular attitudes. A secret report prepared by Samuel Rosenman and his staff advised F.D.R. that recent surveys showed that the American people were almost twice as much interested in domestic affairs as international affairs. Two-thirds of those polled believed that the United States should not furnish aid to foreign countries if such aid would lower the standard of living in postwar America, and about half of those questioned believed that it would.[20]

American isolationism at times threatened to morph into a kind of militant unilateralism. Indeed, by 1944 a number of Britons had concluded that all Americans were imperialists of one sort or another. Minister of State Richard Law, during a trip to New York and Washington in late 1942, was particularly struck with the revival of missionary diplomacy in the United States. There was, he reported, very much an attitude abroad in the land that America had something that the rest of the world needed—whether it knew it or not—and that it was America's duty to export this commodity.[21] Other British students of America claimed to see a more tangible sort of imperialism emerging among conservative nationalists and, ironically, isolationists. Lord Halifax, British ambassador to the United States and his chief political advisor, Ronald Campbell, warned as early as 1942 that such a group was forming around GOP presidential candidate Wendell Wilkie and Wall Street financiers such as Thomas Lamont and Bernard Baruch. Those men saw the world as a vast market for the American producer, industrialist, and trader, Halifax wrote. "They are believers in the American century, energetic technicians and businessmen filled with a romantic... self-confident economic imperialism, eager to convert the world to the American pattern."[22] "There are among the isolationists," Campbell observed, "A type of people I can easily imagine proceeding from their isolationist reasoning to a stage where they will satisfy themselves that in order to isolate themselves properly the United States must rule the roost."[23]

In tacit alliance with the nationalist-isolationists in Congress were Henry Morgenthau, Jr., and his subordinates in the United States Treasury. The Treasury, determined to protect the country from another depression and headed by aggressive bureaucratic imperialists, was determined to preserve America's monopoly on the world's supply of gold and dollars made possible by the war and to take advantage of the nation's superiority in money and material to establish an international financial system dominated by the United States. As John Maynard Keynes was designing in the spring of 1942 an apparatus for international currency stabilization, the United States Treasury advanced its own plans for a stabilization fund and international bank for reconstruction and development. The principal difference between the Keynes plan and the American structures designed by Harry Dexter White was that the former aimed at securing British financial independence while the latter was intended to ensure United States domination of international finance.[24] That the Treasury's primary motive was the transfer of world financial leadership from London to Washington became clear as Morgenthau and White labored throughout 1943 and 1944 to hold British gold and dollar balances to a bare minimum. Needless to say, Treasury policy was immensely popular with nationalists in Congress, and F.D.R. supported not only Treasury's drive to control a postwar monetary union but also its efforts to restrain the growth of Britain's liquid reserves.[25]

After seeing their gold and dollar holdings virtually wiped out by the middle of 1941, the British gradually rebuilt them until they reached $1.2 billion in July 1943. These reserves, as Lord Cherwell reported to Prime Minister Winston Churchill, were likely to reach $2 billion by fall 1944 as American troop concentrations in the United Kingdom increased and as these soldiers spent their wages.[26] In January 1943 the president approved Treasury's recommendation that the United States manipulate lend-lease aid so as to hold British balances between $600 million and $1 billion, and appointed a committee headed by Morgenthau to guide lend-lease policy to this end. When the British protested, the administration replied that it would be preferable to hold British reserves to the absolute minimum rather than for Congress to cut lend-lease.[27]

Washington's campaign to establish U.S. hegemony in international finance reached its climax when delegates from the world's chief trading nations assembled in New Hampshire in mid-1944 for the Bretton Woods Conference. Under the provisions of the International Monetary Fund (IMF) Agreement signed at that meeting, each member country was obligated to establish a par value for its currency fixed in terms of either gold or dollars, and to peg the exchange rate of its currency against other currencies within a range of 10 percent above or below that par value. To help governments deal with pressures on these exchange rates caused by fluctuations in their national economies, the conferees established a $10 billion pool of currencies from which members could borrow. Quotas originally assigned were the U.S., $2750 million; Britain, $1300 million; China, $550 million; and France, $430 million.[28] Because representation on the governing board of the IMF was related directly to quotas, the United States, and specifically the U.S. Treasury, would determine policies of the Fund. American preponderance on the governing board would ensure that dollars and gold would be sold only to finance current transactions and not to build up the gold/dollar reserves of other nations.[29] It should be noted that although Morgenthau was motivated in part by personal and bureaucratic ambition, both he and the president wanted to protect Britain and multilateralism from economic nationalists in Congress.

The Bretton Woods gathering also created the International Bank for Reconstruction and Development (IBRD) and assigned it a working capital of $9.1 billion. The total was to be subscribed by 44 nations with 10 percent paid in immediately and 10 percent on instant call. The United States eventually pledged $3 Billion and Britain $1.5 billion. Again, quotas determined representation on the governing board.[30] Essentially the Bank was to be an underwriting and guaranteeing institution, which would supplement rather than supplant private international investment. After the war if the governments of Greece or Yugoslavia wanted to rebuild their railway systems or restore bombed out port facilities, they could approach American or other institutions for a loan. The ensuing private loan would be guaranteed by both the Bank and the borrowing government.[31]

The Reciprocal Trade Agreements Act, first passed in 1934, was scheduled to expire on June 30, 1945. Under RTAA the executive branch had the authority to lower tariff rates by as much as 50 percent in return for a comparable reduction on an American export to that country. According to the most-favored-nation principle, the reduced rates would apply to all items of the same class for countries with whom the United States had signed trade agreements. As required by law, the government gave advance public notice of its intention to negotiate each agreement and provided full opportunity through public hearings and other means for individuals and businesses to object. After the program began, Congress added the "peril point" provision that authorized the Tariff Commission to recommend higher rates to the president if tariff rates in any case endangered the well-being of an American industry. The renewal legislation would extend the measure for three years and allow an additional 50 percent reduction of rates already negotiated.[32]

The RTAA was reenacted in 1945 by record margins in both houses with the vote cutting across partisan, geographic, and ideological lines. Robert Taft voted for it. So did a number of other conservative Republicans even though it was part of a broad program of action on the international economic front recommended by the State Department.[33] That vote was made possible not by the conversion of economic nationalists and the guardians of special interests to the course of internationalism, but by the success of the multilateralists in convincing them that the trade legislation would not sacrifice America's economic interests, narrowly defined. Designed to placate neo-isolationists and economic nationalists, the renewed measure guaranteed national as opposed to international control of the tariff-making process. RTAA provided for selective, item by item reductions, not across-the-board, percentage cuts dictated by a multilateral convention or authority.[34] Moreover, the legislation contained a mechanism for the protection of domestic interests in every case—hearings coupled with the peril point provision.[35] The key provision of executive control over national trade policy was retained, however.

Meanwhile, the administration continued its assault on Britain's sterling empire. In the fall of 1944, Churchill, Roosevelt, and their advisers gathered in Canada to plan the last stages of the war and to discuss the shape of postwar Europe. Topping Britain's agenda at the Quebec meeting was a request for $7.0 billion in additional lend-lease aid for the second phase of World War II, the period between the end of the war in Europe and final victory over Japan. That aid was necessary in part to enable Britain to begin reconversion of its economy to a civilian footing. If the nation could not start this process in 1944, British economists warned, Britain would lose not only new markets to aggressive American exporters but old ones as well.[36] Franklin Roosevelt came to Canada ready to grant the United Kingdom substantial aid, but he wanted much in return. Following extended discussions, the Americans agreed to provide $3.5 million in munitions and $3.0 million in non-munitions aid following Germany's surrender. Though not as much as Churchill had asked, this new injection of aid would permit at least partial reconversion before war's end. In return, Roosevelt required that the United Kingdom promise full cooperation in the final stages of the war in the Pacific. He also forced Churchill to initial the Morgenthau Plan, thus abandoning British schemes for the quick postwar rehabilitation of Germany. And, finally, Roosevelt made it clear that if Britain failed to ratify the Bretton Woods proposals and refused to abolish empire preferences, the promised lend-lease aid would be withheld.[37]

John Maynard Keynes, famed economist and wartime adviser to the British Treasury, was troubled by the course of Anglo-American commercial and financial negotiations during 1944 and 1945. He understood the dangers inherent in the Bretton Woods structures: that they would strip war-weakened and developing nations, such as his own, of the protective devices necessary to preserve their markets and their currencies. Liquidity was the key to making any multilateral system work, and the Bretton Woods agreements did not provide that liquidity. Instead of protesting the IMF and IBRD, however, he acquiesced in their creation, even claimed them as his own and passionately recommended them to his government. He continued to believe that he could make the Americans see the light and that at the very least the United States would provide Great Britain, sure to be its principal ally in the dangerous postwar world, with the capital necessary to get back to its feet and compete.[38] He was wrong.

Less than a year after the close of the Bretton Woods Conference, the war in Europe was over. In July 1945 Britons elected a new government. Though they valued Churchill's services as wartime leader, British voters believed that his and the Conservative party's laissez-faire, free enterprise philosophy, rendered him unfit to preside over peacetime affairs.[39] They chose instead to give the Labor Party under Clement Attlee a clear majority. Not surprisingly, Laborites, particularly the left wing headed by doctrinaire socialists Aneurin Bevan and Emmanuel Shinwell, were deeply suspicious of multilateralism, seeing in it a plot by American capitalists not only to ensure U.S. dominance of the international economic system but to defeat socialism in Britain as well.[40] The moderate leaders of the party, Attlee and Foreign Secretary Ernest Bevin, were not particularly enamored of the concept either, but they were desperate that the United States not retreat into isolationism, once again leaving Britain alone to deal with economic chaos and potential military aggression on the continent.[41] Moreover, they, like Churchill, recognized that if the public's demand for food, work, and homes was to be met, Britain would have to secure a large postwar loan from the United States.

Throughout the fall and winter of 1945, a team of British financial and commercial experts under Keynes, who remained in his post at Treasury, met in Washington with officials of the new Truman administration to work out details of a postwar credit. What Keynes and his colleagues wanted was a multibillion-dollar interest-free loan that could be used to jump-start the British economy. They promised to remove trade barriers and dismantle exchange controls, but not for at least five years, and then only if Britain showed a favorable balance of trade. What they in fact received in the financial agreement of 1946 was a $3.75 billion loan at an interest rate of 1.62 percent. In return for the credit, the Attlee government agreed to recommend to parliament passage of the Bretton Woods agreements and to accept the full obligations of the system within a year. Congress eventually approved the pact on July 15, 1946, and Britain was thus forced to accept full convertibility of sterling on current account in midsummer 1947.[42] Within six months of convertibility coming into force, British gold and dollar reserves were exhausted; with bankruptcy staring it in the face, the Attlee government made plans for a severe austerity program at home and a strategic retrenchment abroad.

American multilateralists remained committed to their vision of freer world trade in the crucial period from 1944 to 1947. Their zeal to break up the sterling bloc and see empire preference abolished was in accordance with their free trade principles, but the strength of neo-isolationists and economic nationalists in the United States prevented them from providing Britain, its principal partner in the noncommunist trading world, with the time and capital to make the transition from one trading and financial regime to another.

It did not take long for the fruits of a flawed multilateralism to become apparent. Britain had available to it only three means to pay for its imported food and raw materials: money earned from services such as shipping and insurance, from foreign investments, and from manufactured exports. But the war had crippled the nation's merchant marine and forced the liquidation of over half of its foreign investments. At war's end many of Britain's industries, particularly those engaged in production for export, were outmoded and capital poor. By December 1946, despite the American loan and a severe austerity program that included the rationing of bread, Britain had reached only its prewar level of production. At this point, nature chose to demonstrate its indifference to human suffering. The winter of 1946–1947 turned out to be one of the harshest in modern history. Temperatures dropped below zero, and snow fell in record amounts paralyzing the transportation system. By February 1947 more than half the nation's factories lay idle as the mining of coal came to a virtual standstill. World War II and the elements were even less kind to the rest of Europe. The vagaries of the weather hit continental Europe with the same severity it did Britain, just at a time when a yawning dollar gap was opening up: Europe, eager to import U.S. goods, as yet had no means to pay for them. The result was a deep economic crisis that threatened to deliver the coup de grace to the still fragile social fabric of postwar Europe.[43]

Despite neo-isolationism and congressional parsimony, widespread sympathy for Europe's plight developed in the United States in 1946–1947. Accounts appeared in the *New York Times* and other nationally syndicated papers of ragged, starving children, teenaged prostitutes, and disintegrating families; such tales aroused the nation's humanitarian instincts. A number of Americans were aware, moreover, that Europe had been their nation's primary trading partner prior to the war and that an economically enfeebled Europe would retard America's growth. Most important, there were those in the United States, particularly members of Congress and government officials, who believed America would have to come to Europe's rescue to fend off the twin threats of Soviet imperialism and communist subversion. Indeed, the only reason that members of the conservative coalition—Southern Democrats and Republicans—had voted for the financial agreement of 1946 was that the State Department had justified it as necessary to strengthen Britain for the forthcoming struggle against the Soviet Union and the forces of international communism.[44]

By the spring of 1947 Congress and the American people had come grudgingly to support those in Washington who were arguing that modified multilateralism was not sufficient to achieve the reconstruction of Europe. Instead of continuing to press London and the other European capitals to participate in an international economic free-for-all with the United States, officials of the Truman administration set about helping the continent develop an integrated economy modeled on the internal American market. The system would eliminate internal trade barriers and monetary controls and lead to the creation of a European economy that could stand up ideologically and phys ally to the threat posed by international communism and, not coinciden ally, better compete with the United States.[45]

With the economic situation in Western Europe deteriorating daily and the popularity of the Italian and French Communist parties growing apace, Secretary of State George Marshall directed his staff to work out a program of aid. The fruits of their labor, subsequently known as the Marshall Plan, were made public in a commencement address the secretary delivered at Harvard University on June 5, 1947. In his speech, Marshall called upon Britain and the nations of the continent to frame an integrated plan for Europe's recovery and promised "friendly aid" to help bring that scheme to fruition. What emerged from the European–American dialogue that began in 1947 was an economic order that focused first on the rehabilitation of the national economies of Europe with limited moves toward European integration. The IBRD and the IMF were left to deal primarily with the developing world. As Alan Milward and others have pointed out, the $13.3 billion distributed under the Marshall Plan was necessary because multilateralism as modified by the Bretton Woods and Anglo-American financial agreements did not work.[46]

Nonetheless, Roosevelt, Hull and the multilateralists had laid the basis, intellectually and institutionally, for a system of freer if not free trade. FDR and his heirs in the Truman administration were constrained but not defeated by economic nationalism. The World Bank and IBRD have survived. Its policies have been criticized for emphasizing fiscal responsibility at the expense of social justice, but the Bank has played an important role in the development of third world economies.[47] From 1946 through 1948 at conferences in London, Geneva, and Havana the United States and the other major noncommunist trading nations hammered out the structure for an International Trade Organization (ITO). Like RTAA, the ITO was based on the twin principles of bilateral, reciprocal tariff negotiations and the most favored nation (MFN) principle granting to MFN nations the concessions subsequently negotiated in bilateral agreements. Congress, afraid of turning American trade policy over to an international organization, balked at the ITO, but the multilateralists were able to fall back on the General Agreement on Tariffs and Trade concluded in conjunction with the ITO. GATT in many respects represented the internationalization of RTAA. Under its terms, trading nations have been able to negotiate bilateral, reciprocal tariff cuts and employ the MFN mechanism. At the same time, there are provisions that allow national maneuverability in economic planning, protection for import-sensitive industries, and protection against unfair trade practices.[48] Roosevelt, Hull, and the multilateralists did surrender much in the short run, but the institutions and mechanisms that their leadership spawned have had much to do with the globalization that is such a conspicuous aspect of international economics today.

NOTES

1. Carolyn Rhodes, *Reciprocity, U.S. Trade Policy, and the GATT Regime* (Ithaca, NY: Cornell University Press, 1993), 60–63.
2. Richard N. Gardner, *Sterling-Dollar Diplomacy*, 2nd. ed. (New York: McGraw-Hill, 1969); and Alfred Eckes, Jr., "Open Door Expansionism Reconsidered: The World War II Experience," *The Journal of American History* 59, 4, 910–945 (March 1973). See also Minutes of the Executive

Committee on Commercial Policy, 7/20/40 and 10/23/40, RG353, Records of Inter- and Interdepartmental Committees, and Some Problems Raised by the Joint Declaration of August 14, 1941, Files of Harley A. Notter, RG 59, Records of the Department of State, National Archives.

3. Arthur Schlesinger, Jr., *The Age of Roosevelt. Vol. 2, the Coming of the New Deal* (Boston: Houghton Mifflin, 1958), 188–9; and Philip E. Green, "Conflict Over Trade Ideologies During the Early Cold War," Ph.D. dissertation (Duke University, 1978), 7–9. See also Michael Butler, *Cautious Visionary: Cordell Hull and Trade Reform, 1933–1937* (Kent, OH: Kent State University Press, 1998).

4. Quoted in Donald M. McCloskey, "Magnanimous Albion: Free Trade and British National Income, 1811–1881," *Explorations in Economic History* 17, 3 (July, 1980): 303. For a compelling history of the free trade idea, see Douglas A. Irwin, *Against the Tide: An Intellectual History of Free Trade* (Princeton, NJ: Princeton University Press, 1996).

5. See Alfred E. Eckes, Jr., *Opening America's Market: U.S. Foreign Trade Policy Since 1776* (Chapel Hill, NC: University of North Carolina Press, 1995), 142–3.

6. Winant Memorandum, undated, *Foreign Relations of the United States, 1945, Vol. VI* (Washington, DC: U.S. Government. Printing Office, 1960), 22–24 and *Anglo-American Financial Agreement*: *Hearings Before the Committee on Banking and Currency*, U.S. Senate, 79th Congress, Second Session (Washington, DC: U.S. Government. Printing Office, 1946), 193.

7. "Some Economic Problems Raised by the Joint Declaration of August 14, 1941," Notter Files, RG 59, National Archives, College Park, MD.

8. U.S. Draft Memo of Understanding of Financial Matters, October 30, 1945, 611.4131/5–746, RG 59, NA and *Anglo-American Financial Agreement*.

9. *New York Times*, February 13 and 16, 1944 and Richard Law Minute on Article VII Negotiations, February 2, 1945, OF371/45679, Records of the British Foreign Office, Public Record Office, Kew, England.

10. Winant Memorandum, undated, Foreign Relations of the United States, 1945, VI (Washington, DC, 1946), 22–24 and Anglo-American Financial Agreement, 193.

11. Conference Report for Roseman, November 15, 1943, Papers of Samuel Rosenman, Franklin D. Roosevelt Library.

12. For the Anglo-American economic relationship during World War II see Gardner, *Sterling-Dollar Diplomacy*; Alan P. Dobson, *U.S. Wartime Aid to Britain, 1940–1946* (Dover, NH: Croom Helm, 1986), William Roger Louis, *Imperialism at Bay: The United States and Decolonization of the British Empire, 1941–1945* (New York: Oxford University Press, 1978); and Randall B. Woods, *A Changing of the Guard: Anglo-American Relations, 1941–1946* (Chapel Hill, NC: University of North Carolina Press, 1990).

13. Acheson to Winant, September 14, 1945, 740.00119 Council/0–1945, RG 59, Decimal Files, Records of the Department of State, National Archives and Warren F. Kimball, *The Most Unsordid Act: Lend-Lease, 1939–1941* (Baltimore, MD: Johns Hopkins Press, 1969), 119–50.

14. Laughlin Currie to Harry Hopkins, 7/20/44, Box 5, Papers of the Assistant Secretary of State for Economic Affairs (Clayton-Thorp), Harry S. Truman Library; Taft Memo on Phase II Lend-Lease, 8/25/44, Box 10, Papers of Charles P. Taft, Library of Congress; Foreign Capital Position of the U.S. and G.B., 9/29/43, Box 82, Notter Files, RG 59, DOS; and Diary of Henry A. Wallace, 10/15/43, N.B. 24, Box 9, and 10/19/43, N.B. 36, Box 12, University of Iowa.

15. Richard E. Darilek, *A Loyal opposition in Time of War: The Republican Party and the Politics of Foreign Policy from Pearl Harbor to Yalta* (Westport, CT: Greenwood Press, 1976).

16. Ibid., 125–6.

17. Congressional Attitudes Toward the Use of Executive Agreements, July 19, 1943, Records of the Division of British and Commonwealth Affairs, RG 59, Records of the Department of State, National Archive.

18. Darilek, *Loyal Opposition*, 126. See also Hull, Hawkins, Vandenberg and Connally Conference, July 7, 1944, Box 10, Papers of Charles Taft, Library of Congress, Washington, D.C.

19. *New York Times*, February 16, 1944.

20. Conference Report for Rosenman, November 15, 1943, Rosenman Papers, Roosevelt Library.

21. Christopher Thorne, *Allies of a Kind: The United States, Britain and the War Against Japan, 1941–1945* (New York: Oxford University Press, 1978), 138–9.

22. Summary of a Report on Anti-British Feeling in the United States, 1944, T247/72, Papers of John Maynard Keynes, Records of the British Treasury, Public record Office, Kew, England.

23. Ibid.

24. Armand Van Dormael, *Bretton Woods: Birth of a Monetary System* (New York: Holmes & Meier Publishers, 1978), 36–37 and 44–46; Keynes to Caine 4/29/42, T247/67, Keynes Papers, PRO; and Gardner, *Sterling-Dollar Diplomacy*, 73–74.

25. See Stettinius to F.D.R., 2/22/44, Box 49, President's Secretary's File, Papers of Franklin D. Roosevelt, Roosevelt Library and F.D.R. to Churchill, Book 703, Diaries of Henry Morgenthau, Jr., Franklin D. Roosevelt Library. Roosevelt's attitude toward Great Britain is discussed in detail in C. Thorne, *Allies of a Kind*, 95–98, 119–22, 534–5; W.R. Louis, *Imperialism at Bay: The United States and the Decolonization of the British Empire*, 147–58 and 361–5; Robert M. Hathaway, *Ambiguous Partnership: Britain and America, 1944–1947* (New York: Columbia University Press, 1981), 14–15, 104, 129, 203 and 307; and Terry H. Anderson, *The United States, Great Britain, and the Cold War, 1945–1947* (Columbia, MO: University of Missouri Press, 1981), 16–17, 23, and 48.

26. Wallace Diary, undated, N.B. 19, Box 6, Iowa.

27. Lord Cherwell to Prime Minister, 11/11/43, PREM 4/17/5, Records of the Prime Minister, Public Record Office. See also "The British Dollar Balances," undated, Files of John D. Hickerson, RG 59, Department of State, National Archives.

28. A.G. Kenwood and A.L. Lougheed, *The Growth of the International Economy, 1820–1960* (Albany, NY: State University of New York Press, 1972), 240–1.

29. Van Dormael, *Bretton Woods*, 51–54 and Gardner, *Sterling-Dollar Diplomacy*, 73–74.

30. John Morton Blum, *From the Morgenthau Diaries, Vol. III: Years of War* (Boston: Houghton Mifflin, 1962) 274–6.

31. U.S. Delegation Meeting, 7/2/44, Book 749, Morgenthau Diaries, Roosevelt Library.

32. U.S. Congress, *Hearings on the 1945 Extension of the Reciprocal Trade Agreements Act*, House Ways and Means Committee (Washington, DC: U.S. Government. Printing Office, 1946), 11.

33. Ibid., and Acting Secretary of State to Winant, 3/5/45, 840.50/3–545, RG 59, DOS.

34. 1945 Extension of RTAA, 10–14.

35. During the lunch with Raymond Buel of *Fortune* magazine a month after renewal, Charles Taft admitted as much. Luncheon Meeting with Raymond L. Buel and James Angell, 6/25/45, Box 10, Papers of Charles Taft, Library of Congress.

36. Lyttleton to Prime Minister, 8/4/44, PREM 4/18/6, Records of the Prime Minister, Public Record Office and Keynes Memo on United Kingdom's Overseas Financial Position, 7/14/44, T247/124, Keynes Papers, PRO.

37. Diaries of Henry L. Stimson, 9/6/44, Roll 9, Center for Research Libraries; Conversation between Taft and Matthews, 9/20/44, Box 7, C. Taft Papers, L.C.; and Cherwell to Churchill, 9/7/44 and 9/12/44, PREM 4/18/6, PRO.

38. Woods, Changing of the Guard, 350–60.

39. C.J. Bartlett, *A History of Post-War Britain, 1945–1974* (New York: Longman, 1977), 17; and "The Real Issue," *The Economist*, June 23, 1945.

40. Michael Foot, *Aneurin Bevan: A Biography* (London: Four Squre, 1962), 25.

41. Matthew A. Fitzsimmons, *The Foreign Policy of the British Labour Government, 1945–1951* (Notre Dame, IN: University of Notre Dame Press, 1953) 26–27.

42. Wayne S. Knight, "The Nonfraternal Association: Anglo-American Relations and the Breakdown of the Grand Alliance, 1945–1947," Ph.D. dissertation (Washington: American University, 1979), 119–120; and Statement by the President, July 15, 1946, Box 802, Official File, Harry S. Truman Papers, Harry S. Truman Library, Independence, MO.

43. Randall B. Woods, *The Marshall Plan: A forty Year Perspective* (Washington, DC: German Marshall Fund of the United States, 1987), 7–8.

44. James T. Patterson, *Congressional Conservatism and The New Deal: The Growth of the Conservative Coalition in Congress, 1933–1939* (Lexington, KY: University of Kentucky Press, 1967), 13, 15; Bailey to Wallace, October 12, 1945, Notebook 36, Box 12, Wallace Papers, university of Iowa; Kenneth McKellar to Harry S. Truman, 11/6/45, Official File, Truman Library; Taft Address to War Veterans' Club of Ohio, 5/6/44, Box 802, papers of Robert Taft, LC; Knight, "Nonfraternal Association," 110; B.W. Anderson to

Clayton, 1/12/46, Box 1, Clayton-Thorp papers, Truman Library; New York Times, April 18, 1946; and Richard P. Hedlund, "Congress and the British Loan, 1945–46," Ph.D. dissertation (University of Kentucky, 1976), 98.

45. For a comprehensive though conflicting histories of the Marshall Plan, see Michael Hogan, *The Marshall Plan: America, Britain, and the Reconstruction of Western Europe, 1947–1952* (New York: Cambridge University Press, 1987), and Alan S. Milward, *The Reconstruction of Western Europe, 1945–1951* (Berkeley, CA: University of California Press, 1984).

46. Alan S. Milward, "The Reconstruction of Western Europe," in *The Cold War in Europe*, ed. Charles S. Maier (New York: M. Wiener Pub., 1991), 245–6.

47. In civil aviation, advocates of "open skies" made significant headway. At the Chicago Aviation Conference in late 1944, the United States and other current and aspiring air powers voted to establish the International Civil Aviation organization and adopted two accords: the Two Freedoms Agreement granting signatories the right of innocent transit and technical stop and the Five Freedoms Agreement providing for the negotiation of commercial landing rights. Patrick J. Hearden, *Architects of Globalism: Building a New World Order During World War II* (Fayetteville, AR: University of Arkansas Press, 2002), 56–60.

48. Rhodes, *Reciprocity*, 75–77. For a comprehensive history of the origins of GATT, see Thomas W. Zeiler, *Free Trade, Free World: the Advent of GATT* (Chapel Hill, NC: University of North Carolina Press, 1999).

CHAPTER 8

FDR AND THE STRUGGLE FOR A POSTWAR CIVIL AVIATION REGIME: LEGACY OR LOSS?

ALAN P. DOBSON

AS LATE AS 1946, American and British airlines were only allowed two round-trip transatlantic flights a week. And the planes that they flew were not jumbo jets. British and American airlines certainly crisscross the Atlantic more frequently now carrying hordes of passengers, and in March 2007 the EU and the United States reached agreement on the first stage of what is envisaged as a process leading to an Open Aviation Area (OAA) that will deliver a common airline market. This would allow airlines to operate largely free from politically required regulation and become just like any other commercial enterprise. According to one expert assessment, the OAA could increase annual transatlantic passenger numbers from 4 million to 11 million: something of a contrast with the state of civil aviation affairs in 1946.[1]

In many ways the last half century has been the heyday of international commercial aviation, but such a development seemed unlikely in World War II. So, how did the airline industry get from a trickle of transatlantic passengers in 1946 to the current flood? What role did Roosevelt play in all this and what legacy for international civil aviation did he leave?

NOT JUST ANOTHER COMMERCIAL
ENTERPRISE: PROBLEMS WITH CIVIL AVIATION

Civil aviation has operated at the interface of economics and politics ever since the Convention Relating to the Regulation of International Air Navigation in Paris in 1919 asserted national sovereignty over air space. There have always been security, prestige, safety, and public service factors that have led to political interventions and regulation. Also, for many years commercial aviation was thought to be different from other economic activities in that economies of scale did not seem to apply. The result of all this was that aviation was stifled by regulations that insisted on national ownership and control and restricted routes, rates, capacity, and the frequency of flights. Changing that system challenged British and American officials in World War II and ultimately Churchill and Roosevelt. It would be the United States and Britain that determined the postwar civil aviation regime, but unfortunately they had different interests and different ideas about how things should be.

Put simply, the problem was this: the Americans had advanced technology passenger planes and successful airlines that the British did not have; the British had a system of worldwide bases and the United States did not. Before the war the United States already had 80 percent of the international airline market; then, during the war, it developed aeroplanes and airlines that would enable it to become even more dominant, provided the world market could be opened up for competitive commercial activity. The British were fearful that American airlines would sweep all others before them and so strove to reserve a substantial proportion of the world market for British airlines by politically negotiated agreements. Their key card in this game was their ability to exclude American airlines from operating freely to Britain and across the Empire, the Dominions, India, and client states.

From these conflicting interests arose two radically different strategies. The United States wanted a liberal and open regime that would allow U.S. commercial operations to flourish and they pursued this vision through seeking an agreement to what became known as the five freedoms of the air. These allowed (1) innocent passage or overflight; (2) technical stop for repairs or refueling; (3 and 4) the rights to carry passengers to the bilateral partner and pick up passengers for the return flight; and (5), the right to pick up passengers from the bilateral partner's country and carry them forward to a third-party destination. On the American side, while the majority supported this position, they still favored regulation. One should not confuse their position with the later deregulation movement that arose in the States in the 1970s. During World War II, even the most radical U.S. policymakers favored both subsidies when necessary to sustain important routes and provisions for the setting of minimum rates. In contrast, the British wanted a strong international organization to regulate the industry, set rates and allocate market quotas and routes, and regulate capacity and frequencies. Effectively, there would be no competition and no domination by U.S. airlines.

POSITIONS: CHURCHILL
AND THE BRITISH

Churchill was no stranger to aviation. In 1913 he took flying lessons for a while until prevailed upon that it was too dangerous. As First Lord of the Admiralty he supported the development of the Royal Naval Air Service and in the 1930s he was vigorous in his calls for expanding the RAF.[2] During the war, as prime minister, worried by the prospect of America expanding its peacetime dominance of international aviation even further, ironically partly due to an Anglo-American agreement on division of labor that gave transport aircraft development to America, he prioritized the needs of nation and Empire. He wanted to cooperate with the Americans but was also determined that British airlines would have a substantial slice of the market. British anxiety was raised further in 1941 with Henry Luce's talk of an American Century and then later in 1943 when Clare Booth Luce called for overwhelming U.S. power in the air and dubbed internationalist ideas of Eleanor Roosevelt and Vice President Henry Wallace as "globaloney." American Century talk made very vivid the fear that America would monopolize commercial aviation as the only country capable of producing efficient, comfortable, long-range aircraft. One British government committee concluded: "the choice before the world lies between Americanization and internationalization. If this is correct, it is difficult to doubt that it is under the latter system that British interests will best be served."[3] Imperial communications had to be safeguarded and the British wanted a slice of the commercial aviation cake for themselves, and felt that it would be unfair if their war effort were to put them at a disadvantage in this field. And, like the Americans, they were highly sensitive to the interconnections between civil aviation and military air power.[4]

Churchill hoped to strengthen the British position with the help of the Dominions, but Canada was far from being wedded to his strategy. In September 1943, shortly after the First Quebec Conference, Churchill had something of a confrontation with the then Canadian Ambassador to the United States, Lester Pearson. Pearson later recalled:

> He faced me squarely, frowned, waved his cigar, and told me that...there was going to be an early Commonwealth discussion of civil aviation questions before we talked with other countries, whether Canadians wished to attend or not, or whether other powers (he really meant the United States) liked it or

not.... in working out their policies for an air transport fleet adequate to their needs and consistent with their resources, he felt sure that the Commonwealth could present a united front. Anyway, he said, with a final admonitory wagging of his cigar in my direction, they were going to try, with or without Canada.[5]

Unfortunately, from the British perspective there were three outstanding difficulties with their internationalization strategy. The first was its practicality. When Deputy Prime Minister Clement Attlee suggested in the House of Commons that "internationalisation might be considered" for civil aviation, it provoked laughter.[6] MPs seemingly agreed with Luce's epithet "globaloney" for that kind of thing. The second problem was that the British Dominions could not agree to full-blown internationalization, so there was little chance of foisting such a scheme on the Americans.[7] The third problem directly related to the strength of the British position and was the exigency of Britain's economic plight at the war's end. This forced it to become a suitor to the United States for financial assistance. The piper's payment came with requirements for several tunes to be played, including in the civil aviation theatre.

POSITIONS: ROOSEVELT AND THE AMERICAN

When asked: "What quality in your husband do you think was most responsible for his success?" Eleanor Roosevelt responded:

> His patience and his ability to look at things historically. By that I mean that his vision was not limited by the immediate situation, but he was able to see the background and the future of whatever was under consideration. When he made a decision he would patiently wait for the outcome; and if it was wrong or partially wrong, he had the patience to begin again.[8]

These views have resonance with how Franklin Roosevelt developed his vision for civil aviation and the way he dealt with problems that arose in trying to realize that vision.

In contrast to Churchill, Roosevelt was more liberated from terrestrial thinking and had a truly global vision. He wanted international competition, though in a controlled commercial regime. Roosevelt was as clear, if not clearer, in his own mind as Churchill about what he wanted for international aviation, but he had to operate in a more fragmented and contentious environment, which warrants more detailed attention.

Aviation was little different in Roosevelt's mind to other aspects of commercial and human interaction. Where possible it should be allowed to operate freely, but abuses of the marketplace and national security would also have to be pragmatically taken into account. Roosevelt adhered to the broad principles laid out in his famous four freedoms expressed in his annual message to Congress in January 1941: the freedoms of expression and religion and freedoms from want and fear. With Churchill at Placentia Bay, Newfoundland, in August 1941, he affirmed similar principles in the Atlantic Charter, which specifically called for freedom of the seas and non-discriminatory access to trade and commerce. Time and again, whenever feasible, Roosevelt favored freedom. He successively supported: Cordell Hull's Reciprocal Trade Agreements' program and wartime plans for an International Trade Organization for the progressive reduction of tariffs and an end to discrimination; Henry Morgenthau's and Harry Dexter White's designs for freely convertible currencies, though stabilized through the IMF; and freedom of information. In preparatory talks for meetings with British Foreign Secretary Anthony Eden in March 1943, Roosevelt "talked a great deal on [the] ... subject of a United Nations news service. He believed that there should be what he called 'Free Ports of Information' established at strategic points around the world, so that there would be no area wherein the people could be denied access by totalitarian censorship to the same news that was available to all other people."[9]

In domestic civil aviation, Roosevelt's inclination toward a free market was curbed by the need to nurture a viable, coherent, and safe industry that would service national needs as well as those of the travelling public. The regime, which emerged under the aegis of the Civil Aeronautics Board in 1939, was tightly regulated, but this did not prevent Roosevelt from wishing to see a more open system that would allow the development of international routes and enable U.S. airlines to compete with their foreign counterparts. However, it did mean that new policy had to be formulated. Not only was the international system more of a challenge than the domestic because of the sovereign airspace of others, American policymakers would have to work out just how open and competitive they wanted the system to be and how far they could go in persuading other nations, and particularly the British, into accepting their proposals. Americans could not play this game alone. Without the willing collaboration of others, international traffic would be grounded. Things were not going to be easy, not only because of the external dimension and lack of a clear policy model to follow, but also because there were conflicting opinions among U.S. policymakers and a de facto monopoly on U.S. overseas routes held tenaciously by Juan Trippe's Pan American World Airways (PAA). Breaking that monopoly would not be easy because Trippe had influential supporters in Congress and the U.S. government was beholden to PAA for opening up strategically important routes and for working to suppress German aviation influences in Latin America.[10]

Roosevelt abided by general principles, but often changed his ideas on specific policies to deal with difficult contingencies.[11] He was preeminently a practical man.[12] Interestingly, with civil aviation, he was consistent in both the general and the particular, with a few notable exceptions, for example, his move away from initially favoring government control of airlines operating abroad.[13] He consistently opposed PAA's monopoly on overseas routes and favored competition, though moderated, by allocating different U.S. airlines to different operational regions. In April 1941, when American Export Lines attempted to obtain a license to operate a transatlantic service and break PAA's monopoly, he observed that its success would bring "great benefits to the nation, and that it is contrary to the public interest to continue indefinitely unrestricted monopoly in this field."[14] PAA was on notice of change to come. Three months later, Roosevelt emphasized the importance of international aviation policy when he argued that "neither...short term or [sic] long term policy should be neglected at this time."[15] In crafting policies Roosevelt drew on his gift of spatial awareness and sense of globalism and was receptive to the internationalist ideas of Henry Wallace.[16] In March 1943 Wallace said:

> The Atlantic Charter rightly includes freedom of the seas among its cardinal principles. Freedom of the skies will be equally an asset of victory and a pledge of unity for essential international purposes. The two freedoms are in fact complementary. In both fields supremacy must be international. But freedom of the skies is a phrase that requires definition and application. How it is to be achieved and sustained is a problem that the interested nations are required to approach and to solve.[17]

Later in 1943 Roosevelt would also talk of freedom of the skies in an analogous way to freedom of the sea. This was a dominant theme in his thinking, as Adolf A. Berle, assistant secretary of state and a key figure in the development of U.S. wartime civil aviation policy, later recalled:

> The President...had in mind the body of law brought into existence by Hugo Grotius' famous essay on the freedom of the seas and hoped to transpose that doctrine into the field of air communication.[18]

Evidence of how advanced Roosevelt's ideas had become by 1943 comes from comments from his old friend, Admiral Richard E. Byrd. In 1943 Roosevelt asked Byrd to conduct a survey of Pacific islands to determine their civilian and military uses after the war. In April 1944 Byrd duly reported.

> My study shows that you were right—that you were years ahead of all of us, even those concentrating on the overall aspects of post-war strategy and international air commerce.... I found that commerce and political military strategy will be inextricably entwined....[19]

Later analysis of the report indicated that civil aviation would be essential for the development of some strategic routes; it would provide a basis for rearmament and supplement military aircraft; it would help with intelligence gathering; and commercial bases overseas could be used to deny facilities to others.[20] Roosevelt had a sure grasp of civil–military interrelationships and struck a nice balance between them, but even in such a sensitive strategic area as the Pacific, he wanted the maximum freedom possible for civil operations for all countries. In August 1943 Admiral William Brown reported to Roosevelt that:

> I told Admiral Byrd that I had heard the President say repeatedly that except for air bases that may be required for national defense, in general his idea of post-war commercial aviation is that the islands of the Pacific should be open to commercial use by all nationalities....[21]

All this indicates the general terrain and development of Roosevelt's ideas, but just how clear and coherent they were only became fully known in November 1943.

CONTENDING U.S. VIEWS

All parties in Washington wanted to maximize U.S. international aviation interests. However, a fault line separated two ranges of opinion about strategy for achieving that goal. There were those who favored a robust nationalistic policy of bilateral negotiations to bring maximum U.S. leverage to bear and there were those who feared that such an approach would be counterproductive and who were in any case naturally inclined to a more internationalist approach. Trippe epitomized the extreme end of the first range.

> ...we [Americans] should keep ourselves free of any general commitments in favour of reciprocity, that we should seek landing rights without offering them, that we should handle requests for landing rights from countries that have granted them to us, on their merits, and that in practice...we should successfully, and without jeopardising our own position abroad, find plausible reasons to deny most requests and keep our concessions to a minimum.[22]

Welch Pogue, chairman of the CAB and General "Hap" Arnold, chief of the U.S. Army Air Force and close adviser to Roosevelt, were more moderate bilateralists, but they also feared that international agreements would undermine U.S. interests. Pogue was particularly influential because when the Interdepartmental Committee on International Aviation (IDCIA) was set up in 1943 under the chairmanship of Berle, he was put in charge of the main working subcommittee that formulated policy. However, the forces of bilateralism had Berle to contend with, as he was very much in the internationalist camp. So much so that in the autumn of 1943 Pogue felt that he needed to enlist the help of Roosevelt's most intimate confidant and adviser Harry L. Hopkins to counter what he saw as Berle's naïve liberalism. Pogue did not know Hopkins well and their general politics were very different (Pogue was Republican), but they both came from Ohio, which made them "kind of related," Pogue had a good appreciation of just how influential Hopkins could be with Roosevelt, and they both leaned more to bilateralism than internationalism for civil aviation.[23]

After a faltering start, planning for postwar aviation proceeded with increasing pace in 1942 and 1943; however, Roosevelt was determined that policy should not develop beyond a point that he could decisively set its general character. On November 10, 1943 he did just that. He called a meeting with those senior officials most intimately involved in aviation matters—Under Secretary of State Stettinius, Assistant Secretary for War Robert Lovett, Harry Hopkins, Berle, and Pogue. Reading from a memorandum, which he said he had himself prepared, the president proceeded to spell out American policy. He did not want their wartime enemies to be able to fly anything more than a toy plane propelled by an elastic band, but otherwise his proposals were extremely liberal, more so than any of his adviser's, including Berle's. Cabotage, the reservation of domestic traffic exclusively for a state's own airlines, should remain. Subsidies should be allowed where they were necessary for important routes to survive. PAA's monopoly should be broken and U.S. airlines should be allocated regions abroad in which they could operate and compete against foreign carriers but not with each other. But, it was on the principles of commercial operation that Roosevelt's liberal vision really emerged.

> As to air rights, the President said that he wanted a very free interchange. That is, he wanted arrangements by which planes of one country could enter any other country for the purpose of discharging traffic of foreign origin and accepting foreign bound traffic.[24]

Furthermore, Roosevelt went on to demonstrate that he had fully grasped the concept and importance of the 5th freedom rights. A Canadian plane, for example operating from Toronto via Buffalo and Miami to Jamaica, he said, could pick up passengers in Buffalo and carry them to Jamaica (5th freedom traffic), but could not pick up traffic in Buffalo for Miami (cabotage traffic). Roosevelt was no amateur at this. He was determined to create an open competitive system, and with that in mind he kept control of American policy. Interestingly, in October 1944 when Secretary of War Henry Stimson, overlooking the fact that his department had already approved American policy, raised objections with Berle, the latter rather testily replied: "As you are aware, the policy and general method of approach toward the air settlements have been at all times under the direction of the President."[25]

Immediately after the meeting on November 10, Roosevelt's views caused consternation among several groups. The most violent opposition came from PAA and its supporters who favored bilateral negotiations that would only concede the minimum on the U.S. side in return for the widest possible operating rights from others: some even went so far as to suggest military coercion for extracting operating rights for U.S. carriers. However, more telling opposition came from Welch Pogue.

Pogue was distressed by Roosevelt's views and subsequently wrote to Hopkins that neither he nor his subcommittee favored the automatic granting of rights to pick up and put down passengers, as the president had suggested in the meeting.[26] Pogue later explained that he felt that "the trouble with Roosevelt on aviation was he just didn't know what he was doing. He had an idea that we could have a multilateral worldwide agreement because we had a great position in the war. Well that didn't follow at all."[27] Pogue only wanted to grant other countries the "privilege" of operating to the United States if that were essential for getting similar rights for U.S. carriers. He wanted to ensure that any port of entry would not adversely affect U.S. domestic carriers and thought that government should control capacity and rates.[28] He also thought that it would be foolish to wait for an international conference before seeking operating rights from other countries. He felt that this would allow Britain to make deals that would exclude U.S. operations. He explained to Hopkins:

> I am convinced... that the American public would be horrified at the idea of our marking time because the British wanted us to or even agreeing to keeping them informed of everything we are doing in the international field. That just sounds very inept to me politically.
>
> I strongly urge you to stay firmly in this air picture. Rapid progress is absolutely indispensable now; our bargaining position deteriorates day by day.[29]

On this at least Pogue had some success when in 1944 it was decided that the United States would follow a two-track approach: bilateral agreements would be pursued immediately and an international meeting would be sought.

In some ways Pogue was right about the overoptimistic attitude Roosevelt had toward what might be viable, but that did not stop Roosevelt's policy being presented at the Chicago international aviation conference in 1944, and Pogue, as he later acknowledged, "had to sort of play ball because I knew it would fail, but I put forward the transport agreement because that is what

Roosevelt commanded us to do."[30] Matters in fact did come to their first climax at the Chicago Conference held in Chicago between November and December 1944, and Pogue was proved largely correct, at least in the short term: the longer term vision of what might be possible was something else.

THE CHICAGO CONFERENCE

Berle led the U.S. delegation and Lord Swinton led the British. Neither were easy men to get on with. Berle was brilliant but prickly and self-opinionated. He was not over-endowed with interpersonal skills. For his part, Swinton was new to the aviation brief and came across as arrogant and inflexible at Chicago, but it is important to note that he was constrained by a British Government White Paper that had been published in October. It laid out the British case for strong international regulation.[31] At their very first meeting Berle and Swinton took an immediate dislike to each other.[32] Swinton provocatively talked of equitable divisions of traffic. When Berle seemed shocked, Swinton said: "Did you really think that we were going to change our minds?" And with rhetorical flourish demanded to know why traffic division was not fair? Berle's response was simple. He knew it was impossible to keep the 80 percent of international traffic that the United States had before the war, but a 50/50 division that would divert traffic from United States to British airlines was simply unacceptable.[33] The American alternative to the regime proposed by the British was an international organization with a lighter touch that would primarily oversee technical and safety matters and a liberal commercial environment based on a multilateral exchange of the five freedoms.

The conference made progress on technical issues and there eventually emerged widespread support for the right of innocent passage and technical stop, but on commercial operating rights there was impasse between the British and Americans. The British accepted the 3rd, 4th, and even the 5th freedom in principle, but then with regard to the 5th freedom, they hedged it round with safeguards to prevent what they feared would be exploitation of their local European routes by American airlines. From the American perspective, the right to refill their aircraft in London was indispensable for their long-haul flights into Europe and round the world. If the British denied them significant numbers of 5th freedom passengers, then such flights would be commercially unviable. At this point Roosevelt and Churchill reentered the stage, with Roosevelt writing to Churchill on November 21.

> In addition [to the controls agreed], your people are now asking limitations on the number of planes between points regardless of the traffic offering.

This seems to me a form of strangulation. It has been a cardinal point in [U.S.] policy throughout that the ultimate judge should be the passenger and the shipper. The limitations now proposed would, I fear, place a dead hand on the use of the great air trade routes.[34]

Churchill replied that the encroachment into local traffic under the regime proposed by the Americans was just not acceptable.[35] Roosevelt now resorted to the strong-arm tactics long favored by Pogue and the U.S. service departments: he would exploit Britain's dependence on aid from the United States. Disingenuously professing that he would exert his best efforts to meet Britain's Lend-Lease[36] needs he then added: "We will face Congress on that subject in a few weeks and it will not be in a generous mood if it and the people feel that the United Kingdom has not agreed to a generally beneficial agreement."[37] Churchill saw the letter for the blackmail it was and indignantly replied that the British ought not "to be confronted with such very serious contingencies as are set out in your message."[38] He also wrote, in a tone expressing petition more than anger, that he hoped that the American sense of justice would prevail. On November 30 Roosevelt took his lead from Churchill and reassured the prime minister of America's intention to uphold justice and promote fair play, but insisted that agreement remained possible. However, by then in Chicago concessions had already been withdrawn and harder positions adopted.[39] Notwithstanding further exchanges with Churchill, Roosevelt was unable to retrieve a commercial regime for aviation at Chicago.

Britain did not get what it wanted, neither did the United States. Berle tried to claim that great strides forward had been made, but his ex colleague and sometime under secretary of state, Sumner Welles, belied such claims when he wrote in 1946 that "aviation is one field where no success in international co-operation has yet been encountered."[40] This was certainly true regarding commercial operating rights. So far as U.S.–UK civil aviation relations were concerned, an agreement struck in the mid-1930s still governed, which only allowed two return flights a week for each country's airlines.

LEGACY: SHORT TERM

Roosevelt did not live to see Anglo-American agreement on aviation, but he had the consolation of seeing the American hand strengthen. The United States tried to get "as many gateways to Europe as possible and with no limitations on frequencies" and in January 1945 was on the verge of an agreement with Eire, which included 5th freedom rights that raised the spectre for Britain of being bypassed by U.S. airlines refuelling and topping up their passenger numbers in Eire on their way to Europe.[41]

When Churchill learnt of the proposed deal, he was furious, writing to Roosevelt: "I cannot feel sure that this affair has been brought to your notice...." But there was no reply. When the agreement was finalized, Churchill wrote again asking the president to "take the necessary steps to have the agreement annulled." Predictably, Roosevelt said there was no question of that: "I am sorry but there it is."[42] There followed a tense period in which both sides tried to move out into international operations and exclude the other.

Jockeying for position continued, but the British could not offer the economic incentives that the United States could and did not have suitable aircraft to exploit the market. Most crucially of all, with the atom bomb's sudden ending of the war, Britain faced dire economic crisis with industry shattered, export markets depleted, and its currency fragile because of enormous debts. It was increasingly difficult to see how it might weather the storm without U.S. financial assistance.

In January 1946 the British and Americans came together on the island of Bermuda to seek a settlement of their troubled aviation relations. At the time the U.S. Congress was still considering financial help for Britain in the form of the U.S.–UK Loan Agreement that would provide Britain with a line of credit amounting to $3.75 billion. There was hard bargaining at Bermuda, but the outcome was a foregone conclusion. Civil Aviation Minister Lord Winster put his finger on Britain's vulnerability when toward the end of the proceedings he wrote:

> ... if the Cabinet felt that the signing of the agreement was of vital importance from the point of view of our general relations with the United States and the consideration of the loan agreement by Congress, he was willing that our delegation should be authorised to sign.[43]

The United States achieved relatively open skies with few restrictions on capacity and frequency and the exchange of 3rd, 4th, and 5th freedoms. This was not part of a multilateral regime of the kind that Roosevelt had sought, but the Americans held up Bermuda as a model for the future for all other countries to follow: it was the closest they could get to a common international agreement. What had been achieved was a much more liberal and internationalist regime than had existed in the interwar period. It also operated in a more liberal way than either Pogue or the American service departments had argued for, and it helped international aviation to expand and U.S. airlines to thrive, and that was what Roosevelt had sought. While his vision was thus not fully realized, he had been instrumental in crafting an agenda that delivered results in 1946 and which could be used for further liberation from market-hostile regulations in the future.

LEGACY: THE LONG TERM

Much has happened since the Bermuda Agreement, and as one moves away from Roosevelt's time the harder it becomes to talk meaningfully about legacy. Nevertheless, if we examine the postwar years, a legacy picture does emerge through six key developments. These include: the aftermath of Bermuda; U.S. deregulation; Bermuda 2; the creation of the Single European Aviation Market (SEAM); U.S. "open-skies" policy; and the transatlantic OAA.

After Bermuda a two tier system developed. When the United States was party to a bilateral, it embodied the liberal provisions of Bermuda, if it was not, a more regulatory outcome was common. According to one highly experienced official, "airlines and governments sat down and said whatever this agreement [Bermuda] meant to say we aren't going to let you do more than we want to do."[44] The result in Europe was a pattern of government and industry collaboration and collusion. Airlines operated in an environment devoid of competition, full of government-favored instruments (i.e., national flag carrier airlines) in dominant positions, and under regulations that carved up the market and stunted development.[45] This was very different from what Roosevelt had envisaged, but since little of this affected the United States directly, it tolerated it, at least until the mid-1970s. Then things began to change. A second postwar phase began, partly prompted by a growing unease among the Europeans that Bermuda-style bilaterals gave away too much market share to U.S. airlines, but more so by the emergence of economic and political ideas in the United States that advocated deregulation.

In his first message to Congress on March 4, 1977, President Carter urged "…Congress to reduce Federal regulation of the domestic commercial airline industry."[46] Subsequently, the 1978 Airline Regulatory Reform Bill initiated rapid moves to a free untrammelled domestic airline system. It also set in motion forces that soon dispelled the conventional wisdom that economies of scale did not apply to the airline industry.[47]

> What was discovered were economies of scale…, i.e. you organised your system in such a way that you were able to consolidate large amounts of traffic at a point and then redistribute that traffic. For each unit…that you flew, if you had…higher load factors on that piece of equipment in effect you had a more productive piece of equipment—a more productive unit of production.[48]

This was the hub and spoke configuration of routes. Well positioned through their domestic interconnected hubs and their vast number of feeder spokes to assemble large numbers of passengers, domestic U.S. operators now used their dominance over that market, approximately 40 percent of the entire world's, to thrust out their spokes into the international sphere. They did so in the context of two other moves by the Carter Administration: the first was a challenge mounted by Chairman of the CAB Alfred Kahn to IATA price fixing, which gradually but ineluctably led to price competition; and the second was the pursuit of even more liberal ASAs (Air Service Agreements) than Bermuda, promoted by the International Air Transportation Competition Act, 1979.[49]

This U.S. surge toward making international aviation more of a straightforward commercial affair ran into its most serious difficulties with the British. The result was a conference replay of 1946 resulting in Bermuda 2. In 1976, the British were so disgruntled with the market share held by U.S. carriers that they denounced Bermuda 1. The United States and Britain then had under the terms of that agreement twelve months in which to negotiate an alternative. The outcome was to be rued by the Americans for the next thirty years. They were simply out-negotiated and out-maneuvered. The net result as one senior U.S. official put it was that:

> Every city pair market is restricted in terms of entry. Every city pair market is restricted in terms of capacity. Every city pair market is restricted in terms of the fares the airlines may charge the passengers. There is no aspect of the market that is not being regulated pursuant to UK insistence.[50]

Even worse, in follow-up talks in 1980 the Americans fell into more difficulties. The British entwined them in their traffic distribution policy for London airports such that only PAA and TWA or their corporate successors were allowed to fly into Heathrow. This turned out to be the ace in the hole for the British over the following twenty-seven years. When the Americans subsequently argued for a more liberal ASA and most importantly for freer access to Heathrow—the busiest international hub in the world, the British response was always: "Why should competition stop at the water's edge? We'll open up Heathrow and our cabotage if you'll open U.S. cabotage and/or change airline ownership and control rules." Either change would have allowed British airlines to arrange better feeder services for their transatlantic flights by setting up operations within the U.S. domestic market. Without such feeder services the British argued that they could not compete on an even playing field with their U.S. counterparts on the transatlantic, and that reserving 40 percent of the world's entire airline market as U.S. cabotage was simply too protectionist. The British and the Americans never resolved this impasse, at least not by themselves.[51]

While Britain seemed unrelentingly regulatory to Americans, its behavior in Europe was very different. There it took the lead and worked closely with the European Commission toward creating a competitive free aviation market for the European Community (EC). In a series of three packages of reform between 1987 and 1992 the SEAM gradually came into being: it reached internal completion in 1997.[52] The market was subjected, at least in operations within the EC, to common rules. Competitive pricing and liberal licensing rules were adopted and pooling arrangements outlawed, new routes were opened, capacity and frequency controls removed and cabotage abolished, and the concept of Community airlines adopted, which meant any airline from within the EU could operate anywhere in the EU. For all intents and purposes, EU airlines no longer belonged to countries but to the EU. That was fine internally, but it would eventually cause immense problems externally as all existing bilaterals with other countries, including the United States, had national not Community ownership and control clauses.

As the SEAM came into being, the United States became even more aggressive in its overseas aviation policy. Among other things there were nagging fears about the EU becoming an economic fortress, leading to curbs on commercial rights for U.S. airlines. The United States began to pursue what it called open-skies agreements that embodied free pricing and unrestricted 3rd, 4th, and 5th freedoms. They also offered a tempting incentive: antitrust immunity for alliances between U.S. airlines and foreign airlines. This would allow airlines of those countries that entered "open-skies" agreements with the United States to moderate the problem of getting U.S. feeder services that Britain had so often complained about. They could benefit from their U.S. alliance partner's feeder services to international gateways in the United States. The first "open-skies" agreement to be consummated in Europe was with the Netherlands in 1992. Over the years many more followed. Britain alone, among the main aviation nations in Europe, resisted U.S. overtures. Then everything was tipped into turmoil by the European Court of Justice in November 2002. It ruled that bilateral ASAs between the United States and Member States of the EU were illegal because they contained nationality clauses and did not recognize the concept of Community air carriers. It was in the interests of both sides to remove this legal anomaly, but to the astonishment of many, the Europeans came up with the most radical of solutions.[53]

As a matter of urgency the European Council of Ministers granted authority to the Commission to negotiate a new Community-wide agreement with the United States. Full-scale talks began with the Commission delegation led by Michael Ayral and the U.S. side led by Richard Byerly, deputy assistant secretary of state for transportation affairs. The United States had its standard open-skies agenda, including the offer of antitrust immunity for alliances and unlimited 5ths within and beyond the EU: from the European perspective, 5ths within the EU now amounted to cabotage rights. The European agenda was more radical. The Europeans wanted to create an OAA that would merge European and U.S. cabotage, that would permit 100 percent ownership and control of U.S. airlines by Europeans and vice versa, and a harmonization of competition and safety regulations.

The negotiations were long and drawn out, partly because the European Council of Ministers rejected a draft agreement in 2005 on the grounds that it did not go far enough on the crucial issue of ownership and control. The U.S. Department of Transportation now tried to circumvent congressional hostility to changes in ownership and control by an executive reinterpretation of existing rules to make them more liberal, but the political outcry was such that they had to abandon this tactic and talks with the Europeans ground to a halt in the second half of 2006. Then in early February 2007 the Transport Council President Wolfgang Tiefensee and Commissioner for Transport Jacques Barrot went to Washington to see if they could revive things. They succeeded and two rounds of negotiations followed, which resulted in an agreement in March, subject to ratification by the EU Transport Council.

U.S. law on control and cabotage remained unchanged. Europeans were allowed to buy more of an American airline's nonvoting stock, but the limitation on ownership of 25 percent of the controlling voting stock remained. The Americans made concessions elsewhere but did not depart very substantially from traditional U.S. open-skies agreements, except for recognition of the concept of EU Community carriers. Furthermore, the one thing that might have persuaded the United States to embark upon a more radical path appeared to have been given away because the Americans were granted open access to Heathrow. When the agreement came before the European Transport Council the decision was unanimous in favor of acceptance, but the British managed to persuade Jacques Barrot to make clear that if there were no movement on U.S. ownership and control by 2010 in the follow-on stages of negotiations, then the EU would have the option of withdrawing from the agreement.

*   *   *

Where would Roosevelt have stood on all of this and to what extent do these developments naturally flow from the regime that he promoted in World War II?

Roosevelt's use of the term "free air" is not all that far removed from the idea of "open-skies," particularly when one also recalls his admonitions to colleagues in November 1943 that they must aim for a "very free interchange" that would allow airlines to take on and discharge passengers in other states. He wanted international agreement on the liberal operation of the five freedoms. In many ways, at least prior to the OAA, he was still ahead of developments in his talk of multilateral agreements automatically granting freedoms that would allow international commercial aviation to flourish. It was not until the SEAM and the OAA that anything approaching that vision was achieved.

Regarding his notions on competition and pricing, the picture is more ambiguous. Roosevelt had opposed PAA's monopoly, but he conceived of U.S. airlines being allocated regions within which to operate and compete against foreign airlines. Head-to-head competition by U.S. airlines on the same routes was beyond his vision in 1943 and 1944. Also on pricing, although the Americans ducked and weaved on this with the British and tried to give the impression that they were granting a concession on price fixing, in fact they were never entirely hostile to some price regulation and became even less so after trouble with PAA and what amounted to predatory pricing in 1945. All this is a far cry from the current situation. However, during the Chicago Conference, Roosevelt argued with Churchill that "It has been a cardinal point in [U.S.] policy throughout that the ultimate judge should be the passenger and the shipper."[54] In other words, let the market decide. If one were to imagine him remaining steadfast to that principle as aviation developed over the following decades, it does not seem too fanciful to imagine that Roosevelt would have found little difficulty with head-to-head competition between U.S. airlines and competitive pricing. Indeed, one might imagine him championing such developments.

Finally, cabotage and ownership and control: these two areas are the ones in which the Europeans, after trailing on U.S. liberal coattails for so long, have taken the lead. The EU's demand for common cabotage and ownership and control rules were not acceptable to the United States. This is partly to do with the protectionism of labor, the pilots, and some members of Congress, but also hinges on widespread concerns about defense and security. U.S. airlines play an important role through the Civil Reserve Air Fleet, which is employed to transport U.S. troops and supplies in times of hostilities and war. There are also other traditional advantages to be reaped for defense and security from civilian airlines. During the war, internationalist proposals for the free operation of airlines were dubbed "globaloney" or met with mirth, as in the British House of Commons, but such "globaloney" rarely went so far as to consider the idea of opening cabotage and abolishing national ownership and control regulations. In that sense they were beyond the ken of most policymakers at that time, including Roosevelt. So, it might be stretching things to suggest that Roosevelt ever seriously entertained such radical proposals. And yet during the war he argued for liberal access for all nations' civil airlines to islands in the Pacific, an extremely sensitive strategic area for the United States. If strategic concerns in the Pacific did not trump commercial needs for Roosevelt in 1944, is it beyond the bounds of credibility that similar strategic concerns would have failed to override the temptation to open U.S. cabotage and change U.S. ownership and control rules in 2007? After all, these changes would have created a truly open and free transatlantic commercial aviation market, which would chime harmoniously with Roosevelt's general and many of his specific views on civil aviation.

This chapter has tried to make clear what Roosevelt thought about civil aviation, what policies he favored and tried to nurture, how he struggled with Churchill, and what emerged from all this at the war's end. It has also tried to identify Roosevelt's legacy in later developments. The commercial civil aviation regime that we now have seems, from some perspectives at least, to owe much to Roosevelt and his vision for postwar civil aviation. There is a discernible thread that runs through, albeit with various snags along the way, from his ideas in 1943 to 2007. What one makes of those snags will largely determine views of the extent to which Roosevelt bequeathed a legacy to the industry and how much of his vision was lost or changed in the political battles of what have been termed elsewhere as "peaceful air warfare."[55]

NOTES

1. Brattle Group, "The Economic Impact of an EU–U.S. Open Aviation Area," report for DG TREN, 2002.

2. P. Addison, *Churchill: The Unexpected Hero* (Oxford: Oxford University Press, 2005), 61–62.

3. CAB 87/2, RP(42)48, "Internationalisation of Civil Aviation after the War," December 15, 1942.

4. Examples that illustrate the civilian–military connections both before and after the war can be found in M.R. Megaw, "The Scramble for the Pacific: Anglo-American Rivalry in the 1930s," *Historical Studies* 17 (1977): 458–73. D.J. Mrozec, "The Truman Administration and the Enlistment of the Aviation Industry in Post-war Defence," *Business History Review* 48 (1974): 73–94.

5. Lester Pearson, *Memoirs 1897–1948: Through Diplomacy to Politics* (London: Victor Gallanz, 1973), 231–2.

6. *Hansard*, June 1, 1943, vol. 390, col. 99.

7. CAB 65/34, WM88(43), June 24, 1943; Alan P. Dobson, *Peaceful Air Warfare: The United States, Britain and the Politics of International Aviation* (Oxford: Clarendon Press, 1991), 163; CAB 65/44, 148(44)3, November 8, 1944.

8. Eleanor Roosevelt, *If You Ask Me* (London: Hutchinson, 1946), 96.

9. R.E. Sherwood, *The White House Papers of Harry L. Hopkins: An Intimate History*, 2 vols. (London: Eyre and Spottiswoode, 1949), vol. 2, 705.

10. See R. Daley, *An American Saga: Juan Trippe and His Pan American Empire* (New York, Random House, 1980), chapter 39.

11. For a thoughtful and penetrating interrogation of Roosevelt's principles and his modus operandi see generally the collection of essays by Warren F. Kimball, *The Juggler: Franklin Roosevelt as Wartime Statesman* (Princeton: Princeton University Press, 1991).

12. J.M. Burns, *Roosevelt the Lion and the Fox 1882–1940* (New York, Harcourt Brace and World, 1956).

13. Roosevelt Library, FDR, PSF Subject File, box 92, file: American Export Line, James Rowe Jr. to Roosevelt, January 31, 1941.

14. Roosevelt Library, FDR OF box 2, folder 1941, Roosevelt to Whitney of PAA 25 April 1941.

15. Ibid., Roosevelt to Acting Secretary of State, Postmaster General and Chairman CAB, July 31, 1941. This was prompted by the fact that although American Export Lines had been issued a route license, PAA had rallied its supporters in the Congress and they had blocked the allocation of funds for the route.

16. See Alan K. Henrikson, "Roosevelt and the 'World-Wide Arena,'" paper for Conference: *In the Shadow of FDR* (Franklin and Eleanor Roosevelt Institute, September 2005).

17. *The Times*, March 11, 1943, quoted from P.F.M. Fellowes, "Freedom of the Skies," in Philip Gibbs, ed., *Bridging the Atlantic: Anglo-American Fellowship as the Way to World Peace: A Survey from Both Sides* (London: Hutchinson, 1945), 235.

18. Roosevelt Library, Berle Papers, Box 169, Articles and Book Reviews 1964–1967, folder Articles and Book Reviews 1965, "The International Civil Aviation Treaties Twenty Years later," Columbia University, March 1965.

19. Roosevelt Library, FDR MR box 162, folder 5 sect. A4–2 Air Routes, Byrd to Dear Franklin, April 14, 1944.

20. Ibid., box 207, Senior members' Review of Byrd Report.

21. Ibid., box 162, folder: 5 sect. A4–2—Air Routes, memo. for file, Rear Admiral Wilson Brown, naval aide to Roosevelt, August 27, 1943.

22. Berle Papers, box 54, folder: aviation international 1942–1943, R.G.H. Jr. to Berle, June 15, 1943.

23. Interview with Welch Pogue, conducted by the author August 1, 2000.

24. U.S. National Archives, State Department decimal file 800.796/495, memo. of conversation by Berle, November 11, 1943. Curiously, in Berle's edited papers there is an inadvertently inaccurate summary of this: "6. As to air and landing rights...he wanted a very free interchange...he thought planes should have general right of free transit and right of technical stop—that is, the right to land at any field and get fuel and service, without however, taking on or discharging traffic....," B.B. Berle and T.B. Jacobs, *Navigating the Rapids 1918–1971: From the papers of Adolf A. Berle* (New York: Harcourt Brace Jovanovich, 1973), 483–4.

25. Berle Papers, box 59, State Department Subject File 1938–1945, folder International Civil Aviation Conference Chicago November 1944 Business Correspondence, Notes, Appointments, Diaries, Berle to Stimson undated (probably October 16 or 18) reply to Stimson's letter of October 11, 1944.

26. Roosevelt Library, Hopkins Papers, box 336, folder: air conference 1, Pogue to Hopkins, November 21, 1943.

27. Interview with Welch Pogue conducted by the author, August 1, 2000.

28. Roosevelt Library, FDR, PSF, box 93, file: Aviation 1944, International Air Transport Policy: Special Report CAB, April 12, 1944.

29. Hopkins Papers, box 335, folder: Air Conference 2, Pogue to Hopkins, August 26, 1944.

30. Ibid.

31. Cmd. 6561, "International Air Transport," October 1944; see also J.A. Cross, *Lord Swinton* (Oxford: Oxford University Press, 1982), and Viscount Swinton, *I Remember* (London: Hutchinson, 1946).

32. Ibid.

33. Roosevelt Library, FDR, PSF, box 93, file: Aviation 1944, "Berle to Roosevelt, Report on Chicago," December 7, 1944; Berle, *Navigating the Rapids*, entry November 2, 1944, 499.

34. W.F. Kimball, ed., *Churchill and Roosevelt: The Complete Correspondence*, 3 vols. (Princeton: Princeton University Press, 1984), vol. 3, Roosevelt to Churchill, November 21, 1944, 402–3.

35. Ibid., Churchill to Roosevelt November 22, 1944, 404–5 and CAB 65/44, 153(44)2, November 22, 1944.

36. Lend-Lease was a scheme by which the United States provided wartime aid to Britain in vast quantities: see Alan P. Dobson, *US Wartime Aid To Britain* (London: Croom Helm, 1986).

37. Kimball, *Correspondence*, vol. 3, Roosevelt to Churchill, November 24, 1944, 407–8.

38. Ibid., Churchill to Roosevelt, November 28, 1944, 419–21.

39. Ibid., Roosevelt to Churchill, November 30, 1944, 424–5.

40. Sumner Welles, *Where Are We Heading?* (New York: Harper Brothers, 1946), 33.

41. State Department files, 811.79641D/1–2945, Grew to U.S. Legation, Dublin.

42. Kimball, *Correspondence*, vol. 3, Churchill to Roosevelt, January 27 and 6 March 6, 1945 and Roosevelt's reply, March 15, 1945, 519–20 and 566–7.

43. CAB 128/5, 11(46)8, February 4, 1946 considering memos. CP37(46) by Winster.

44. Interview with Robert Ebdon, Head of Government Affairs, British Airways, conducted by the author, August 5, 1991.

45. The Treaty of Rome, 1957, Article 3, Title 4 Transport Articles 74–84, and Rules on Competition Articles 85–102.

46. Jimmy Carter Library, Staff Offices, Domestic Policy Staff, Eizenstat box 148, folder: Aviation Airline Regulatory Reform, Message to Congress, March 4, 1977, attached to Eizenstat to Carter, February 22, 1977.

47. For the story of deregulation see Alan P. Dobson, *Flying in the Face of Competition: The Policies and Diplomacy of Airline Regulatory Reform in Britain, the USA and the European Community 1968–94* (Aldershot: Avebury, 1995).

48. Interview with Cyril Murphy, Vice President for International Affairs, United Airlines, conducted by the author, July 1, 1991.

49. An important coda needs to be added here. None of this would have been possible without a quantum leap forward in the technology of computers. The complexity of running an airline on a hub and spoke system was intimidating. Ensuring that passengers fed in through multiple spokes for a common destination and then speedily fed out on the relevant spoke to that destination could not have been done without computers. By the mid 1980s the major computer reservation systems could "juggle one hundred million fares at a single time." B.S. Peterson, *Bluestreak: Inside Jetblue, the Upstart that Rocked the Industry* (New York: Portfolio, 2004), 101.

50. Interview with Jeffery Shane, Assistant Secretary for Policy and International Affairs, U.S. Department of Transportation, conducted by the author, April 5, 1991.

51. For various aspects of the troubled U.S.–UK aviation relations in this period, see Alan P. Dobson, "Regulation or Competition? Negotiating the Anglo-American Air Service Agreement of 1977," *The Journal of Transport History* 15, 2 (1994): 144–65; "Aspects of Anglo-American Aviation Diplomacy 1976–93," *Diplomacy and Statecraft* 4, 2 (1993): 235–57; "The USA, Hegemony and Airline Market Access to Britain and Western Europe, 1945–96," *Diplomacy and Statecraft* 9, 2 (1998): 129–59.

52. For the story of reform in Europe, see Alan P. Dobson, *Globalization and a Regional Response: The Origins, Development and Impact of the Single European Aviation Market* (London: Routledge, 2007).

53. See COM(2002)649, Final, "Communication from the Commission on the consequences of the Court judgements of 5 November for the European air transport policy," November 19, 2002.

54. Kimball, *Correspondence,* vol. 3, Roosevelt to Churchill, November 21, 1944, 402–3.

55. Dobson, *Peaceful Air Warfare.*

CHAPTER 9

FDR'S WORLDVIEWS, 1941–1945

WALTER LaFEBER

AMIDST THE GLOBAL BLOODSHED, national upheavals, attempts of racial extermination, and the massive movement of what turned out to be historic political, economic, and social movements in a period of just five years, Franklin D. Roosevelt accomplished a great deal—enough to rank him, along with Lincoln, Washington, and Jefferson, in the highest echelon of American leaders. Battling the last throes of isolationism during the later years of the 1930s, FDR finally took a unified nation into war in 1941. During the conflict, his administration did a remarkable job of maintaining a pro-war consensus and convincing Americans—most of whom had indicated only a few years earlier that they would not allow their sons and daughters to fight and die abroad, especially after Roosevelt himself had said as late as 1940 that such sacrifice might not be necessary—to participate wholeheartedly in a conflict that covered much of the globe, mobilized more than sixteen million American men and women, and killed in battle 292,000 of them.[1]

Roosevelt was a great war leader at home, an accomplishment perhaps only properly appreciated after noting how Presidents Harry Truman in 1950–1951, Lyndon Johnson between 1965 and 1968, Richard Nixon during 1970 to 1974, and George W. Bush after 9/11 fell far short of FDR's performance. In each case, these later chief executives paid heavily for their failures in both election results and the history books. As Alan K. Henrikson's chapter in this volume explains, Roosevelt not only carried on an intense and quite successful educational campaign to teach Americans that global geography, especially when viewed from the poles, required an international—not simply a Pan-American—perspective and set of foreign policies. He also filled that new conceptualization on January 6, 1941 (that is, nearly a year before the United States entered the war) when he spoke to Congress and the American people, declaring that a properly functioning international community must now require "a world founded upon four essential human freedoms": freedom of speech "everywhere in the world," "freedom of every person to worship God in his own way, everywhere in the world," "freedom from want...everywhere in the world," and "freedom from fear...anywhere in the world." As Henrikson notes, the speech's global reach was remarkable considering the previous decades of American political withdrawal. Equally remarkable were other parts of the speech in which FDR argued that the safety of the previous "ninety-nine years" had ended. "Without regard to partisanship," he told Congress eleven months before the Pearl Harbor attack, "we are committed to full support of all those resolute peoples, everywhere, who are resisting aggression.... By this support, we express our determination that the democratic cause shall prevail."[2]

When Roosevelt died on April 12, 1945, however, the world looked quite different than the one he had prophesied four years earlier. The "democratic cause" was deeply endangered in Central Europe, Eastern Europe, Southeast Asia, and China. By this time the Four Freedoms speech seemed less an accurate forecast of the next century—the "American Century" as many thought it would be—than an ideological call to action against an immediate, possibly fatal, danger posed by the Axis powers.[3]

Henrikson instructively traces what happened in the wake of Roosevelt's Four Freedoms speech: a historic conceptual shift in American History from the regional perspective of the Monroe Doctrine that marked the 1930s and before, to a global perspective characterized by a commitment to the United Nations in 1945. This geographic shift (and considerable enlargement) formed the major link between the failed movement toward globalization during the 1870 to 1914 years (a movement that remained submerged for the next half century because of the traumatic effects of World War I), and the ongoing acceleration toward globalization after the 1960s.[4] The conceptual shift outlined by Henrikson was thus by no means completed by 1945—or even by 1965. Instead of the Four Freedoms "everywhere in the world," as Roosevelt had prophesied, the Cold War endangered, and in many areas removed, his Four Freedoms and the "democratic" cause.

The problem was not his large view, which Roosevelt seldom lacked, but the absence of an integrated worldview. Such a worldview had to be both realistic in terms of military strategy and in recognizing the probable results of that strategy. At the same time, it had to be defensible when it became involved with both the onrushing debate of American politics and the demands of a full-throttle American economic engine that produced half the world's gross national product by 1945.

This lack of integration meant FDR was never able to forge a workable, ongoing, realistic worldview. His attempts could be followed through the "Four Freedoms…everywhere" global vision of 1941–1942, complemented by his launching of the United Nations idea in 1942; through his belief, particularly in 1943–1944, that Three Policemen—the United States, Great Britain, and the Soviet Union—should order the postwar world (or sometimes Four Policemen whenever the president wanted to bring China into the club, often to taunt Churchill and his colonial aspirations in Asia); followed by his efforts later in the war to cut secret deals on territorial boundaries and the composition of governments of newly liberated areas during the Teheran and Yalta conferences of 1943 and early 1945—deals shaped not by the Four Freedoms or the United Nations principles, but by the realities of Soviet military power—and these shifts by no means form the complete list.

In October 1944, Churchill suddenly flew to Moscow to protect British interests by negotiating with Stalin private territorial deals involving the Balkans and Eastern Mediterranean. Roosevelt continued to hope that—somehow—this arrangement of the de facto spheres of influence could be made amenable to his earlier concept of open economic doors, democratic regimes, and the Four Freedoms. At this point, in the autumn of 1944, he also continued to hope that—somehow—both British and French colonies would become decolonized, perhaps come under international trusteeship, and in any case become open to increasingly dependent United States exporters. A possible exception might be the British crown jewel of India, which FDR finally decided, after much Churchillian upbraiding and hectoring, to leave alone for the time being. But by early 1945, the president's strong anticolonial sentiments were ruptured when FDR essentially allowed the French and British armies to reenter colonial areas of Southeast Asia.[5] The Four Freedoms of 1941 had metastasized into colonialism, or more accurately attempted colonialism.

Significant and indeed fundamental shifts also occurred when Roosevelt attempted to deal with Germany, Europe's dynamic, industrial and militaristic core. At Quebec during the autumn of 1944, FDR stood aside while his secretary of treasury, Henry Morgenthau, bludgeoned Churchill into accepting the idea for a postwar deindustrialized, economically emasculated Germany. No sooner than the president returned to Washington, however, than he reversed the Quebec agreement after Secretary of State Cordell Hull and Secretary of War Henry Stimson convinced him that a healthy noncommunist Europe required a healthy, capitalist Germany at its center. FDR's worldview in October 1944, which had a supposedly pastoral postwar

Germany at the center of Europe (the kind of Germany which most pleased Stalin), had become by December a worldview resting on a Germany that was by necessity united and industrialized. Indeed, so much so that at Yalta, during February 1945, he refused in discussions with Stalin to agree to any specifics that might mean either a long-term division of the country or heavy reparations that would ruin the possibility of German economic viability.

The president thus held at one point to certain laudable principles, such as the Four Freedoms, a UN structure, and an economic open door to begin restoring the pre-1914 globalization drive. But he could come up with no consistent foreign policy framework that might have helped him systematically and tactically move toward the realization of these principles. As Warren Kimball argues in this volume, Roosevelt was convinced throughout the war that "Great Power cooperation took precedence." That was Plan A. If, however, the Soviets placed their own idea of Russian security ahead of cooperation with Washington in handling, say, Eastern Europe, or if Great Britain and France defied FDR's anticolonial hopes in Asia, there was no coherent Plan B. Eastern Europe fell outside the open-door principles, Indochina and Hong Kong fell back inside European colonial empires, and FDR's vision of a world based on "four essential human freedoms" lay shattered.

The chapters in this volume and the two conferences that inspired it explain why Roosevelt encountered overwhelming problems in his attempt to evolve a workable, tactical worldview that would realize his Four Freedoms dream. One obvious difficulty was that the one world/Four Freedoms/American Century concept necessary to obtain American consent to leave the 1930s behind and become internationalists bore little resemblance to the Three (or Four) Policemen/secret boundary/political arrangements horse trading FDR believed he had to make at Teheran in 1943 and during the period from the Yalta conference until his death in April 1945. A contradiction existed at the center of his vision, one that he was less able to remove as Soviet armies moved westward and British and French armies became the only forces capable of ejecting Japan out of parts of South and Southeast Asia.

Mark Stoler's close examination of the president's relationship with, and control over, the U.S. military during the war richly reveals why Roosevelt faced these contradictions in his worldview. On one level he established solid institutional decision-making structures that were overseen and shaped by General George Marshall, who tried to keep competing military demands—such as FDR's preference for giving the European war zone priority over the Asian—in order, thus ensuring efficient execution of policies. The successful evolution of this "National Security Establishment," combined with Roosevelt's "enormous expansions of executive power in this realm," Stoler argues, "constitute Roosevelt's true legacy in military affairs for the postwar era."

To translate these military plans into a workable, broad-based foreign policy, however, FDR made himself "the sole coordinating link," to quote historian William Emerson's phrase. (Emerson knew the president's career particularly well because he served as director of the Franklin D. Roosevelt Presidential Library.) As U.S. policies traveled across this link from the military options to the foreign policy objectives, there was no institutionalized foreign policy establishment, no viable and recognized set of institutions for evaluating, vetting, concluding, and implementing foreign policies. Indeed, one of the most remarkable aspects of the two conferences that gave rise to this book is the lack of mention of the State Department in the many papers, comments, and discussions that took place. There only was, as Emerson and Stoler argue, the president. He had isolated Secretary of State Hull while limiting him to the pursuit of Hull's Wilsonian dream of unimpeded international trade and international political organizations. Roosevelt meanwhile largely ignored Secretary of War Stimson, who not only had a worldview (which, unlike Hull's, placed priority on the importance of the several great powers) but also thirty years of international experience. Hull and Stimson won their fight in late 1944 to break Roosevelt's commitment to the Morgenthau Plan for Germany, but on other issues the president largely went his own way, as evidenced by his decision to ask neither his secretary of state nor his secretary of war to accompany him to meetings with Stalin, Churchill, and Chiang Kai-shek.

The U.S. military establishment operated under FDR's guidance effectively and victoriously between 1941 and 1945. Given the extent of the losses suffered at Pearl Harbor in 1941 and the South Pacific Theatre in early 1942, such rapid success was hardly guaranteed. But when this military machine had to be integrated into the foreign policy apparatus to help achieve a Four Freedoms world, Roosevelt—the "sole coordinating link," to repeat the Emerson–Stoler phrase—could not act as a viable long-term bridge. Thus, as several of this volume's chapters discuss, U.S. troops could not reach much of Germany ahead of Russians to ensure an integrated, capitalist Central Europe. And, as Lloyd Gardner superbly outlines, U.S. military capabilities could never be matched with Roosevelt's anticolonization stance to ensure that Indochina, Indonesia, and Hong Kong would move toward independence, instead of, as in the first two instances, many years of warfare generated by anticolonial revolutions.

Gardner observes that some experts in the late 1940s and 1950s argued that had FDR's anticolonial beliefs been upheld after his death, the thirty-year Vietnam War would have been avoided. But, as observed above, the president was never able to construct an overall operative foreign policy complete with the necessary power to accomplish this goal. In early 1945, he instead had to turn his head while European armies moved to regain power. "The problem with all this ruminating about Roosevelt's supposed plans, of course," Gardner concludes, "is that we do not know how he would have moved to implement any of his ideas, or, which ideas he would have pursued." Gardner pointedly recounts the highly revealing story of how FDR courted the Saudi Arabian King and his unsurpassed reservoirs of oil by assuring the Saudi ruler that the open-door principles of the United States—not the closed-off spheres of influence of European colonials—could ensure that Saudi wealth would be open to everyone, with monopolies for no one. The postwar reality, nevertheless, was that U.S. troops and dollars could enforce an open door for American oil companies to the wealth of Saudi Arabia, but, given the overall military situation, could not force open the door to Soviet-dominated Eastern and Central Europe or to parts of Asia.

In Asian affairs, FDR hoped during 1943 to mid-1944 that Chiang Kai-shek's Nationalist leadership in China would be the U.S.-supported force that could stabilize the vast region while guaranteeing its openness to a resumption of economic globalization, led, of course, by the United States. Here, Roosevelt's worldview (with a Nationalist led China as one of the Four Policemen, but necessarily dependent on U.S. aid and wishes) rested on mere hope. Americans and Chinese "would police Asia," FDR mused aloud to an aide, while Great Britain and Brazil [sic] stabilized Africa, and the British and Russians kept Europe in proper order."[6]

Another of FDR's forecasts, however, was actually pretty much on course when he told a British diplomat that "We should probably see in China, in the next 50 years, a development similar to that of Japan in the later years of the 19th-century." He even foresaw that "China, in any serious conflict of policy with Russia, would undoubtedly line up on our side."[7] But the China that rose from the devastation of World War II turned out to be quite different, and as early as 1944 it had become clear that FDR's vision of U.S.-Chinese cooperation in Asia had all but collapsed, with terrible consequences rippling down through a communist takeover, the Korean War, and the Vietnam conflict.

Ironically, this collapse was triggered by the presence of U.S. air bases in China and the Japanese decision in early 1944 to launch an offensive targeting them. Roosevelt responded by pushing Chiang to allow General Joseph ("Vinegar Joe") Stilwell to assume command over Chinese armies for a counterattack. "The Peanut," as Stilwell dismissively, and privately, called Chiang, rejected the president's plea and forced FDR to recall Stilwell. Michael Schaller's chapter in this volume well summarizes this historic turn: "While Roosevelt spoke of promoting China as a 'great power,' General Stilwell and his staff dealt with a crumbling army, corrupt leaders, and incipient civil war."

FDR's hopes for postwar Asia never recovered. "The tensions between Roosevelt's grand strategy and the military–diplomatic realities of China," Schaller succinctly concludes, "contributed to eventual disaster." As for the hope of Soviet cooperation in an area where Russians had claimed crucial interests for a century, Schaller believes that as early as the 1943 Teheran Conference, when Stalin and FDR reached some agreement on a deal to bring the USSR into the war against Japan at a later time, "Roosevelt recognized that the final stages of the Pacific War might simply pass China by." The Fourth Policeman, in other words, would be of little use to FDR's once-hopeful plans for an American Century in the Far East. Once again, however, Roosevelt paid for ignoring State Department advice he did not particularly want to hear. Schaller notes how U.S. Ambassador Clarence Gauss, "a grouchy State Department veteran," well understood that Chiang suffered from "unreality," that the Chinese leader was supporting reactionary colleagues, and that the best U.S. hope was to work with more moderate and liberal elements—a highly complex, ultimately impossible goal for an outsider to achieve and, not surprisingly, a goal FDR was never able to reach.

In dealing with boundary, colonial, and governmental issues involving liberated, transitional regimes, the president could act secretly, often in team with the two other members of the Big Three, and on the basis of what at the time was his own worldview; or, as events unfolded, an evolving series of worldviews. In putting the wrecked world economy back together, however, he had to work with the U.S. Congress and a maze of both public and private overseas interests. FDR raised the power of the imperial to new heights when he acted at the closed meetings in Teheran, Quebec, and Yalta. But those powers rapidly melted when he had to approach Congress, which, after all, constitutionally controlled the power over commerce and finance, even in wartime. They also tended to melt when he encountered the economic demands of a maze of other nations and interests, many of them threatening to veer to the left to find safety if economic help was not forthcoming in order to piece together a new international commercial framework. The prewar framework, such as it was, had not only been destroyed by war, but utterly discredited by the post-1929 economic chaos.

Randall Woods's chapter in this volume analyzes the many participants who were involved with trying to put a peacetime structure back together again. On the most crucial part of this policy, Americans were pretty much united. Led by their president, and in this case the zeal of his secretary of state, Cordell Hull, they swore to break down once and for all the Imperial Preference System the British had drawn around their empire in 1931–1932 as a means to keep U.S. exports out of such potentially lucrative markets as Canada, India, and South Africa. As Woods details the process, U.S. officials knew the war would end with a bankrupt Great Britain dependent on American aid, and they used this handle to coerce London to accept their ideas for the postwar economy, including the rapid dismantling of the Imperial Preference System.

Woods emphasizes the most important conclusion that arose out of this process: although the resulting global (outside the Soviet-controlled bloc) trade structure was termed multilateral, theoretical multilateralism in reality gave way to a Washington-designed system that was largely based on Hull's Reciprocal Trade Agreements program that funneled benefits primarily to the United States. One objective was to pump life as rapidly as possible into parts of war-torn Europe and Asia that could absorb the growing flood of U.S. exports and make these areas—as they were before the war—an important part of the world economy. Washington officials hoped to do good while doing well. By the early 1950s, particularly with the help of sudden military spending during the Korean War scare, this objective began to be realized. Another American objective was to break down the European colonial systems' protective tariff walls. This target, as Roosevelt learned in South and Southeast Asia in 1944–1945, proved tougher to hit and it would not be until well into the 1950s that these barriers would begin to come down.

As the chapters of Warren Kimball and Randall Woods explain, Roosevelt's internationalism, in both the political and economic realms, turned out to be regionalism. The beginnings of an establishment of a Communist empire by Stalin in Eastern Europe and Central Europe assured that U.S. policies resting on democratically elected governments and open-door economics would not be realized in a large and economically strategic part of the globe. Roosevelt, as Kimball details, clearly told the British that the great powers would make the important decisions and policies, while the UN General Assembly would act as an escape valve where "the smaller powers...blow off steam." FDR even told the press that the General Assembly "is not really of any great importance." Such words indicated that the president was being reduced to talk with some certainty about tactics and means. His worldview, that is, how U.S. global objectives were to be realized by those three—or four—great powers, moved off in so many different directions that by April 1945 he was working with a fragmented, if to some colorful, spectrum of objectives that had either little coherence or little relationship to the ideas he pursued and promoted from 1941 to early 1944.

David Reynolds's valuable chapter demonstrates the ongoing post-1945 debate through which Americans and many others came to evaluate Roosevelt's vision, or visions. The much publicized publication in 1955 of the volume of documents on the Yalta Conference of ten years earlier proved curiously unexciting and anticlimactic, especially given the expectations of conservative Republicans and others who disliked Roosevelt. The volume revealed no sellouts by the president, no massive errors that could be traced to his rapidly declining health in early 1945. Instead, he tried to open Russian controlled Poland and the Balkans to open elections and trade— and, not surprisingly, failed, given the presence of the Red Army in those areas. He tried to protect Germany's economic health, as Stimson and Hull had convinced him he must, but he had to settle for an overly general agreement that did little in the immediate postwar years to secure this goal. FDR ensured Stalin's entry into the Pacific War three months after Hitler's defeat by giving the dictator valuable territory and rights then held by Japan—and historically held by Roosevelt's supposed fellow Policeman, China.[8]

Reynolds argues that for all the attention the Yalta records received (and the disappointment they produced for Roosevelt's critics), the conference was less important than the Big Three meeting at Teheran in 1943. It was there, particularly in regards to the German question, that FDR's Four Freedoms/ UN approach designed to create an open, democratically based world ran into the immovable contradiction of the Four Policeman idea, now happily accepted by Stalin because it could mean the Soviet domination of Eastern and parts of Central Europe. Similar ominous disagreements arose over the Polish question. Warren Kimball has concluded elsewhere that at Teheran, FDR, Stalin, and Churchill finally tried "a kind of diplomatic papering over cracks in the [Allied] wall." But the emerging postwar world with all its considerable cracks and divisions was difficult to conceal, even as early as the fall of 1943.[9]

Throughout this period, Roosevelt tried to hold to his 1941–1942 vision of a Four Freedoms/UN world, then a Three (or Four) Policeman-patrolled globe that would meld big power cooperation into a restored and open international system whose open-door economy would not be threatened by colonial systems. But by 1944, the "cracks" and contradictions began to weaken his hold. Within less than two years, FDR's conception of how the world could be reunited and economically reenergized became more scrambled, aimless, and confused. Stalin ruthlessly pursued his objectives of a weak (or at least, divided) Germany, a Soviet-dominated Eastern Europe, and the recovery of the Czar's long-lost prizes in Asia, especially Manchuria. Churchill, meanwhile, went after a restoration of the British and French colonies, so necessary, he fervently believed, for the economic survival of the colonial powers. At the same time he made his own deals with Stalin to ensure a British hold on strategic parts of the eastern Mediterranean, especially Greece. He also clung to the unrequited hope that the cause for which England ostensibly went to war, Poland, could somehow remain outside the Soviet empire. Churchill as well countered the United States when he, along with his famous economic guru, Lord Maynard Keynes, attempted to set up in 1944–1945 an international commercial system that protected, rather than exploited, a nearly bankrupt Britain. Given Churchill's relative weakness, when compared with his two fellow Policemen in 1945, batting .400 by obtaining two of the five was not bad. But his achievement of these two objectives in Asia and the eastern Mediterranean ran counter to Roosevelt's thinking and hence served to undermine the president's concurrent efforts to impose his own Four Freedoms/Four Policeman vision on the postwar world.

The president meanwhile obtained a good part of what he wished for in the postwar economic system, but by 1946 the final product would not have any application to large areas of Communist occupied Europe and Asia. He began to see the power of the Policemen, but at least one of them had no interest in the Four Freedoms or open economic doors, and the interest of another, the British, was, to say the least, greatly qualified. The Fourth Policeman, Chiang Kai-shek, survived the war with his country's longtime enemy, Japan, destroyed. But as FDR clearly saw as early as mid-1944, Chiang was in no position to act as a U.S. ally or even keep his own country together in the face of rising Chinese Communist power. At one point in 1942–1943, Roosevelt's worldview even included using China to liberate and then oversee the European colonies in Asia so the old colonialism could not be restored. Perhaps remembering the 1000 years of wars between the Chinese and Vietnamese, which produced more bloodshed than happiness for China, Chiang politely declined FDR's offer.[10] The president never found another way of taking the colonial areas away from the Europeans. In early 1945 he quietly surrendered to the French and British in regard to Southeast Asia and Hong Kong, largely gave up on Chiang, and tried desperately but unsuccessfully to piece together some kind of postwar vision, particularly in regard to Eastern Europe, which contained the American principles and international vibrancy of his 1941–1943 worldviews but many fewer of the contradictions.

Hence, Roosevelt, by 1945, did not have a worldview—no plan B on which to fall back. When the assumptions and hopes of his first worldview did not work out, he devised another, then another, until they finally tended to disappear beneath his post-Yalta generalizations and his recognition of the power held by the other two (even three) Policemen who disagreed throughout the war with the major principles he had so eloquently articulated in the early years of the conflict.

FDR was a great wartime leader at home. He also was essential to holding together an ultimately triumphant wartime coalition whose partners during the twenty-two years before 1941 had often been at each other's throats. But extending New Deal benefits, Wilsonian democracy, and U.S.-style capitalism abroad has not been accepted by some powerful antagonists either before 1939 or after 1989. To this day, Americans have had a hard time understanding or accepting this. As Eric Alternman, Frank Castiglio,

Gary Clifford, William Roger Louis, and Anders Stephanson pointed out in their comments at the original conference that gave rise to this book, Wilsonianism has so shaped our language and our assumptions for the twentieth and twenty-first centuries that most Americans are used to hearing and believing that democracy can easily travel; that democratic institutions, such as an independent judiciary, can be established without undue difficulties; that other people want to be like Americans—once, as Lloyd Gardner has pointed out, the bad people are removed. Driven by this impulse, Americans have come to believe, in Wilson's own phrase, we can do no other than to spread American principals throughout the world. This is what Randal Woods called the American messianic impulse. But this Wilsonian language has turned out not to be a policy, it's a disease that essentially dictates America's view of the world. And it was a disease that not even FDR—searching for a consensus for policies in 1945 he knew would not work—was immune to.

FDR may have been more farseeing than his post-1898 predecessors or his post-1945 successors. But he, like they, nevertheless learned, often bitterly, the limits of American power, both military and diplomatic, during wartime.

NOTES

1. A good overview of FDR's views about, and use of, public opinion at this time is in Hadley Cantril, *The Human Dimension: Experience in Policy Research* (New Brunswick, NJ: Rutgers University Press, 1967), 35–42. A useful context for this turn is provided in Robert A. Divine, *Foreign Policy and U.S. Presidential Elections, 1940–1948* (New York: New Viewpoints, 1974), esp. 82–83.

2. This speech, remarkable at this particular time for its globalism, is available on the Franklin D. Roosevelt Presidential Library and Museum's Web site, www.fdrlibrary.marist.edu/od4freed.html. Accessed October 20, 2006.

3. The classic small, widely read treatise laying out, in the months before the U.S. entry into the war, the great American expectations for the postwar world is Henry Luce, *The American Century* (New York: Farrar & Rinehart, 1941), notably 5–40.

4. For more on the early and unsuccessful attempts to develop a "global economy," see Carolyn Rhodes, *Reciprocity, U.S. Trade Policy, and the GATT Regime* (Ithaca, NY: Cornell University Press, 1993).

5. For a pivotal document that helps mark the transition of Roosevelt's anticolonial worldview to a view that contained considerably more sympathy for the colonialists because of the new Soviet and Communist dangers in the Pacific theater, note Averell Harriman to Harry Hopkins, September 10, 1944, box 96, Harriman file, Harry Hopkins Papers, Franklin D. Roosevelt Library, Hyde Park, New York. This document is provocatively placed in a much

larger context in a pioneering and important account of Harriman's turn and his influence, or lack thereof, on Roosevelt: Frank Costigliola, "'I had Come as a Friend': Emotion, Culture, and Ambiguity in the Formation of the Cold War, 1943–45," *Cold War History* 1 (August 2000): 103–28. An especially significant study of FDR's shift on the colonial issue is Christopher Thorne, "Indochina and Anglo-American Relations, 1942–1945," *Pacific Historical Review* 45 (February 1976): 73–96; see also "Roosevelt, Churchill and Indochina: 1942–1945," *The American Historical Review* 80, 5 (December 1975): 1277–95.

6. William D. Hassett, *Off the Record with FDR, 1942–1945* (New Brunswick, NJ: Rutgers University Press, 1958), 166.

7. Roosevelt quoted in a minute by William Strang, March 29, 1943, PRO, FO371 F1878/25/10, Public Record Office, Kew, England.

8. Diane Shaver Clemens, *Yalta* (New York: Oxford University Press, 1970), esp. 82–95, which discuss the military situation at the time of the conference, and 275–82 for German questions, remains a superb, succinct analysis.

9. Warren Kimball, ed., *Churchill and Roosevelt: The Complete Correspondence*, 3 vols. (Princeton, NJ: Princeton University Press, 1984), vol. 2, 612.

10. Important documents on the Chiang–FDR exchange, and the President's views, can be found in U.S. Government, *Foreign Relations of the United States: The conferences at Cairo and Tehran, 1943* (Washington, DC, 1961), 325 especially; and Samuel I. Rosenman, ed., *The Public Papers and Addresses of Franklin D. Roosevelt, 1944–1945* (New York: Harper, 1950), 562–3, which provides FDR's later view of Chiang's response.

Epilogue:
FDR: Reflections on Legacy and Leadership—The View from 2008

David B. Woolner

On April 12, 1945, a stunned world learned that Franklin D. Roosevelt was dead.[1] President for twelve of the most tumultuous years in the history of the United States, it seemed impossible that this strong figure, who had become for many the embodiment of the struggle against fascism, was no longer there to lead the Allies to final victory. The universal comment among American fighting men, recorded on innumerable occasions, was that FDR's death was like losing one's own father. And for the men, women, and children on the home front the loss was equally great. Thousands upon thousands lined the route of his funeral train as it made its way from Warm Springs to Washington and then to Hyde Park. In London and the other capitols of Europe, expressions of grief were equally intense. Winston Churchill wept as he told the more than two thousand people who filled St. Paul's Cathedral and thousands of others who stood outside listening to his memorial service on loud speakers that Roosevelt's death was "a bitter loss to humanity."[2] Churchill expressed an equally profound personal sense of loss in a private note to King George VI, when he remarked that with FDR gone "ties have been shorn asunder which years had woven."[3] In Moscow FDR was honored as no foreigner had been honored before—with memorial broadcasts, extensive front-page press coverage in the official Soviet press, and with black bordered flags flying above the Kremlin.[4]

Certainly this unprecedented outpouring of grief—matched only by Abraham Lincoln's funeral eighty years before—tells a great deal about the quality of FDR's leadership. Yet it is important to remember that FDR was and will always remain a controversial and enigmatic figure. He was often—as the chapters in this volume make clear—difficult to read. And the principles he professed to follow frequently clashed with the policies he eventually pursued. There were, as Walter LaFeber points out, "contradictions" in his thinking that are difficult to reconcile: the tension between his belief in fundamental human rights and the realities of geopolitics; his need to protect American interests while promoting international understanding and cooperation; his sense of a world community based on universally shared values and aspirations versus the realization that the potent and often pernicious forces of nationalism were here to stay. These tensions—and the many others he faced—formed the framework within which FDR had to operate. Equally important was his realization of the limits of American power, particularly military power, in the face of a rapidly changing world. Taken together, these tensions and limitations forced FDR to narrow his focus and to concentrate on the issues that he believed were fundamental to the preservation of postwar peace: Great Power cooperation; the creation of an international institution to facilitate that cooperation; a reordering of the world's economic structure; and the continuation of American moral, political, and military leadership in the postwar world. In FDR's view, these were the critical elements necessary for the prevention of another, even more cataclysmic, war, and if the achievement of these fundamental objectives required him to back off or reassess his previously held positions, on such an issue as colonialism, for example, then perhaps his shift in stance is understandable.

But does this really diminish FDR as a man and as a leader? Does this indicate that his convictions were not as strongly held as we might imagine or that the private FDR was a much less inspired figure than the public FDR? And what about the question of legacy? Did the necessity for him to compromise his principles in the face of global political and military reality compromise his legacy as well? I would argue that the short answer to these questions—an answer confirmed by many of the observations in this book—is no.

Franklin Roosevelt faced a crisis unlike any other in American—or world—history. He understood that it was his duty as a leader to inspire the American people to live up to their international responsibilities. He also understood that if he were successful in convincing the American people of the merits of international engagement, the United States, by virtue of its enormous—but not unlimited—power, had the potential to reverse the tragic events of the 1930s and 1940s by providing the leadership necessary to lay the foundations for a better world. Moreover, having lived through the Great Depression and the unparalleled violence of World War understood that the world was in desperate need of serious s... reform, reform that would only be possible if he were able to create the sort of postwar environment that would allow the United States—under his leadership—to advance the causes he cared so deeply about.

Given this reality, FDR found himself having to become a master of two tasks simultaneously: the critical need to keep the American people and other like-minded individuals around the world inspired and committed to his progressive ideals, versus the equally difficult and hard hitting task of maintaining Great Power cooperation as the Allies made the transition from coalition warfare to victory. It was this "juggling" of the public need to promote the sorts of progressive values he felt were critical to the future, versus the private diplomacy of coalition warfare—along with his tendency to keep his thoughts to himself—which at best has rendered his legacy difficult to fathom, and at worst has contributed to the notion that FDR was a duplicitous and deceitful figure whose willingness to compromise his principles has rendered them—and his legacy—meaningless. Yet, as the chapters in this volume show, it is possible to point to at least five major areas or spheres in the political, military-strategic, diplomatic, economic, and moral realms where I would argue FDR's wartime leadership—and convictions—had a profound impact on the postwar world.

The first major area involves the political. Here we learn through Alan Henrikson's work, "FDR and the World-Wide Arena," that FDR literally changed the way Americans view the world, taking the American public from a hemispheric focus that encouraged the idea that the United States, positioned as it was between two oceans, was set apart from the other continents, to a global vision (based largely on polar map projections) that saw the United States as intimately linked with the rest of humanity. Moreover, this shift involved far more than merely a change in the way Americans interpret geography or view the placement of North America on a map; it also involved a psychological shift that encouraged not only "global thinking on the geographical plane," but also universal thinking on an "ideological plane." In this sense, Henrikson argues, FDR's "world picture," a picture that he purposefully painted for all those who would listen, became a "world philosophy" based on the common aspirations of people everywhere to enjoy a life based on universally shared values, values best articulated in his famous Four Freedoms address of January 1941. Hence the struggle to help America's allies defeat the Axis on other continents became synonymous with the struggle to defend America and American values wherever that need may arise. The two, in short, were indistinguishable as it was impossible in "One World" to separate American security needs from those of other peoples.

Based on these concepts, FDR was able to argue that "isolationism" (what Warren Kimball correctly defines as unilateralism or the noninvolvement in the affairs of others) was not only naive but also dangerous, for it was imperative in the wake of the twin crises that struck the world in the 1930s and 1940s for the United States to stay actively engaged with the rest of the world.

Closely related to FDR's conviction that it was impossible for the United States to act unilaterally was his conviction that Great Power cooperation was essential to the preservation of world peace. This made it necessary not only to work with the British, but also to recognize that one of the key—if not *the* key—elements of postwar stability and security lay in cooperation with the Soviet Union. This brought the United States head-to-head with the twin realities of Soviet power and its need for security, as made manifest in Stalin's wartime demands for a revision of the Soviet Union's western borders and for the establishment of friendly governments in Eastern and Central Europe after the war. Given FDR's professed support for democracy and self determination, as articulated in the Atlantic Charter, Stalin's security requirements placed him (and Churchill) in something of a dilemma, but as Warren Kimball makes clear in "The Sheriffs: FDR's Postwar World," Roosevelt's means of solving this dilemma tells us a great deal about his wartime diplomacy, political skills, and approach to the postwar world.

First and foremost of course was his conviction that the use of force was not an option in dealing with the Soviets because this might lead to a third world war. Indeed, direct confrontation or the use of military force to solve a *political* problem was antithetical to Roosevelt's thinking. So the president opted in the short term to do all he could to persuade Stalin to accept the terms of the Atlantic Charter via the Declaration of Librated Europe and other provisions, while at the same time stressing the need for long-term cooperation. In other words, FDR accepted the premise that both during and after the war, it was critical to work with rather than against the Soviet Union.

Contrary to later public perceptions, this approach was not based on ignorance or naiveté, but rather on the firm recognition that Soviet power was here to stay. It was also based on the equally realistic understanding that the Great Powers have a need—in Roosevelt's terms—to feel comfortable in their own neighborhoods. Out of these basic ideas flowed the two concepts that Kimball argues stood at the base of FDR's thinking about the postwar world: "regionalized cooperative internationalism," which involved the creation of global structure in which the Great Powers—or four policemen—would keep the peace; and "Americanism," which Kimball defines as "shorthand for everything else in Roosevelt's geopolitical thinking," including the internationalization of the New Deal, his conviction that leadership and persuasion were the means of creating peaceful relationships, and his calm and unshakable belief in the American democratic tradition.

Consistent with FDR's view that it was imperative to change the way Americans viewed their place in the world, as described in Henrikson's analysis, both these concepts required the American people to reject "isolationism" (Kimball's unilateralism) and embrace internationalism. This meant that the American people had to learn to accept the idea that the United States—as one of the four policemen—had no choice but to continue to play a leading role in world affairs, by which FDR meant a firm commitment to the United Nations Organization (the institution through which FDR expected the Great Powers to cooperate), active involvement in the newly created International Monetary Fund and International Bank for Reconstruction and Development (later the World Bank); and internationally focused engagement on a host of other political and economic issues. Given that the United States has stood at the forefront of the international community—with one or two notable exceptions—for the past sixty years, it seems reasonable to argue that this commitment to internationalism has become a permanent fixture of FDR's wartime leadership, and hence one of his most important legacies.

FDR's belief in the need for American world leadership—a belief that greatly intensified with the outbreak of World War II—soon led him to the conclusion that it was necessary to develop a new means of developing and executing American foreign policy. This realization brings us to the second major area where FDR's wartime leadership has had a profound impact on the postwar world—in the military-strategic sphere. In "FDR and the Rise of the National Security State," Mark Stoler shows us that FDR was "determined to be a very strong and active Commander-in-Chief..." As such, he made a number of moves to consolidate his leadership of the military. In 1939, for example, FDR personally selected a new chief of naval operations, Admiral Harold R. Stark, and a new army chief of staff, General George C. Marshall. He then transferred the offices of the Joint Army–Navy Board, within which they served, from the existing Navy and War Departments to the newly created Executive Offices of the President. This shift, which was carried out so as to create a direct link between the president and his service chiefs (thus enabling him to bypass his civilian secretaries of war and navy, as well as his secretary of state), created America's first true national strategy body and rendered the members of the Joint Army–Navy Board (later the Joint Chiefs of Staff) "the president's foremost and immediate strategic advisors." Equally important, it also made FDR "the sole coordinating link between U.S. military strategies and foreign policies."

These moves—and others, such as the creation and expansion of the Joint Chiefs of Staff, the numerous military boards to support this new entity, and the appointment of the first White House Chief of Staff—represented a significant consolidation of power inside the White House, a consolidation that was carried out by design. They made it possible for the president to merge foreign and military policies and to become much more intimately involved in the design and development of what we now call "National Security Policy." They also led to a permanent restructuring of America's foreign, intelligence, and military policymaking establishment, formalized in the immediate postwar years through the creation of such institutions as the National Security Council, the National Security Advisor, the Central Intelligence Agency, and the Department of Defense. It is, of course, ironic, given FDR's love of ad hoc arrangements, that the "institutional revolution" that gave rise to this massive national security structure was largely his work, but we should not let FDR's methods conceal his motives. It was his strong desire to personally direct U.S. foreign and military policy. Doing so, in the midst of a global war, required not only a fundamental shift in the U.S. approach to foreign policy and the definition of what it means to be "Commander-in-Chief," but also the creation of a massive national security structure to support this new approach. Taken together, these two moves—the replacement of traditional foreign policy with the new concept of national security policy and the creation of the infrastructure to carry it out—stand as one of the most profound legacies of his leadership, a legacy that remains largely intact and is with us to this day.

In the diplomatic sphere, where FDR dealt with such issues as colonialism and China, his legacy is more ambiguous. On the question of colonialism, this stems in part from the fact that by the end of the war FDR had largely given up on the notion of forcing his European Allies to give up their colonial possessions in favor of trusteeships. But as Lloyd Gardner argues in "FDR and the Colonial Question," this did not necessarily mean that Roosevelt's antipathy to colonialism had diminished or that he had given up on the idea entirely. The problem, of course, is that FDR died before the war in the Pacific reached its climax and as such we will never know how he might have handled the transition from war to peace in such areas as Vietnam. What is clear, however, is Roosevelt's prescience with respect to the long-term trend: he understood that the aspirations of colonial peoples for independence was not going to fade away after the war; he also understood that it was in America's best interest to identify itself with these aspirations through such instruments as the Atlantic Charter and the Cairo Declaration. In this sense, one could argue that FDR helped accelerate the desire for independence or at the very least *the promise* of independence among colonial peoples worldwide and hence helped precipitate—and sustain—the largely successful postwar drive for the decolonization of Asia and Africa. Certainly, FDR would be happy to identify himself with such a legacy, but as Gardner so succinctly points out, not necessarily the means by which this goal was often achieved—through violence and war, especially violence and war that was perpetuated by the United States. It is here that the question of FDR's death becomes acute, for as we now know, a tragic shift occurred when America's wartime anticolonialism was replaced by postwar anticommunism, as this ultimately led the United States to abandon a pronationalist solution to the question of who should govern such areas as Indochina. FDR, in contrast, was not so troubled by ideology—or by the fear of a worldwide Soviet-inspired communist conspiracy—and may have been more inclined to work with, rather than against, nationalist-communists, be they in Yugoslavia, China, or Vietnam. Gardner hints that these twin attributes may have produced a far different postwar scenario had FDR lived, especially in Vietnam, but sadly FDR's untimely death and the onset of the Cold War rendered this hope impossible. Nevertheless, FDR's willingness to speak openly about the need for the European powers to give up their imperial possessions, and his professions of support for the aspirations of colonial peoples, does constitute something of a legacy, for it helped inspire the belief among the colonial peoples of Asia and Africa that change was inevitable and that with or without American support the march for national self determination must go forward.

The same prescience that FDR possessed with respect to the issue of colonialism can be found in his view of China. He understood that China was destined to become one of the world's leading powers and he entertained great hopes that that power might begin to manifest itself in the joint American–Chinese struggle against the Japanese during World War II. Through Michael Schaller's work, we know that by 1945 FDR's hopes for China as a wartime ally had all but faded, and that this disillusionment played a major role in FDR's decision to pressure the Russians to invade Manchuria at the Yalta conference. But this did not mean that FDR had abandoned his view that China would ultimately achieve Great Power status or that she might one day prove useful as a counterweight to the expansion of Soviet power in the postwar world. On the contrary, FDR well understood the need to keep China engaged and in the war, and even after he had abandoned his wartime military aspirations for China, he continued to place a great deal of emphasis on U.S.–Chinese relations. The problem was that—thanks in large part to the machinations of men like Patrick Hurley—FDR was ultimately persuaded to cut all links to the Chinese Communists and deal only with the Chinese Nationalist under the corrupt and inept leadership of Chiang Kai-shek. This placed the United States firmly in the Nationalist camp and made it much more difficult, if not impossible, for the United States to act as an honest broker between the two parties in any potential effort to stave off or stop a civil war.[5]

Having built up China's wartime image through numerous references to China as a key U.S. ally and one of the Four Policemen who would help maintain the peace after the defeat of the Axis, it is not surprising that the resumption of the civil war in 1946 and the defeat of the Nationalists at the hands of the Communists three years later would be regarded as a major blow to U.S. foreign policy. In this sense, one could argue that FDR's legacy with respect to China is negative—particularly in light of the oft expressed wartime fear that we might "lose" China as an ally (through a separately negotiated Sino–Japanese peace) if we did not make a concerted effort to keep her in the war.

But did the Nationalists' defeat really mean that we had "lost" China? Certainly in the geopolitical sense the answer to this question is no. Once again, FDR's basic assumptions were correct, some would say tragically correct. China—communist or not—was indeed more likely to line up with the Americans than with the Soviets in any major showdown among the Great Powers, as Richard Nixon and Henry Kissinger were to discover some thirty years later. China, for good or for ill, would also emerge as one of the world's leading postwar powers, and in spite of the difficulty that the United States has had with China in the intervening years (as exemplified in the Korean war and elsewhere), it is obvious today that without the engagement of the Chinese government on a host of international issues—from the environment to nuclear proliferation—progress will be difficult if not impossible.

It is perhaps in the fourth area—the economic sphere— that we find FDR left the strongest wartime legacy. Indeed the roots of today's global economy come straight out of Roosevelt era, and as Randall Woods indicates, this was no accident. By September 1939, FDR had firmly embraced the notion—put forward by U.S. Secretary of State Cordell Hull and others—that the dislocation of trade caused by high tariffs and preferential agreements, such as the British system of Imperial Preference, had been a major cause of the global economic crisis of the 1930s and the concomitant rise of fascism in Europe and Asia and hence the war itself. Based on this analysis, the Roosevelt administration was determined to establish a new postwar multilateral trading system based on freer trade and the free movement of capital. It was also determined to use the massive economic power it accumulated as a result of the war (as exercised through lend lease and other forms of wartime aide) to try to force Great Britain—which still possessed a vast empire and remained the world's second largest trading nation—to abandon Imperial Preference and other impediments to freer trade, including the currency exchange controls in use throughout the sterling area, so as to ensure the success of its postwar economic plans.[6]

By the summer of 1944, the Roosevelt Administration had tackled the first of these two major requirements—the free movement of capital—through the successful negotiation of the Bretton Woods agreements, which, among other things, called upon Great Britain to accept the full convertibility of sterling. British concurrence to the Bretton Woods accords, however, was made in the expectation that Great Britain would receive up to an additional $7 billion in Lend-Lease aid to help the British make the transition from a wartime to a peacetime economy. Franklin Roosevelt was sympathetic to the British position and as late as September 1944 had promised Churchill an additional $6.5 billion in Lend-Lease aid as the war shifted from Europe to the Pacific.[7] But the U.S. Congress was not so compassionate, and in the months following FDR's death, the promised aid was converted to a loan and cut by roughly half. As Woods notes, the twin blows of reduced aid and the forced convertibility of sterling soon led the British into bankruptcy, making it much more difficult, if not impossible, for Great Britain to transition from one trading regime to another.

In the meantime, U.S. efforts to negotiate a truly multilateral trade agreement ran into similar difficulties. Congress may have been willing to support a renewal of Hull's Reciprocal Trade Agreements Act in 1945, but the establishment of an international trade regime was another matter.[8] This skepticism not only made it impossible for the multilateralists within the Roosevelt or Truman Administrations to obtain a fully negotiated multilateral trading mechanism during the war, it also rendered it impossible for them to achieve it in the immediate postwar years, as made manifest in their failure to get Congress to endorse the establishment of an International Trade Organization in the late 1940s and early 1950s. But as Woods makes clear, the successful negotiation of the General Agreement on Tariff and Trade or GATT, which came out of the negotiations for the ITO, and which, like the RTAA, was based on reciprocal, rather than across the board, multilateral reductions in tariff rates (and hence was much more acceptable to the U.S. Congress), was a major success. Taken together, these two measures—the Bretton Woods accords and the GATT—represented a profound change in global economic policy that formed the basis for what we now call globalization.[9]

One obvious element of the new global economy is the vast increase in air travel, which today allows millions of people worldwide to move about the planet. As is the case with the international economic restructuring that occurred in the mid- to late 1940s, this expansion of civil aviation owes a great deal to the leadership of FDR and his administration. Indeed, as Alan Dobson articulates in "FDR and Post-War Commercial Aviation: Legacy or Loss?" FDR took a great deal of interest in civil aviation, which is perhaps not surprising given his global perspective and his strong belief in the need to internationalize key elements of the New Deal, particularly with respect to its call for regulated yet nondiscriminatory access to trade and commerce.

Under his leadership, the United States embarked on a concerted effort to negotiate an international civil aviation agreement with the British, who with their enormous empire controlled much of the world's skies. As was the case with the negotiation of a multilateral trade agreement, however, these negotiations fell short of their mark, and the two sides were unable to come to a complete understanding during the course of the war.

Still, like the failed attempt to establish the ITO, the negotiations themselves proved enormously useful, and in 1946 the two sides were able to achieve a compromise settlement on the island of Bermuda, which was held up as a model for the rest of the world to follow. Here, the United States achieved what Dobson calls "relatively open skies" through a much more liberal and internationalist regime than had existed in the prewar period. Moreover, although the Bermuda accords fell short of the multilateral regime that the Roosevelt Administration sought, they nevertheless laid the basis for a significant expansion of postwar international aviation, an expansion which allowed U.S. airlines to thrive.

One question that has persistently plagued historians is whether or not FDR's attempts to reshape American foreign policy in the military, diplomatic, economic, and political spheres described above were essentially reactive or purposeful in nature, and if the latter, whether these efforts, taken together, constitute a consistent integrated "worldview." In other words, was FDR guided by an overall vision and does this vision in some way represent his greatest legacy?

In struggling with this difficult question, which brings us to our fifth area, the moral dimension of FDR's leadership, Walter LaFeber draws on the observations of the other contributors to this book, as well as his own profound understanding of the deep currents of American history. Here, he notes for example that FDR was unquestionably one of the greatest of all war leaders at home—on par with the likes of Washington and Lincoln. He was also the key figure in the Grand Alliance and deserves much of the credit for holding together "an ultimately triumphant wartime coalition whose partners during the twenty two years before 1941 had often been at each other's throats."

But on the question of FDR's worldview, LaFeber is less sanguine. He concludes that FDR did not have a single worldview, but in fact had multiple worldviews that changed with the changing circumstances of the war. Early in the conflict, for instance, LaFeber insists that FDR's vision was centered on a global extension of the ideas contained in his famous Four Freedoms address, complemented by his launching of the United Nations ideal in 1942. This was followed in 1943–1944 by his Four Policemen concept, after which FDR turned to the less laudable attempts in 1945 "to cut secret deals on territorial boundaries and the compositions of governments of newly liberated areas...deals shaped not by the Four Freedoms or United Nations principles, but by the realities of Soviet Military power..."

LaFeber notes that these "significant shifts" in policy were in many ways a natural reaction to the shifting circumstances and "overwhelming problems" of a global war, all of which made it very hard for the president to maintain a workable, ongoing, realistic worldview. But other factors were at play as well, including FDR's tendency to make himself the "sole coordinating link" between "military options and foreign policy objectives," alluded to in Stoler's work, as well as the absence of the State Department in the formulation of most policy—an absence that ultimately meant "there was no institutionalized foreign policy establishment, no viable set of institutions for evaluating, vetting, concluding and implementing foreign policies." This left only the president, whose ability to conceptualize and articulate larger ideas, unfortunately, did not result in the establishment of the type of integrated foreign policy framework that could realize his Four Freedoms dream. By 1945, this inability to translate his larger ideas into tangible policy meant that for practical purposes FDR ended the war (and his life) without a coherent worldview in place.

This may be a harsh judgment, but LaFeber's assessment of FDR's lack of a consistent worldview brings up another important question—a question that David Reynolds wrestles with in the opening chapter of this book. To what extent is history and legacy shaped by historians and the historical actors themselves? Or, to put it another way, is our assessment of FDR somehow clouded by the immediate postwar polemics that guided much of the writing of history in the first decade after the war?

In this fascinating examination of history and memory, Reynolds argues that many of the issues and positions staked out in the first postwar decade—from the controversy swirling over the attack on Pearl Harbor to the decision to drop the atomic bomb—have shaped historical debate ever since. In light of this, Reynolds reminds us that in any attempt to assess FDR's legacy, it is important for the contemporary historian to consider how the historical image of Roosevelt's war leadership took shape in this critical period. Here, we learn for example that the publication of the official State Department record on the Yalta Conference (Foreign Relations of the United States, or FRUS) was hurriedly pushed through in the early 1950s by a Republican controlled Congress and White House that in the wake of the 1948 electoral defeat had decided to adopt a partisan approach to foreign policy, which included the charge that the Democrats had "lost China" in 1949 and "appeased" the Soviet Union at Yalta. As a consequence the FRUS volume on the Yalta Conference (which tended to support the position that FDR did not cave in to the Russians) was published in 1955, but with the Democrats regaining control of both houses in January of the same year, further publication of the official wartime conferences was delayed. This meant that for a considerable period the FRUS volume on Yalta stood alone. One result, Reynolds argues, is that historical writing on wartime diplomacy—and the public interpretation of that diplomacy—has continued to focus more on the Yalta conference than is historically justified, as we now know from our examination of the documentary record of the wartime summit meetings that the Tehran conference, for example, was far more substantive and important.

The same type of shift in emphasis has had a similar influence on our interpretation of Anglo-American strategy regarding the opening of a second front in Europe; the debate over the Pearl Harbor attack and the "end" of isolationism; the doctrine of unconditional surrender and treatment of the Axis; and the decision to drop the atomic bomb. In all of these areas, numerous factors came to play in the writing and recording of these events—partisan politics, contemporary diplomacy, the intensification of the Cold War, even the desire to take advantage of lucrative publishing contracts. No doubt, the same types of influences continue to play their part in our own interpretation of the past, for as Reynolds reminds us, the "light of history is, of course, ever-changing."

*   *   *

So where does this leave the legacy of Franklin Roosevelt? Sixty plus years after his death, can we speak of a consistent and meaningful legacy? Are there any threads that run through all the facets of his policies and thinking that do indeed add up to a thematic whole? The chapters in this book certainly point toward a number of consistent themes that taken together form the basis of his thinking and his legacy.

First and foremost was FDR's desire to be the "sole coordinating link" in the design and execution of U.S. foreign and military policies. This desire to place himself at the helm of all facets of the decision-making process has led to a significant expansion of presidential power in the execution of American foreign policy, which has rendered it much easier for the president as the "Commander-in-Chief" to commit American forces to battle without a congressional declaration of war. This may not have been FDR's intent, but it nevertheless stands as one of the consequences of his leadership. It has also led to replacement of traditional foreign policy with the new concept of National Security Policy and the development of a massive bureaucratic infrastructure to support it. Viewed from the perspective of sixty plus years, we can now see that the creation of this national security infrastructure and FDR's tendency to concentrate the decision-making process inside the White House has frequently resulted in the marginalization of the State Department in the formulation of U.S. foreign policy. LaFeber is correct when he argues that this tendency carries a certain element of risk—as numerous events since 1945 have shown—but it was FDR's intent to carry out this concentration of power and it remains a key characteristic of the contemporary office of the Presidency.

Second, and equal in importance, was FDR's desire to destroy what at the time was called "isolationism" (unilateralism). FDR firmly believed in the value of American leadership—especially if that leadership was being carried out under his tenure. It was critical, therefore, to change the way the American people perceived their position in the world—not as an isolated or insulated continent, but as an entity physically and philosophically connected to the rest of humanity. Closely linked to this change in perception was his realization that the one sure means to keep the peace was to facilitate Great Power cooperation. This also required American leadership—and hence a commitment to internationalism on the part of the American people, which made it doubly important that he characterize America's commitment to the world community in terms that the American people would accept and understand, through such concepts as the Four Freedoms and the building of an international organization—the United Nations—that would help realize the twin dreams of peace through Great Power cooperation and the steady expansion of human rights.

Third was his conviction that colonialism was doomed and consigned to the past. Much like his efforts to convince the American people to embrace internationalism, this required the public identification of the United States as being in step with the march of history—even though the need for Great Power cooperation, which by definition had to take precedence over colonialism, sometimes required the American Government to quietly and perhaps temporarily acquiesce in the continuation of colonial regimes. The same recognition of historical inevitability of the demise of colonialism led FDR to argue that China must ultimately be regarded as one of the world's Great Powers—a great power that must be reckoned with, and which, if handled correctly, would more often than not align itself with American as opposed to Soviet interests.

Fourth was his firm belief in the need to reorder the world economic order so as to improve America's and the world's standard of living. This was necessary not only to prevent a reversion to economic nationalism at home—which might precipitate a return to the hated policy of "isolationism"—but also as a means to prevent a renewal of the antidemocratic conditions that gave rise to fascism in Europe and Asia prior to the war. The subtext of this effort, and in many respects one of the most important subtexts of the war—and of this book—was the need to get the British to go along with the American economic agenda (which included an element of anticolonialism, since colonial empires tended to restrict access—especially

American access—to trade and raw materials). American willingness to use its economic power as leverage in this effort renders the notion of a "special relationship" more complex and difficult than might be immediately apparent—especially in light of the rhetoric of Winston Churchill and others who, as David Reynolds reminds us, were the first interpreters of the history of the war.

Finally, there is FDR's belief in moral leadership. Here, it seems reasonable to argue that in spite of the difficulties FDR experienced in trying to formulate and execute a consistent worldview—thanks in large part to the vagaries of war—FDR nevertheless believed and understood that in the long term, the ability of the United States to secure a safe and productive place for itself in the world depended not on military or economic power or the combination of the two, but rather on moral persuasion. On the ability of the American government and people to articulate and promote the sorts of values that all peoples—"everywhere in the world"—could embrace. Indeed, without such moral underpinnings, FDR knew that military and economic power were ultimately useless. Surely this is a lesson, and a legacy, that can serve as an enduring light to illuminate our way forward for the future.

NOTES

1. The author would like to thank David Reynolds, Warren Kimball and Christopher Breiseth for taking the time to read advanced copies of this chapter. He would also like to thank Marist College and the Franklin and Eleanor Roosevelt Institute for the sabbatical leave that made it possible for him to complete this chapter and the editing of this book; and Churchill College and the Churchill Archives Centre at Cambridge University for the grant of an Archives By-Fellowship in support of this and other projects.

2. *New York Times*, April 18, 1945, 1–2.

3. Churchill to King George VI, April 13, 1945, Churchill Papers, Churchill Archives, CHAR 20/193B/185–186.

4. Time Magazine, *World's Man*, April 23, 1945. It was traditional in the Soviet Press that all foreign news must occupy the back pages of newspapers. This tradition was broken in the case of FDR's death, which was widely reported as front-page news.

5. As was the case in the 1945–1947 Marshall Mission to China, a diplomatic attempt by U.S. General George C. Marshall under the direction of U.S. President Harry Truman, to bring the Chinese Communists and Nationalists together into a unified government.

6. The Sterling Area or "bloc" refers to the group of countries, most often colonies and Dominions of the British Empire, which used the Pound Sterling as their currency or linked their currency to the British Pound.

7. For more on Lend-Lease and the state of Anglo-American relations in September 1944, see David B. Woolner, ed., *The Second Quebec Conference*

Revisited: Waging War, Formulating Peace; Canada, Great Britain and the United States in 1944–1945 (New York, Palgrave/St. Martins Press, 1998).

8. The Reciprocal Trade Agreements Act (RTAA) was first passed by the U.S. Congress in March 1934. It gave the Executive Branch of the U.S. government the power to enter into bilateral talks with America's trading partners and to negotiate up to a 50 percent reduction (or increase) in the existing U.S. tariff rates in exchange for a reciprocal reduction by the trading partner. The act was to remain in force for three years, after which it was subject to renewal by the U.S. Congress.

9. For further information on the link between Hull's RTAA and the globalization of the world's economy, see David B. Woolner, "Cordell Hull, Anthony Eden and the Search for Anglo-American Cooperation, 1933–1938," (Westport, CT: Praeger Press; forthcoming); Alan P. Dobson, *U.S. Wartime Aid to Britain, 1940–1946* (London: Croom Helm, 1986); Randall Bennet Woods, *A Changing of the Guard* (Chapel Hill, NC: University of North Carolina Press, 1990); and Thomas W. Zeiler, *Free Trade/Free World* (Chapel Hill, NC: University of North Carolina Press, 1999).

CONTRIBUTORS

Alan P. Dobson is professor of Politics and director of the Institute for Transatlantic European and American Studies at the University of Dundee, Scotland. He is editor of the *Journal of Transatlantic Studies* and cochairs the Transatlantic Studies Association. His most recent publications include *Globalization and Regional Integration: the Origins, Development and Impact of the Single European Aviation Market* (London/New York: Routledge, 2007); and *US Economic Statecraft for Survival 1933–1991* (London/New York: Routledge, 2002). He is also the coauthor with Steve Marsh of *US Foreign Policy since 1945* 2nd edition (London: Routledge, 2006).

Lloyd Gardner received his Ph.D. from the University of Wisconsin in 1960 and has taught at Rutgers University since 1963. He is the author or editor of over a dozen books on U.S. foreign policy, including *Pay Any Price: Lyndon Johnson and the Wars for Vietnam* (Chicago: Ivan R. Dee, 1997), and most recently an edited volume with Marilyn Young, *Iraq and the Lessons of Vietnam* (New York: New Press, 2007; Distributed by W.W. Norton & Co.). He is a past president of the Society of American Historians of Foreign Relations.

Alan K. Henrikson is director of Diplomatic Studies at The Fletcher School of Law and Diplomacy, Tufts University. Among his recent publications are: *What Can Public Diplomacy Achieve?* (The Hague, Netherlands: Clingendael, 2006); "Niche Diplomacy in the World Public Arena: The Global 'Corners' of Canada and Norway," in *The New Public Diplomacy: Soft Power in International Relations* (New York: Palgrave Macmillan, 2005); "The Geography of Diplomacy," in *The Geography of War and Peace* (New York: Oxford University Press, 2005); and "Good Neighbour Diplomacy Revisited," in *Holding the Line: Borders in a Global World* (Vancouver: University of British Columbia Press, 2005).

Warren F. Kimball is author of *Forged in War: Roosevelt, Churchill, and the Second World War* (New York: W. Morrow, 1997), *The Juggler: Franklin Roosevelt as Wartime Statesman* (Princeton, NJ: Princeton University Press,

1991), and editor of *Churchill & Roosevelt: The Complete Correspondence*, 3 vols. (Princeton, NJ: Princeton University Press, 1984). He is on the Board of Governors of the Franklin and Eleanor Roosevelt Institute and is an academic adviser to the Churchill Centre. While he still tries to unwrap the true "riddle wrapped in a mystery inside an enigma"—FDR—he is writing an institutional history of the U.S. Tennis Association and is the USTA historian.

Walter LaFeber is the Andrew and James Tisch University professor emeritus at Cornell University and a Weiss Presidential Teaching fellow. His recent books include *America, Russia and the Cold War, 1945–2006*, 10th Edition (Boston: McGraw Hill, 2006); *The Clash: U.S.–Japanese Relations since the 1850s* (New York: W.W. Norton, 1998); and *The American Age: U.S. Foreign Relations at Home and Abroad since 1750*, 2nd Edition (New York: W.W. Norton, 1994).

David Reynolds is professor of International History at Cambridge University and a fellow of the British Academy. His books include *Summits: Six Meetings That Shaped the 20th Century* (New York: Basic Books, 2007); *In Command of History: Churchill Fighting and Writing the Second World War* (New York: Random House, 2005); *From World War to Cold War: Churchill, Roosevelt and the International History of the 1940s* (New York: Oxford University Press, 2006); and *From Munich to Pearl Harbor: Roosevelt's America and the Origins of the Second World War* (Chicago: Ivan R. Dee, 2001).

Michael Schaller is Regents professor of History at the University of Arizona. Among his several publications are *The United States and China into the Twenty-First Century* (New York: Oxford University Press, 2002); *Douglas MacArthur: The Far Eastern General* (New York: Oxford University Press, 1989); *The American Occupation of Japan: The Origins of the Cold War in Asia* (New York: Oxford University Press, 1985); and *The U.S. Crusade in China, 1938–1945* (New York: Columbia University Press, 1979).

Mark A. Stoler is professor emeritus of History at the University of Vermont. His publications include *Allies in War: Britain and America Against the Axis Powers, 1940–1945* (London: Hodder-Arnold, 2005); *Debating Franklin D. Roosevelt's Foreign Policies, 1933–1945*, with Justus Doenecke (Lanham, MD: Rowman and Littlefield, 2005); *Allies and Adversaries: The Joint Chiefs of Staff, the Grand Alliance, and U.S. Strategy in World War II* (Chapel Hill: University of North Carolina Press, 2000); and *The Politics of the Second Front: American Military Planning and Diplomacy in Coalition Warfare, 1941–1943* (Westport, CT: Greenwood, 1977).

Randall B. Woods is the John A. Cooper distinguished professor of History at the University of Arkansas, and former dean of Arts and Sciences. His publications include *LBJ Architect of American Ambition* (New York: Free Press, 2006); *Vietnam and the American Political Tradition: The Politics of Dissent* (New York: Cambridge University Press, 2003); and *A Changing of the Guard: Anglo-American Relations, 1941–1946* (Chapel Hill: University of North Carolina Press, 1990).

David B. Woolner is associate professor of History at Marist College and executive director of the Franklin and Eleanor Roosevelt Institute. He is the author of *The Frustrated Idealists: Cordell Hull, Anthony Eden and the Search for Anglo-American Cooperation, 1933–1938* (forthcoming from Praeger Press); coeditor of *FDR and the Environment* (New York: Palgrave Macmillan, 2005); *FDR, the Vatican and the Roman Catholic Church in America, 1933–1945* (New York: Palgrave Macmillan, 2003); and editor of *The Second Quebec Conference Revisited: Waging War, Formulating Peace; Canada, Great Britain and the United States in 1944–1945* (New York: St. Martin's Press, 1998). In the fall of 2007, he was named an archives by-fellow at Churchill College, Cambridge.

INDEX

(Please note that page numbers appearing in *italics* indicate end notes.)